THE SCOTS IMAGINATION AND MODERN MEMORY

THE SCOTS IMAGINATION AND MODERN MEMORY

ANDREW BLAIKIE

EDINBURGH UNIVERSITY PRESS

Edinburgh University Press Ltd
22 George Square, Edinburgh
www.euppublishing.com

Typeset in Goudy Old Style by
Servis Filmsetting Ltd, Stockport, Cheshire, and
printed and bound in Great Britain by
CPI Antony Rowe, Chippenham and Eastbourne

A CIP record for this book is available from the British Library

ISBN   978 0 7486 1786 9 (hardback)

Contents

Figures

Acknowledgements

Curiosity rarely follows a straightforward path. Conceived as an idea about memory and visual sources that stemmed from the fragile liaison between individual biographies and collective historical accounts, and eventually born as something concerning visions of belonging and place, this book has had an unusual gestation during which I have learned a great deal. In the course of what has often been a tentative progress, I am grateful to many individuals for their support and encouragement, more especially perhaps for the moments when a look or a remark indicated that they understood my point or wanted to ask a pertinent question. Such signals told me that I might be getting somewhere and gave me the confidence to continue. It remains for the reader to decide whether or not I have reached an interesting destination, or way-station on the road to a better understanding.

Drafts of various parts of this book were presented to conference and seminar audiences in Chicago, Edinburgh, Glasgow, Guelph, Istanbul, Manchester, St Andrews, Toronto and Wellington, and I am indebted to each for their constructive remarks. Elements of Chapter 2 were aired amongst colleagues in Aberdeen, and I am grateful to John Brewer and David Inglis for the opportunity to discuss these. More generally, I wish to record my appreciation to Tom Devine and Cairns Craig of the Research Institute for Irish and Scottish Studies, and the College of Arts and Social Sciences, University of Aberdeen for providing the wherewithal to support two inter-disciplinary seminar series on Memory, History and Society, which proved extremely stimulating in the development of notions of memory. In particular, I would like to thank Enda Delaney whose idea they were in the first place and with whom I have had a very enjoyable, fruitful dialogue.

Research took me further afield and I wish to extend my gratitude to the

Nuffield Foundation whose grant enabled visits to the following reposi-tories: the Scottish Ethnological Archive, Edinburgh; Orkney Library, Kirkwall (Horne, Hourston, Kent, Robertson and Wood Collections); Noel Hill Collection, Kirkwall; Shetland Museum and Archives, Lerwick (Halcrow prints). Likewise, the National Museum for Photography, Film and Television, Bradford, which houses Jarché's photographs as part of the *Daily Herald* archive. I am grateful to its erstwhile curator, Roger Taylor, for providing extremely helpful advice. The staff of the Grierson Archive, University of Stirling were also most accommodating.

Pamela Cranston, Noor Ebrahim, Tim Edensor, Duncan Forbes, Tim Ingold, Owen Logan, Hayden Lorimer, Liam McIlvanney, Tom Normand, Vee Pollock, Joe Schaffers and Matt Sillars furnished me with specific items of information which are much appreciated. Any errors of fact or interpretation are, of course, the responsibility of the author.

Parts of Chapter 6 appeared as 'Photographs in the cultural account: contested narratives and collective memory in the Scottish islands', *Sociological Review*, 49 (3), pp. 345–67, and parts of Chapter 7 as 'Photography, childhood and urban poverty: remembering "The Forgotten Gorbals"', *Visual Culture in Britain*, 7 (2), pp. 47–68. I wish to thank Wiley-Blackwell and Manchester University Press respectively for permission to reproduce these articles in adapted form. Thanks also to Rob Aitken for allowing me to quote from his draft article in Chapter 3. Permissions covering illustrations are acknowledged in the credit line adjacent to each figure. All reasonable efforts have been made to trace copyright holders and obtain their permission for the use of copyright material.

CHAPTER I

Scotland and the places of memory

INTRODUCTION

Cramond, Edinburgh . . .

> Rebus lit a cigarette, smoked in the uncompanionable silence. He could still see St Andrews as it had been to him nearly half a century before. He knew it represented something extraordinary, but couldn't have said what. The words didn't quite exist. It was as though loss and permanence had mingled and become some new entity, the one tasting of the other.[1]

A fictional Scots detective gives fleeting pause for thought, stubs out his Silk Cut, moves on quickly to more pressing, practical matters, the conundrum lingering only as long as the pause in his conversation with a disagreeable colleague. The plot moves on. I finished the novel, but marked the page, wanting to dwell some more on the frisson where 'loss and permanence had mingled and become some new entity'. What, quite, could this 'something extraordinary' be and what was new about that 'new entity'? A momentary reverie points to a difficult issue: memories link people with places in enigmatic ways. Sometimes we find the vivid equivalent of Proust's madeleines – smells, sights, sounds, flavours of childhood – to catalyse the connection. But at others there is only the inchoate sensation of something known but inexpressible. If this is how it is for individuals – real as well as make-believe – can it also be true for whole societies? In what ways, for instance, do such moments affect how Scots remember Scotland? Is there something peculiar about the Scots, rather than the English or the French or whoever? Are memories simply unmediated personal recollections, and has it always been thus; or is there a shared, contemporary manner in which remembrance is recalled? What is modern memory and how does it affect the ways we see the nation?

Grossly, a people is of a place, but to explore what this means is to discover a highly complicated range of attachments, accommodations and associations, from the primordial to the postmodern, blood-and-soil ethnic nationalism to hyperreal cultural bricolage. Nevertheless, as a sociologist I am persuaded by Charles Taylor's contention that 'the number one problem of modern social science has been modernity itself'. This phenomenon, which he defines as an 'historically unprecedented amalgam of new practices and institutional forms (science, technology, industrial production, urbanisation), of new ways of living (individualism, secularisation, instrumental rationality), and of new forms of social malaise (alienation, meaninglessness, a sense of impending social dissolution)', has undoubtedly impacted upon how we see the social.[2] Our social imagination – fragmented and multifarious, certainly plural – means not only that each of us, Scots-born or otherwise, perceives this place in a particular way, but also that in establishing our belonging to the country we identify connections to the past through specific kinds of narratives. Such articulation has been explored through the analysis of creative cultural production in literature and art and in the problematisation of Scottish historiography, while alternative voices seek prominence in poly-cultural, gendered, oral and other accounts.[3] Equally, the explosion of genealogical interest and roots-tourism testifies to an increasingly popular desire to 'construct and substantiate meaningful self-narratives . . . and so recover a more secure sense of home and identity'.[4] Scholars have sought guidance in the analysis of cultural practice by studying the memories incorporated in rituals of embodied performance.[5] Others address the meaning of 'space' in states and nations by aggregating all the sites of memory (lieux de mémoire) – geological, cartographical, statistical, and historical – through which they have been captured.[6] All of these approaches offer theoretical and methodological perspectives through which researchers may study the relationship between nations and their pasts. Yet there is something missing, and it is a vision thing. In trying to understand how people sense belonging through memory, of how they interpret their past experiences,[7] we need first to consider their implication within the present. What constitutes the social imagination through which the world may be perceived?

The history of memory has seen shifts from oral transmission to documentary recording and increasingly sophisticated forms of visual media. The printing press, Romanticism, mass literacy, and latterly electronic image processing have, since the Renaissance, ensured a proliferation of forms of commemoration – from postage stamps to museums – through which efforts have been made to develop shared national memories and by which such representations might now be deconstructed. In the encounter with modernity, new ways of seeing developed. These, in turn, affected the ways in which societies could remember. This book explores some examples using the Scottish case, a choice that is not fortuitous, for it is here, very arguably, that the notion of modernity was conceived. In 1770 no less a figure than David Hume wrote proudly of his country: 'I believe this is the historical Age and this the historical Nation'.[8] In similar vein, but with the benefit of 230 years' hindsight, Herman contends that being Scottish is – among other things – 'a state of mind, a way of viewing the world . . . It is a self-consciously modern view, so deeply rooted in the assumptions and institutions that govern our lives today that we often miss its significance, not to mention its origin . . . the Scottish Enlightenment created the basic idea of modernity . . . created the lens through which we see the final product'.[9] He elaborates: 'In presenting man [sic] as a creature of his environment, the product of history', Hutcheson, Kames, Robertson, and above all Adam Ferguson were 'the true inventors of what we today call the social sciences'.[10] This view finds support from present-day commentators, for instance Brewer, who avers: 'sociological discourse finds its origin partly in a special type of history [that] began to be deployed by Ferguson in eighteenth century Scotland because it enabled analytical discussion of social change in Scotland. Therefore, the "making of Scotland" was also in part the "making of sociology", for in placing Scotland's transformations within the wider framework of the history of civil society, Ferguson achieved a radical reconceptualisation of the general features of society and social life'.[11] Because Ferguson and others saw the development of 'civil society' through a stage-based model, the social structure became 'simultaneously both a topic whose origins and development needed to be explained and the source of an array of explanatory variables used in causal analysis'.[12] Herman goes on to argue that 'understanding the character of those different stages, and identifying the crucial moving parts in each, would become the task of the Scottish imagination for the next hundred years . . . It defined the fields of comparative anthropology and sociology for two hundred years'.[13] While this assertion is certainly open to dispute, it is nonetheless interesting to ponder Ferguson's legacy in the context of a general tendency for sociologists to see their subject as being 'born' with Comte in the 1830s, thereby rendering its 'pre-history' practically forgettable.[14] Although this oft-neglected genealogy includes contributions by Aristotle, Hobbes, Rousseau and Ibn Khaldun among several others, in engaging with such key themes as exploitation, alienation, private property, political subordination, and the division of labour – all of which directly influenced Hegel and Marx, thereby Gramsci and after – Ferguson can, at least, lay claim to a seminal role as the 'Father of Modern Sociology'.[15]

It is the 'modern' aspect that concerns us here, because, of course, the idea that nations are coterminous with modernity is no less contentious than assuming a particular point of origin for sociology. One cannot just claim that because sociology as a way of understanding society and the modern Scottish nation happened at the same time, our national consciousness simply occurs as a local version of what Taylor calls the 'modern social imaginary'.[16] That would be sociology as tautology. If modernity changed perceptions, older visions also persisted and interacted with these. Others contend that the Scottish Enlightenment 'wasn't Scottish at all, or rather it represented the belated intellectual fruits of the Union. Operating on a much bigger stage before a larger and more sophisticated audience, it was "strikingly non-nationalist – so detached from the People, so intellectual and universalising in its assumptions, so Olympian in its attitudes."'[17]

THE MODERN NATION

Debates about the relationship between modernity and national identity are of particular interest here because they raise issues over the ways in which people understand places and their connection to them. The emergence of the discourse of modernity from, *inter alia*, the stage model of history, created a dichotomy between 'modern' and 'traditional' societies, and in sociology – or, at least, for Marx, Weber, Tönnies, Simmel and other foundational theorists – the conditions of modernity effected a break from older ideas like 'community'. Whatever its periodisation, the birth of the modern signified a rupture, a discontinuity,[18] hence the overplayed chronological distinction between the old static, feudal world and the urbanised, and rapidly changing framework of industrialised capitalism.

For those pursuing a functionalist line of thought, materialist transformation prompts political thinking – 'nationalism is an ideational product of modernity'[19] – which, in turn, invents the nation. Thus Gellner contends that by the later eighteenth century economic development in Western Europe entailed both the demise of universal religious world-views and the collapse of dynastic realms of rule.[20] In Scotland, the economic and political changes brought about by the suppression of the clan system in the Highlands, infrastructural 'improvement' and the consolidation of industrial development in the Central Belt, all paradoxically aided in no small part by the Act of Union, provided the necessary preconditions for nationalism to thrive. A shift from hierarchical to egalitarian society occurred, with an increasingly deep division of labour, greater specialisation and a system of occupational and social mobility, which, although firmly class-based, replaced ascribed status with the possibility of equality of opportunity. Economic expansion, technological innovation and migration brought contact with strangers, replacing fixed social ranking with the presumption of a free market requiring that people learn to communicate in ways that were context-free but culturally standardised. The precondition of employability, full citizenship and acceptable social identity became a common level of literacy in a single common language that could only be realised through education. And, crucially, this society-wide socialisation system then provided a single cultural and linguistic apparatus through which a shared view of the history of the nation, a singular Scotland, was promoted. Ironically, therefore, despite the break implied by the advent of modernity, the modernisation process succeeded in claiming the historical continuity of an entity – the nation – that was in effect contrived. This constructionist model finds analytical application in the putative invention of traditions, like the kilt and Ossianic poetry, and in Walter Scott's re-imagining of Highland history prior to 1745.

Clearly such thinking contrasts with the primordialist view that ethnic groups form national realities stretching back many thousands of years. However, Smith argues for a third, ethno-symbolist perspective, where the existence of national identification requires a shared sense of sacred memories, customs and events in a fixed homeland; that is, the idea of a mythic homeland is rather more significant than its actual geographic territory.[21] Self-determination is justified by remembrance of battles and the extolling of 'ancestral polities and founding charters'[22], such as the Declaration of Arbroath (1320). While many modernists castigate attachment to such myths and symbols as false consciousness, others consider nations as 'products of powerful and usually protracted experiences, occurring well before the modern period'.[23] Moreover, Hutchinson perceives 'contradictory impulses in our attitude to the national past' evident in a tension between the 'desire to emancipate . . . societies from the authority of myth' and the 'desire to find in the past a meaning and direction'. Several implications follow. Firstly, since claims for the continuing salience of 'older ethno-communal identities' or 'ethno-historical memories (real or imagined)'[24] cannot be discounted, any argument for national identity predicated on a post-eighteenth century, civic modern Scotland set against a pre-modern, non-national world of ethnic communities is questionable. Secondly, if some kind of ethnic substratum endures beneath the modernist national project, then this is only contingently connected to the state. Thirdly, if such persistence were characterised by multiple and conflictual heritages, this would undermine the modernist assumption of cultural homogeneity; instead of a high culture of intellectuals forging a consensus over belonging, we would find plural, dynamic and adaptable tendencies generating rival symbolic nationalisms.

Arguably, because modernity relies upon a before-and-after historical framing, the idea of a modern public sphere has rendered invisible the continuing importance of traditional fora, such as the Presbyterian kirk, or the moral economy of local minorities, where values and ways of being might constitute something of 'a dissident genealogy that reveals a hidden history of continuities and alternatives'.[25] If so, contemporary devolved Scotland in fact represents a 'hybrid assemblage', challenging the modernist notion of linear transformation.[26] Yet, by the same token, the project of modernity surely entailed 'shifts in the imagination and the gaze that prepare[d] the ground for the later reorganisation of knowledge'.[27] The Enlightenment project drew the contours of a new cultural landscape. As McCrone indicates, cultures provide systems for framing ways of seeing: 'the key point is that there is a Scottish "frame of reference"'.[28] The question, then, is not What, Why or When was Scotland?[29] – in the sense of establishing a time and space in which the nation might justifiably exist, either as a fixed idea or something more malleable and contested – but How have these relations between people, place and identity been configured?

Let us consider the proposition that 'societies are to be distinguished . . . by the style in which they are imagined'.[30] Here Anderson invokes the idea of the nation as an imagined community, imagined in that, firstly, although its members may claim ties of kinship and common descent 'members of even the smallest nation will never know most of their fellow-members'. Imagined does not mean 'false' or 'fictitious', simply that all social groups larger than the smallest village are 'imagined' and that any large social body that exists over more than one generation is 'imagined'. Secondly, this imagined community is limited in having finite boundaries: nations always have 'others' against which they define themselves, as 'Scotland' continually sets itself against 'England'. Positive images of those within the community logically require negative images of those outside it, hence an often defensive or aggressive – not to say offensively racist – stance towards those outside its fraternity or motherland. Thirdly, the nation is a sovereign political unit. It is only in the eighteenth century, with the collapse of dynastic monarchies, and the Enlightenment, French and American Revolutions, that the space is created for the rise of the nation above which there is no greater power. Finally, the nation is a community, a fellowship of equals: 'regardless of the actual inequality and exploitation that may prevail in each, the nation is always conceived as a deep, horizontal comradeship'.[31] The post-Reformation decline of religiously imagined communities based on Latin, coupled with the diffusion of vernacular print capitalism to increasingly literate societies understanding time in a calendrical modern sense meant that the readers of books, newspapers and novels could perceive themselves as simultaneously part of a common culture shared by other readers.

This latter theory has been criticised for being 'obsessively engaged with the notion of the fulfilment of national identity as the achievement of unity'.[32] For instance, Anderson claims that by singing national anthems together at ceremonial events people who do not know one another 'utter the same verses to the same melody . . . the echoed physical realisation of the imagined community'.[33] Although the *frisson* accompanying the singing of 'Flower of Scotland' at Hampden or Murrayfield remains a vivid reminder for many of the passions that may be aroused by nationalism, in making central such 'unisonal' experiences, Anderson privileges 'sacred' occasions of collective effervescence over the everyday dialectic of dissonant voices and internal fracturing within the nation. Meanwhile, the 'ninety-minute nationalist' jibe suggests that, for many, such moments represent the sum-total of their nationalist fervour. By contrast, Billig contends that nationalism is banal in that it is habitually, unspectacularly and unselfconsciously reproduced in popular culture through 'habitual assumptions about belonging that permeate the media, where the term "we" is unreflexively used as a signifier of "us" as members of the nation'.[34] Unlike Renan's 'clearly expressed desire to continue a common life', such everyday acceptance is unexamined, thus difficult to access.[35] Moreover, as Edensor's lists of institutions, qualities, people, objects and practices taken by individuals to exhibit Britishness indicate, national identity is contested and multiple, 'the fluid and the hybrid seem to prevail over the "unchanging" and the "pure"'.[36] To a degree these identifications qualify the overarching influence of everyday media while warning against imposing notions of imagined community 'from above'. As McCrone notes, nation-ness is not 'out there' but 'in here', not just passively consumed but multi-vocal and actively interpreted by individuals. The existence of a nation 'depends upon people defining a community as such'.[37] Thus Scotland exists because people recognise in it an affirmation of their social experience. A particular combination of images, objects, symbols and descriptions will evoke 'Scottishness' or 'being Scottish'. All of which nevertheless confirms an abiding point: namely, that the nation is knowable through its representations but never in itself.

Scotland is a physical place, but it is also a landscape of the mind: when we consider it as a country we think not just about the objective facts of its geography but also of the images that are evoked and the emotions that belonging conjures up. Such projections and intuitions are not naïve reflexes; instead, they signal historically specific categories of thought. The significant property of the nation is how it is perceived as a collective form of social life. It is here that modernity again raises its head, for 'Western modernity on this view is inseparable from a certain kind of social imaginary'.[38] Contrary to the pre-modern social hierarchy, which corresponded to that of the cosmos, the modern social imaginary involves a novel perception of the moral order of society centred upon three social forms – the market economy, the public sphere, and the self-governing people. It is this concatenation that 'provides the hermeneutic clue to understanding the real', for although modernisation is characterised by displacement of 'community' through the rise of individualism, a new comprehension of sociality also emerges. While 'the implicit map of social space has deep fissures, which are profoundly anchored in culture and imaginary, beyond the reach of correction by better theory', large groups of people share images, stories and legends that frame a 'common understanding that makes possible common practices and a widely shared sense of legitimacy'. Not only do stadial theories of history and attendant ideals of civility and 'sensibility' diffuse throughout society, but what were once the warring moral economies of 'dispersed publications and small group local exchanges come to be construed as one big debate'.[39] This common space of discussion, the extra-political, secular and mediated public sphere, is an imagined community in that it has to be imagined before it can exist,[40] and, crucially, this process is underlain by changes in how people imagine belonging. Whereas previously people could only envisage belonging to a larger whole like a kingdom or a religion through 'the imbrication of more immediate, understandable units of belonging – parish, lord – into the greater entity', modernity heralds 'a revolution in our social imaginary, the relegation of such forms of mediacy to the margins and the diffusion of images of direct access', of unfettered participation in nationwide dialogue. Like Gellner, Taylor links 'modes of imagined direct access' to the abolition of hierarchical belonging, as the individual, rather than ceasing to belong in the anomic sense, imagines him or herself as part of increasingly broad entities such as the state or humankind.[41]

This is not to say that the shift from 'network' and 'relational' identities to 'categorical' ones,[42] produces uniformity of outlook, for identity – personal, social or national – is necessarily relational in another sense. Who we are is constituted by our relations with who we are not: Lowlanders are defined as not-Highland, Scots as not-English. The transformation wrought by modernity means that any such identities will be perceived through the lens of nationhood as a universally understood filter. Yet for all this drift towards universalism, the civic versus ethnic origins of the nation will remain disputed.

The invention and self-definition of 'the people' as 'a self constituting group that exists prior to, and independent of, any formal political constitution'[43] develops an idea rather different from that of a nation constituted in a mythic, ancestral era. However, Taylor also concedes that 'a sovereign people, to have the unity needed for collective agency, had already to have an antecedent unity, of culture, history, or . . . language . . . behind the political nation, there had to stand a pre-existing cultural (sometimes ethnic) nation'.[44] And it is difficult to conceive of any such 'antecedent unity' that was not itself mythical. Thus a Kantian condition of existence for nationalism is 'the ability to represent history in an extremely partial and digestible manner'.[45] Two requirements follow. Firstly, it is useful to distinguish between myth and memory. Secondly, in doing this, rather than debating the nation as a conceptual category, it is useful to look at how identities have developed.[46]

MEMORY AND MYTH

Bell's social agency approach considers memory to be 'the socially-framed property of individual minds,' and collective memory is therefore a consequence of actual social interaction, wherein individuals articulate their personal recollections.[47] This narrow definition means that memories, albeit reliant 'to a large degree on pre-constituted discursive elements, images, vocabularies to . . . make sense of experience', are not transmissible from one generation to the next; nor can they be enshrined in stone or other forms of memorialisation. From this perspective, memory is 'an under-theorised and yet grossly over-employed term'.[48] This stance appears antithetical to Zerubavel's 'sociobiographical memory', the view that memory has the function of socialising individuals to 'mnemonic traditions' via 'mnemonic communities'. By this latter, broad definition, 'being social presupposes the ability to experience events that happened to groups and communities to which we belong long before we joined them as if they were part of our own past'; hence the orientation of historically-situated individuals to the emotive pull of family, school, group and nation – their collective pride, pain and so on. It is to 'remember' much that we have never experienced personally.[49] Precisely for this reason, Bell argues that our shared understandings, conceptualisations and representations of past events – critical to group identity – are *not* strictly mnemonic, since they do not arise, at least for the most part, from discussion of individual experiences. They are instead mythical. By the same token that imagined communities and the modern social imaginary are imagined because we cannot possibly know more than a fraction of those we include, everything beyond the limits of our interaction 'remains either to be internalised as individual memory or shared ("imagined") in terms of mythology'.[50] On the basis of this division, he talks of a national 'mythscape', a discursive realm involving mythologies of both place and 'temporal depth' (where claims of age enhance claims of 'authenticity'), and through which 'the struggle for control of people's memories and the formation of nationalist myths is debated'.[51]

Elegant though these distinctions may be, they occlude much of the complex ambiguity around memory as a shared cultural entity. Misztal remarks that 'memory is a special kind of knowledge about the past, which stresses the continuity, the personal and the unmediated'. Yet she also proffers a somewhat more social, and socially constructed, definition of memory as 'experience of the past mediated by representation'.[52] This apparent contradiction can be resolved by recourse to the sociology of knowledge, which entails an inter-subjective requirement; that is, the language used to narrate remembrance depends upon a common vocabulary through which assorted recollections may be understood, shared or debated.[53] It is in society that people 'recall, recognise, and localise their memories', and it is in the construction of images that their meanings are retold and retailed.[54] Such representations are of a different order of articulation than personal memories, and indeed point to the limitations of social memory. Compared to the near-infinite range of unarticulated or provisional individual memories, only a few schematic images are ever shared, 'transmitted only if they are conventionalised and simplified; conventionalised, because the image has to be meaningful for an entire group; simplified, because in order to be generally meaningful and capable of transmission, the complexity of the image must be reduced'.[55] In this conceptualisation, the idea of memory traverses a spectrum from trillions of individualised impressions to a handful of global myths, the common factor being that it is the medium through which identities may be constructed. If our concern is with social or national consciousness, it might then be thought that 'involuntary' psychological recollections of the sort conveyed by Proust, Freud, Bergson, or indeed by Rankin in our epigraph, are not significant, whereas 'voluntary' or active uses of memory to construct representations at the macro-level are.[56] But this would surely be to deny 'the dialectical tensions between personal and social constructions of the past' and thereby to fail, as did Halbwachs, to explain the sociological *dynamics* of social memory.[57] The danger is not one of missing the contest of counter-memories, which will be evident anyway in the claims of different social groups, but in ignoring the frequent disjunction between personal biography and conventional stereotype. There has to be a way in which, say, a remembered Glasgow childhood that does not fit the accepted model of tenement life may be addressed and interpreted; otherwise, how can we make sense of, and indeed render visible, memories that are not accounted for by either popular mythology or the erstwhile historical record?[58] If the historian's function 'is to insist that there are always exceptions',[59] memory research has an ethical obligation to unearth instances where what is wrong is not the personal biography but the history or the theory that makes it appear erroneous.[60] In this manner, the mythical character of imagined community will stand revealed.

Just how it might be exposed is a complex matter. Because memories 'can and do cut across the abridging logic of mythology' most will 'fall instead into the private, silenced tideways of time'.[61] Certainly, rather more has been said about the mythology of nations than about how people individually and severally connect with nations, events, experiences and others through memories. And, of course, the places and sensations that we identify with may in themselves be mythical, or at least mythologised. Memory is not a naïve, pure thing; for it is awkward in that, firstly, we have two types – the personal and the social – the latter tending toward myth but analytically separate, and secondly, because when people belong to or identify with something, that something is already constituted in representational form, as an image of itself. Furthermore, the long march of history has witnessed what Le Goff refers to as a 'progressive exteriorisation of individual memory'[62] as changes in how we record and transmit information – from oral recitation and *ars memoria*, through the impact of print and literacy to the manipulation and reiterability of virtual imagery – have altered the way societies remember. The 'custodianship of remembering' has undoubtedly shifted over time 'from the religious authorities, through the state to the media', with the result that memory-construction and memory-keeping are increasingly dependent upon media representations[63]. Fresh modes of conceptualisation are linked to shifts in media technology and, importantly, archival organisation and rationale. At the same time, the contexts in which memory work occurs are paramount. Misztal indicates 'the disintegration of collective memory in modern societies' due to 'the destruction of a social framework that ensured the transmission of collective memories from one generation to the next; a process brought about by the contemporary fragmentation of space, time and institutions, as well as the growing number and plurality of groups to which individuals belong'. Consequently, memory has itself been denationalised, fragmented and democratised as comprehensive narratives have declined and 'community-based small memories, which absorb the need for identities' have proliferated alongside the rise of global, extra-territorial ones. We each know who we are by virtue of what we remember about ourselves and how, by extension, we make sense of the past. If thereby, 'memory tends to underpin the search for identity', then in this fractured, late-modern context the connection between personal identity and national identity has become increasingly attenuated. Instead of being based wholly, or even mostly upon real memories of shared experience, 'being Scottish' is about having roots in 'a common heritage which "distils the past into icons of identity, bonding us with procurers and progenitors, with our own earlier selves, and with our promised successors"'.[64] We remain in the realm of representation, of national memory as fabricated, 'top-down' signification, not 'authentic' lived remembrance.

IDENTITIES AND ICONS

In exploring this tension 'between official self-representation [of the nation] and what goes on in the privacy of collective introspection', Herzfeld attempts to 'probe behind the façades of national unanimity'. He argues that accounts of the nation projected for and consumed by outsiders, such as tourists, paradoxically use marginal communities to 'embody the national quintessence'. 'This disjuncture', he continues:

> creates a perennial embarrassment: how is tradition to be recast as modernity, and rebelliousness as a love of (national) independence? For, as the state appropriates for its own purposes the local idioms of morality, custom, and the solidarity of kinship, it diminishes the local renditions themselves as conservative survivals, picturesque tradition, and familism, respectively – all serious obstacles to the European nation-state's rationalist vision of modernity.[65]

Herzfeld studies the Greek case, but his remarks are resoundingly pertinent to Scotland, where the stereotyped Highland whimsy of Rob Roy, kilts, bens and glens that prevails in popular imagery, causes many a Scot to cringe. Just how many and which Scots presents a bone of contention. If one assumes that only an educated, culturally enlightened minority suffers in this manner then the way is open to accept Nairn's assertion that working-class Scots internalise such kitsch unreflexively, thus proving falsely conscious – a function of the dominance of British high culture weaning away Scots intellectuals and leaving only a lumpen cultural sub-nationalism.[66] This is not Herzfeld's point at all; rather, he would claim that most people in a nation-state (and Scotland being a nation subsumed within the British nation-state sharpens this sensitivity) are fully self-aware regarding the contrived outwards representation of themselves. It is simply that to regard this representation as synonymous with a popular self-image is to miss 'this rueful self-recognition, this inward acknowledgement of cultural intimacy'. By cultural intimacy, Herzfeld means 'the recognition of those aspects of a cultural identity that are considered a source of external embarrassment but that nevertheless provide insiders with their assurance of common sociality'. Thus, interpreting how Scots come to terms with images of themselves that they acknowledge to be semiotic inventions becomes an exercise in exploring how members of different social groups 'fashion and refashion their imagined iconicity'[67]. This is not merely to say that Scots or Greeks are uncomfortable about how the world sees them but happy enough about this 'behind closed doors' (although an element of this may exist), but that their 'imagined iconicity' provides, when reworked, a sufficient vocabulary from which to devise a suitable, nonetheless ironic, sense of their own narrative.

Again, there is agreement that a national frame of reference must exist for there to be a competent nationhood. What is of interest here is how representations of the nation are re-appropriated to create competing accounts, counter-inventions of tradition, alternative readings that contest the official story.[68] While different groups with varying cultural or political agendas might 'deploy the debris of the past for all kinds of present purposes', for those with an eye to the main chance the fruits of tartanry, the Kailyard, Clydesidism, or Highlandism are continually re-branded and marketed.[69] Despite the diversity this might imply, at the same time a singular rhetoric of *the* nation does exist, for not only will groups oppositional to the nation still invoke it, they will think about it through the same categories. In other words, the nation is both reified and essentialised. Ethnic emblems may be deployed as part of a cultural strategy to create the simplified semiotic illusion of homogeneity,[70] a unified national culture, thereby rendering what are in fact socially and historically contingent claims as eternal realities 'by removing them from the domain social practice to that of cultural essence'. In this way, 'nationalism shifts emphasis from indexicality to iconicity – from social relations refracting cultural difference to socially atomised cultural homogeneity', the research challenge being 'to reverse the process, to see what indexical social ploys lurk behind the seemingly imperturbable iconicities of an officially unified culture'.[71]

The distinction between icon and index bears further examination in so far as it affects the sources of representation used in analysis.[72] For, Herzfeld:

> an icon signifies something by virtue of a perceived similarity: a photograph is an icon of its subject . . . Iconicity seems natural and is therefore an effective way of creating self-evidence. But it is in fact culturally constituted in the sense that the ability to recognise resemblance depends to a large degree on [both] prior aesthetic criteria . . . Perhaps because persuasive visual images possess a 'redemptive power' by virtue of their reproducibility, they directly serve nationalism's twin preoccupations with infinite human reproduction and collective immortality.[73]

On the other hand, by indexicality he intends something broader than the semiotic, a reference to the orientational, context-specific patterns of language, behaviour and self-representation of social groups. In turn, the cultural meaning of evidence will depend upon, and will vary with, the context in which it is produced. In the same way that people speak in different registers depending upon whether they are among friends or in a more formal situation, or a restricted language code may be used in a vernacular or sub-cultural setting, but an elaborated one to discuss the same material in a more 'official' environment,[74] so with the manner in which identification and belonging are expressed. The code used will be that which suits the context.[75]

This is the stuff of ethnography: the researcher aims to interpret the utterances of her subjects according to her perception of their perception of the situation in which and of which they are talking. For example, when discussing the 'gregarious, ambassadorial and consciously non-violent' behaviour adopted by football fans when travelling abroad to support the international football team, Giulianotti notes: 'Scottish football fans, media commentators and politicians tend to view the ambassadorial Tartan Army as indexing the dominant, internationalist form of Scottish national identity'.[76] As his interviews with individual fans reveal, however, this code is one adapted to the specific circumstances of Tartan Army travel and is not one that characterises the more confrontational atmosphere associated with the domestic league: 'The informal rule that club shirts should not be worn in the Tartan Army helps to ensure that rivalries and feuds between different club fans do not surface'.[77] Similarly, Petersoo considers deictic language positions – how the word 'we' is used to signify meanings of Scottishness – amongst broadsheet newspapers during the periods of the 1979 and 1997 devolution referenda. She finds three main uses of 'we'– a 'newspaper "we"', where 'we' denotes the newspaper, including the speaker but excluding the addressee; a 'Scottish "we"' referring to and including the newspaper and its readers in Scotland; and a 'British "we"'(as with Scottish but pertaining to all of Britain) – and that the frame of reference, or type of 'we' used varies according to topic and context. Thus, *pace* Billig's contention that readers could 'really be expected to (unconsciously and easily) recognise their national selves in the media', she finds a 'wandering "we"' that 'makes the question *Who are we?* rather difficult to answer'.[78]

Likewise with attempts to resolve the question of who is or is not a Scot. Superficially, Scottishness appears to be much more about having a sense of place than having a 'sense of tribe'.[79] McCrone argues thus: 'Scotland's best-selling tabloid newspaper has run a campaign using car stickers proclaiming "I am a real Scot from [place]" . . . "Real-ness" is defined by residence in any town or city in the country . . . It is enough to come from the town of Bathgate, for example, rather than to have a grandmother who came from Bathgate'. He continues: 'By implication, best of all to have a granny who came from Bathgate, and to come from Bathgate yourself'.[80] In this interpretation place as territory has some resonance, but it is the 'coming from' that matters: not just where one lives now, but where one hails from. And surely, issues of assignment by others are important here. For example, would a Spaniard from Bathgate count as a 'real Scot'? As the research of Kiely et al. demonstrates, being Scottish is more a pragmatic issue of where one was born than a matter of descent, 'of birth-place rather than birth-blood'. Whereas ties of blood are ancestral and retrospective, invoking forbears, claims to Scottishness based on being 'born and brought up' in the country are prospective and focus on early socialisation, notably schooling. But there are also those, among them English and Irish immigrants, whose claim of identity relies on belonging through commitment – by residence they have discovered cultural and emotional attachments through later cultural socialisation, '*living* the identity' and finding, if not explicitly demanding, an acquired, rather than ascribed Scottish status.[81] Equally, identities are attributed to people, often rendering the receipt of such claims problematic and undermining them, as with the identification of 'the English' in Scotland as fundamentally 'the other'.[82] There are rules of claim, attribution and receipt, meaning that markers of identity are contestable. For example, 'a nationality claim can be made that does not involve birth if the person can demonstrate that it was an "accident" or if they can successfully avoid making their birthplace known'. Those hearing this claim can either uphold or challenge it, although it is likely to succeed because attributions, unlike claims, are made by guessing on the basis of limited information.[83] On the other hand, simply because they sound English, people with English accents often have great difficulty in being accepted as Scots. Suffice to say here that imagination is not enough. Owen Dudley Edwards remarks: 'I discovered I had become Scottish long before I arrived here. To be Scottish was to enter the world of Scottish imagination'.[84] While this assertion sits well with much I have already said, arguably one cannot become Scottish wholly of one's own volition: he, like me, must also be accepted as such by others.

While these studies problematise the grounds on which some people are regarded as Scottish or not, it is also apparent that people mobilise varying markers of identity in line with appropriate readings of the situation. Despite the desires of politicians that constitutional change would see the rise of a civic sense of Scottishness 'based on belonging rather than birth', researchers find that birth is the most significant marker. Nevertheless, both birthplace and belonging criteria share in emphasising the key significance of becoming rather than simply being Scots. Claims of birth, blood and belonging do not map straightforwardly onto the dichotomous alternatives of civic versus ethnic nationalism; rather, they indicate that 'the praxis of "doing Scottishness" involves . . . accepting a claim for the purpose in hand in a particular context'.[85]

This shifting, relational capacity encourages sensitivity to the circumstantial development, negotiation and expression of identities, to their interactional sites of salience. We might plausibly assume, therefore, that the same may be said for representations. However, a notable effect of postmodernity has been the tearing apart of images from their social anchorage. As simulation and rapid information technology detach images from any real-world context, turning them into floating signifiers that can mean whatever we choose them to mean, so the 'passing of memory into history as we lose a living relation to the past' means that 'our only recourse is to represent and invent what we can no longer experience'.[86] Memory is conveyed via explicit signs rather than implicit meanings.

In such disconcerting circumstances, there is indeed a crisis of representation. But this does not invalidate attempts to examine relations between images, narratives, memory and belonging by historical analysis. Transformations in the media of cultural production, notably the development of photography in the early Victorian period in which Scots played a leading role, facilitated the recording of memories in new ways that were initially considered authentic, not in the sense of being exact, unmodified representations, but as elements in 'a scopic regime that equate[d] seeing with knowledge'.[87] Modernity is the era of the sign, and in this ocularcentric comprehension has had profound implications for national consciousness, MacDonald going so far as to aver that 'photography has, in short, transformed – one might also say produced – the meaning of Scotland'.[88] Undoubtedly, the country's iconography has been fashioned in this way, but is neither singular – since it reflects multiple sites of memory – nor coherent. And what is disputable is the pattern of this incoherence. If we follow the Geertzian logic of knowledge being ineluctably shaped by local experience and reference,[89] then many forms of observation will occur, not just across and outside the nation, but within far more circumscribed milieux, 'each one refashioning space under a different scopic regime'. It follows that, 'the situated character of visual knowledge is therefore best understood by the study of a locality'.[90] However, since the connection between representation and memory would appear to have been severed, surely these forms of observation are no longer credible or trustworthy.[91] As Nora avers, 'there are *lieux de mémoire*, sites of memory, because there are no longer *milieux de mémoire*, real environments of memory'.[92]

Contemporary memory manifests a paradoxical relationship to change. Cultural anxiety over the rupture between past and present – the great discontinuity wrought by modernity – prompts a presentism of remembrance and forgetting organised so as to authorise tradition: 'the underlying argument is that a stable identity, personal or national, rests on awareness of continuity with a beloved past'. To the extent that 'real' collective memory of the nation has collapsed, it has been supplanted by widespread fascination with 'community-based small memories,' arguably offering 'comforting collective scripts capable of replacing a lost sense of community'.[93] Pursuing evidence of what the people, places and events of the past meant is already complicated when the filter of representation – a 'record' of what was said or seen – requires second-guessing one's subjects, particularly in historical research where death has rendered them inarticulate. Here, as Petersoo's example might suggest, methods like contents analysis allow for the interrogation of intentions, while triangulation between different sources can provide clues to their comparable *representativeness*. However, when the potential evidence loses its referential grounding, as with the detached digital image, faith in its credibility as a trace of the real wears perilously thin. Yet this does not mean that just because museums, memorials, oral history projects, blogs and interpretation centres exist putatively to conserve and remember our 'heritage' in different ways, we cannot study such milieux. On the contrary, the archive provides access to crucial sources of information.

The task is one of stripping away layers: firstly, to interrogate our own relationship to the meaning of such material; secondly, to deconstruct the processes or recording and classifying; and, thirdly, to attempt to interpret the significance of these data for their subjects.

This said, in concentrating on construction, deconstruction and reconstruction, there is a danger of ignoring the reception or effectiveness of representations, [94] a process that depends upon how culture 'works'. Schudson asks why it is that sometimes a photograph profoundly changes the way a person sees the world, sometimes not?[95] He seeks an answer via Sperber's 'epidemiology of representations' approach. People's susceptibility to an image will depend upon the retrievability of the picture in question, how accessible it is to memory because of its dramatic qualities and the relative recency or topicality of what it represents. Events or things are made memorable by their rhetorical force relative to that of potentially competing entities and instances – some are more resonant than others. Although available, effective and resonant, cultural objects and representations also require a degree of institutional capture and retention, a form of insinuation that socially certifies them, for '[I]f they never turn up in a school classroom, never become part of common reference, never enter into the knowledge formally required for citizenship or job-holding or social acceptability, their power will be limited'.[96] The cultural reception of mediated material – not only the visual, but also literature, oral accounts, popular rituals and official histories – thus relates to those mnemonic forms of socialisation already discussed in that they require the framework of institutions and social structures to function as representational practices. In this way, commemorations, memorial sites, museums, history curricula, novels, films, magazines and the Internet all act to make remembering in common a possibility. In other words, though the interpretation of representations must be multi-perspectival, while acknowledging fluidity, perceptual standpoints are necessarily expressed by reference to a culturally organised inter-subjective frame of reference. This; or, as with most people's memories most of the time, they remain forever unarticulated.

With such fragments as do exist, it is necessary to reconstruct before we can deconstruct. Memory provides a research resource because its traces, in registering loss, simultaneously record the imprint of that loss.[97] But, again, there is a problem because so many representations of recall have been devalued by losing their referentiality. The first task is to restore confidence in images, narratives and impressions, not as somehow 'authentic' representations, but as feasible sources of evidence.[98] And the only way in which this can be done is by re-assembling the idiomatic contexts in which they were produced and through which their appeals may still echo.

WAYS OF LOOKING

To that end, the chapters in this volume confront issues of sociality, nationhood, modernity, representation and remembrance from different angles and in widely varying contexts. The resultant picture is anything but comprehensive; rather, the analysis aims to demonstrate some ways in which belonging connects – or does not connect – with aspects of modern memory. My focus is upon the representations from which senses of place, be they personal, local or national, have been evoked, images that are inflected by the disciplinary self-comprehension of sociology (Chapter 2) and anthropology (Chapter 6), the impact of the documentary vision (Chapters 3 and 7), by characterisations of community in literature, popular and otherwise (Chapter 4), and by attempts to reflect the meaning of landscape through photography (Chapter 5). Visual sources feature in the analysis.[99] For instance, in Chapter 7 the multiple contexts through which an image may be understood indicate the problems of treating a photograph as merely 'iconic'. Similarly, Chapter 6 demonstrates that while an emic/etic division might have heuristic utility in situating 'insider' interpretations of images of place within a meaningful cultural framework, it would be seriously flawed to regard 'outsider' accounts as in any way culturally neutral.[100] Getting beyond these difficulties requires the development of more nuanced approaches to understanding how representations articulate and calibrate identities.

At the same time, it is important to probe the social thought underpinning what is understood by a nation and how its culture and society function. Our discussion begins, therefore, by pondering the meaning of civil society and looking at its origins in the Scottish Enlightenment (Chapter 2), while Chapter 3 pursues the changing visualisation of the social within the framework of an emerging documentary tradition. These essays, on Adam Ferguson and John Grierson respectively, are not intended to set a frame for the remaining chapters; rather, they point to the range of ideas, indeed novel ways of seeing, subsumed under the rubric of a Scottish social imaginary. Yet for all the vision displayed in the works of these Great Men, respectively the 'Father of Modern Sociology' and the 'Father of Documentary', neither captures the abiding significance of images of local community in understanding the meaning of nationhood. While such representations have been regarded as pivotal in explaining a certain 'cultural sub-nationalism'[101] in the Scots psyche, Chapter 4 challenges the negativity that this view promotes, arguing – albeit just as speculatively – that those consuming and, to some extent themselves shaping popular culture should not be dismissed as political dupes, but considered, à la Herzfeld, as capable of a rather more self-aware, ironic and even strategic grasp of mediated representations of national identity. Conventional readings of Scottish popular literature castigate an apparent tradition of Kailyard and couthiness that at once celebrates a backward-looking idealisation of community, while denying the brute facts of a modernisation process that destroyed actual communities. Although there is much truth in this characterisation, nevertheless there must be strong reasons why what I term the 'parish paradigm' has prevailed. Not least of these, it is contended, is the deep-seated desire in times of uncertainty, such as produced by industrialisation and urbanisation, for what has become known as ontological security – the conferment of a coherent sense of selfhood underlain by continuity in the moral virtues of neighbourly social relations.

Chapter 5 complements this interpretation of the ideational and emotive bond of place and past by considering relationships between landscape and identity, again finding traces of belonging in the remembrance of places as they once reputedly were. In the Scottish case, the 'natural' has been culturally constructed so as to present a 'wilderness' devoid of people, while those who inhabit the country's peripheral shores and islands have been defined as at best differently civilised in their putatively greater closeness to the wild. As already indicated, Chapter 6 plays on this theme by considering the different cultural accounts that have emerged to explain the social anatomies of the Northern and Western Isles in the recent past. The geographical contrast marked in Chapter 7 by shifting the locus to the mythology of the slum is not, however, complemented by as marked a difference in vision as one might expect, for like the islanders of St Kilda the tenement dwellers of the Gorbals have been mythologised as fascinatingly 'other'. And, while deconstructing this categorisation of difference, the analysis again seeks to evaluate the multiple perspectives that alternative accounts of social life engender. 'Community', as ever, provides the key.

To conclude that both belonging to and alienation from place and nation relate to feelings for appropriate social moralities might sound like so much repetition of the obvious. But what is intriguing about Scotland in recent times, is the way in which modernity has inflected the imagined relationships of connection or severance by conditioning the manner in which memory operates. As Chapter 8 suggests, remembrance of the modern nation as time advances is redolent with diverse interpretations and imaginings, but these experiences, at once both personal and social, are far from random or chaotic. They are conditioned by the needs of relative strangers who wish either to maintain some collective sociological grasp of the present, or who feel confronted by its very absence. Such is the illumination cast by the Scottish social imaginary.

NOTES

1. I. Rankin, *Set in Darkness* (London: Orion Books, 2001), p. 203.
2. C. Taylor, 'Modern social imaginaries', *Public Culture*, 14 (1), 2002, pp. 91–124 (p. 91).
3. C. Craig, *The Modern Scottish Novel: Narrative and the National Imagination* (Edinburgh: Edinburgh University Press, 1999); J. Morrison, *Painting the Nation: Identity and Nationalism in Scottish Painting, 1800–1920* (Edinburgh: Edinburgh University Press, 2003); M. Ash, *The Strange Death of Scottish History* (Edinburgh: Ramsay Head Press, 1980); C. Kidd, *Subverting Scotland's Past: Scottish Whig Historians and the Creation of an Anglo-British Identity, 1689–c.1830* (Cambridge: Cambridge University Press, 1993).
4. P. Basu, *Highland Homecomings: Genealogy and Heritage-Tourism in the Scottish Highland Diaspora* (London: Routledge, 2007), p. i.
5. P. Connerton, *How Societies Remember* (Cambridge: Cambridge University Press, 1989).
6. P. Nora, ed., *Rethinking France: Les Lieux de Mémoire: Space v. 2* (Chicago: University of Chicago Press, 2006).
7. P. Wagner, *Modernity as Experience and Interpretation* (Cambridge: Polity, 2008).
8. J. Y. T. Greig, ed., *The Letters of David Hume, vol. 2* (Oxford: Clarendon Press, 1932), p. 230.
9. A. Herman, *The Scottish Enlightenment: The Scots' Invention of the Modern World* (London: Harper Perennial, 2006), p. vii.
10. Ibid. p. 61. He might also have included John Millar and Adam Smith.
11. J. D. Brewer, 'Conjectural history, sociology and social change in eighteenth century Scotland: Adam Ferguson and the division of labour', in D. McCrone, S. Kendrick and P. Straw (eds), *The Making of Scotland: Nation, Culture and Social Change* (Edinburgh: Edinburgh University Press, 1989), pp. 13–30 (p. 14).
12. Ibid. p. 16.
13. Herman, *Scottish Enlightenment*, pp. 97, 99.
14. Intriguingly, given the discussion that follows, it has been argued that such partitioning of the past may be conceived of as 'mnemonic socialisation'; that is, the institution of sociology socialises its members to a particular memory of the discipline (E. Zerubavel, 'Social memories: steps to a sociology of the past', *Qualitative Sociology*, 19 (3), 1996, pp. 283–99 (p. 287); E. Zerubavel, *Social Mindscapes: An Invitation to Cognitive Sociology* (Cambridge, MA: Harvard University Press, 1999), p. 85; see also H. J. Gans, 'Sociological amnesia: the non-cumulation of normal social science', *Sociological Forum*, 7, 1992, pp. 701–10 and B. Eriksson, 'The first formulation of sociology: a discursive innovation of the 18th century, *American Journal of Sociology*, 34 (2), 1993, pp. 251–76, who talks of 'proto-sociology'.

15. L. Hill, *The Passionate Society: The Social, Political and Moral Thought of Adam Ferguson* (Dordrecht: Springer, 2006), p. 4.

16. C. Taylor, *Modern Social Imaginaries* (Durham, NC and London: Duke University Press, 2004).

17. D. McCrone (2004), 'Cultural capital in an understated nation: the case of Scotland', http://www.institute–of–governance.org/onlinepub/mccrone/culturalcapi tal.html (Accessed June 2009), quoting T. Nairn, *The Break-Up of Britain: Crisis and Neonationalism* (London: New Left Books, 1977), p. 140.

18. The timing of the advent of modernity, as against the avowed process of modernisation in the West, cannot indisputably be established by reference to the Enlightenment, Scottish or otherwise, or, indeed, to any one great cultural shift. Todorov, for example, 'identifies 1492 as the birthmark of modernity, arguing that the linking of knowledge with dispossession and subjugation triggered by the colonisation of the Americas must be seen as a central feature of modern reason' (C. Venn and M. Featherstone, 'Modernity', *Theory, Culture and Society*, 23(2–3), 2006, pp. 457–76 (p. 458), citing M. Todorov, *The Conquest of America*, trans. R . Howard (New York: Harper Perennial, 1992).

19. D. Bell, 'Mythscapes: memory, mythology, and national identity', *British Journal of Sociology*, 54 (1), 2003, pp. 63–81 (p. 68).

20. E. Gellner, *Nations and Nationalism* (Oxford: Blackwell, 1983).

21. A. Smith, *Myths and Memories of the Nation* (Oxford: Oxford University Press, 1999).

22. J. Hutchinson, *Nations as Zones of Conflict* (London: Sage, 2004), p. 8.

23. Ibid. p. 2.

24. Ibid. pp. 1, 6, 2–3.

25. Venn and Featherstone, 'Modernity', p. 457. Notions of such persistence have engaged social historians ever since Hill, Hobsbawm and Thompson revised the understanding of English history along Marxist lines. See especially E. P. Thompson, 'The moral economy of the English crowd in the eighteenth century', *Past and Present*, 50, 1971, pp. 76–136.

26. B. Latour, *We Have Never Been Modern*, trans. C. Porter (Cambridge, MA: Harvard University Press, 1993).

27. Venn and Featherstone, 'Modernity', p. 458.

28. McCrone, 'Cultural capital'. M. Schudson, 'How culture works: perspectives from media studies on the efficacy of symbols', *Theory and Society*, 18, 1989, pp. 153–80 (p. 157), suggests, discussing the Biblical 'exodus' story, that 'the power of the story is not so much that there are limits to the number of plausible interpretations but that the interpretations we encounter are of *it* and not of some other story'. The same argument applies to national histories, where, regardless of factional disputes over how 'we' should think of 'ourselves', a national *topos* is identified as the taken for granted 'reality of "us", the people in its national place' (M. Billig, *Banal Nationalism* (London: Sage, 1995), p. 96).

29. Cf. G. A. Williams, *When was Wales?: A History of the Welsh* (Harmondsworth: Penguin, 1985). Much, anyway, boils down to perspectivalism: 'the objective modernity of nations to the historian's eye vs. their subjective antiquity in the eyes of nationalists' (B. Anderson, *Imagined Communities: Reflections on the Origin and Spread of Nationalism* (London: Verso, 1991), p. 5).

30. Anderson, *Imagined Communities*, p. 6.

31. Ibid. p. 7.
32. Craig, *Modern Scottish Novel*, p. 115.
33. Anderson, *Imagined Communities*, p. 145.
34. T. Edensor, *National Identity, Popular Culture and Everyday Life* (Oxford: Berg, 2002), after Billig, *Banal Nationalism*.
35. E. Renan, 'What is a Nation?' [orig. 1882] in G. Eley and R. G. Suny (eds), *Becoming National: A Reader* (Oxford: Oxford University Press, 1996), pp. 41–55 (p. 49). He continues: 'a nation is a soul, a spiritual principle . . . a large-scale solidarity, constituted by the feeling of the sacrifices that one has made in the past and of those that one is prepared to make in the future . . . it is summarised, however, in the present by a tangible fact, namely, consent, the clearly expressed desire to continue a common life. A nation's existence is, if you will pardon the metaphor, a daily plebiscite' (p. 53).
36. Edensor, *National Identity*, p. 189.
37. What Cohen, following T.S. Eliot, refers to as the 'objective correlative' (A. P. Cohen, 'Peripheral vision: nationalism, national identity and the objective correlative in Scotland', in A. P. Cohen (ed.), *Signifying Identities* (London: Routledge, 2000), pp. 145–61); McCrone, 'Cultural capital; D. McCrone, *Understanding Scotland: The Sociology of a Nation* (London: Routledge, 2001), p. 52.
38. C. Taylor, *Modern Social Imaginaries*, p. 1. Taylor describes the social imaginary as: 'the ways people imagine their social existence, how they fit together with others, how things go on between them and their fellows, the expectations that are normally met, and the deeper normative notions and images that underlie these expectations' (p. 23).
39. Ibid. pp. 7, 198–9, 23, 83.
40. Ibid. p. 85; J. Habermas, *The Structural Transformation of the Public Sphere* (Cambridge, MA: MIT Press, 1989).
41. Taylor, *Modern Social Imaginaries*, pp. 159–60.
42. Ibid. p. 212 n. 3. See the discussion of this classification in C. Calhoun, 'Nationalism and ethnicity', *Annual Review of Sociology*, 19, 1993, pp. 211–39.
43. S. Crocker, Review of C. Taylor, *Modern Social Imaginaries*, *Canadian Journal of Sociology Online*, January–February 2005, p. 3.
44. Taylor, *Modern Social Imaginaries*, pp. 190–1.
45. Bell, 'Mythscapes', p. 67. The story of how a national version of Scottish history came to overwhelm other ways of writing about the country's past, not least the local particularism of the *Statistical Accounts*, is critical here.
46. D. McCrone, *The Sociology of Nationalism: Tomorrow's Ancestors* (Routledge: London, 1998), p. 40, argues that the study of so called national identity has been more concerned with debating the concept of 'nation' as a category than with identities and how they are forged and reproduced.
47. Bell, 'Mythscapes', p. 65, defines collective memory/remembrance as 'an experientially formatted inter-subjective phenomenon'.
48. Ibid. pp. 72, 74.
49. J. K. Olick and J. Robbins, 'Social memory studies: from "collective memory" to the historical sociology of mnemonic practices', *Annual Review of Sociology*, 24, 1998, pp. 105–40 (p. 123), citing E. Zerubavel, 'Social memories: steps to a sociology of the past', *Qualitative Sociology*, 19 (3), 1996, pp. 283–300.
50. Bell, 'Mythscapes', pp. 78–9 (n. 3).

51. Ibid. p. 66.
52. B. Misztal, *Theories of Social Remembering* (Maidenhead: Open University Press, 2003), pp. 107–9, 119.
53. The philosophical debt here is to Kant's conception of schema (I. Kant, *The Critique of Pure Reason* [1781] (Cambridge: Cambridge University Press, 1999). Note, however, D. E. Wellbery, *The Specular Moment: Goethe's Early Lyric and the Beginnings of Romanticism* (Palo Alto, CA: Stanford University Press, 1996), p. 361: 'Kant himself did not count aesthetic representations as schematic. In his view, the application of schemata obeys rules determined by a concept, whereas the specificity of aesthetic representations resides precisely in the fact that they cannot be subsumed beneath a single concept'.
54. M. Halbwachs, *On Collective Memory*, trans. /ed. L. A. Coser (Chicago: University of Chicago Press, 1992, p. 38), cited in Olick and Robbins, 'Social memory studies', p. 109.
55. J. Fentress and C. Wickham, *Social Memory* (Oxford: Blackwell, 1992), p. 49, cited in Misztal, *Theories of Social Remembering*, p. 119.
56. Olick and Robbins, 'Social memory studies', p. 114.
57. Misztal, *Theories of Social Remembering*, p. 54.
58. C. Steedman, *Landscape for a Good Woman: A Story of Two Lives* (London: Virago, 1986) problematises this issue.
59. J. G. A. Pocock, 'The politics of history: the subaltern and the subversive', *Journal of Political Philosophy*, 6 (3), 1998, pp. 219–34 (p. 229).
60. Hence what Misztal (*Theories of Social Remembering*, p. 68) calls the 'dynamic perspective', memory being located 'in the space between an imposed ideology and the possibility of an alternative way of understanding experience' (S. Radstone, 'Working with memory: an introduction', in S. Radstone (ed.), *Memory and Methodology* (Oxford: Berg, 2000), pp. 1–24 (p. 18)).
61. Bell, 'Mythscapes', p. 77.
62. J. Le Goff, *History and Memory* (New York: Columbia University Press, 1992), cited in Olick and Robbins, 'Social memory studies', p. 115.
63. Misztal, *Theories of Social Remembering*, p. 48. Since he is concerned with collective impressions, Halbwachs argues that memories need some form of externalisation or they wither. Misztal sees this as forcing attention upon 'rationalisation' rather than the imagination. This would appear to equate individual introspection with 'imagination' but social memory with something more reasoned. However, it is unclear what is intended since the articulation of intersubjective ideas and images always operates within the constraints of a collective social imaginary.
64. Ibid. pp. 46, 157, 135, quoting D. Lowenthal, 'Identity, heritage and history', in J. R. Gillis (ed.), *Commemorations; The Politics of National Identity* (Princeton: Princeton University Press, 1994) pp. 40–57 (p. 43).
65. M. Herzfeld, *Cultural Intimacy: Social Poetics in the Nation-State* (New York and London: Routledge, 1997), pp. 14, 1, 7. See also p. 110, where he refers to the 'paradoxical strategy of simultaneously exoticising their own past and pointing to it as the source of their national character'.
66. Nairn, *The Break-Up of Britain*.
67. Herzfeld, *Cultural Intimacy*, pp. 6, 3, 154. A process he refers to as 'understanding the social life of stereotypes from within' (p. 156). As Hearn remarks, Scots have at once both 'a sophisticated and ironic understanding of the meanings surrounding tartanry'

(J. Hearn, *Claiming Scotland: National Identity and Liberal Culture* (Edinburgh: Polygon, 2000), p. 179).

68. In this respect, as Schudson puts it, 'culture is not a set of ideas imposed but a set of ideas and symbols available for use' ('How culture works', p. 155).

69. Herzfeld, *Cultural Intimacy*, p. 24; see D. McCrone, A. Morris and R. Kiely, *Scotland the Brand: The Making of Scottish Heritage* (Edinburgh: Edinburgh University Press, 1995).

70. A process known as strategic essentialism, and first outlined by Gayatri Spivak (G. Spivak, *In Other Worlds: Essays in Cultural Politics* (London: Routledge, 1987), p. 205).

71. Herzfeld, *Cultural Intimacy*, pp. 140, 29.

72. Conventionally, discussion alludes to the semiotic typology derived from Charles Peirce, whereby three types of sign are identified (C. S. Peirce, 'On a new list of categories', *Proceedings of the American Academy of Arts and Sciences*, 7, 1867, pp. 287–98). Whereas an indexical sign reflects an inherent, culturally specific relationship between signifier and signified, an iconic sign is based on resemblance, it bears a direct likeness. Meanwhile, a symbol represents a conventional but arbitrary relationship between signifier and signified (G. Rose, *Visual Methodologies* (London: Sage, 2007), p. 83).

73. Herzfeld, *Cultural Intimacy*, p. 27.

74. B. Bernstein, *Class, Codes and Control* (London: Routledge, 1971), on restricted and elaborated codes, is perhaps the best-known sociological example.

75. Significantly, of course, writers often use the idiom and vocabulary of varieties of Scots to express meaning in ways that reflect both the context being referred to and that of the intended audience. In this, the nation is 'a space of dialogue, a place of dissonant voices . . . constituted not by the autonomous unity of its language or its culture but by its inner debates and by the dialectic of its dialects' (Craig, *Modern Scottish Novel*, p. 116).

76. R. Giulianotti, 'The sociability of sport: Scotland football supporters as interpreted through the sociology of Georg Simmel', *International Review for the Sociology of Sport*, 40 (3), 2005, pp. 289–306 (p. 291).

77. Ibid. p. 296.

78. P. Petersoo, 'What does "we" mean? National deixis in the media', *Journal of Language and Politics*, 6 (3), 2007, pp. 419–36 (pp. 424, 429).

79. T. C. Smout, 'Perspectives on the Scottish identity', *Scottish Affairs*, 6, 1994, pp. 101–13.

80. D. McCrone, *The Sociology of Nationalism*, p. 42.

81. R. Kiely, F. Bechhofer and D. McCrone, 'Birth, blood and belonging: identity claims in post-devolution Scotland', *Sociological Review*, 53 (1), 2005, pp. 150–71 (pp.170, 152–3).

82. I. McIntosh, D. Sim, D. Robertson, '"We hate the English, except for you, cos you're our pal": identification of the "English" in Scotland', *Sociology*, 38 (1), 2004, pp. 43–59; R. Bond, 'Belonging and becoming: national identity and exclusion', *Sociology*, 40 (4), 2006, pp. 609–26.

83. R. Kiely, F. Bechhofer, R. Stewart and D. McCrone, 'The markers and rulers of Scottish national identity', *Sociological Review*, 49 (1), 2001, pp. 33–55 (pp. 44, 50, 48).

84. T. Devine and P. Logue (eds), *Being Scottish: Personal Reflections on Scottish Identity Today* (Edinburgh: Edinburgh University Press, 2002), p. 67.

85. Kiely et al., 'Birth, blood and belonging', pp. 170, 152–3. See also Hearn, *Claiming Scotland*.

86. Misztal, *Theories of Social Remembering*, p. 121.

87. Rose, *Visual Methodologies*, p. 3, suggests, following Virilio (p. 4), that 'new visualising technologies have created "the vision machine" in which we are all caught', while in a postmodern world 'the modern relation between seeing and true knowing has been broken'. It has become impossible to distinguish what is real from simulacra, since 'images ha[ve] become detached from any certain relation to a real world'. See P. Virilio, *The Vision Machine* (London: BFI, 1994); J. Baudrillard, *Selected Writings*, ed. M. Poster (Cambridge: Polity, 1988).

88. F. MacDonald, 'Geographies of Vision and Modernity: Things Seen in the Scottish Highlands', unpublished D.Phil. thesis, University of Oxford, 2003, p. 3. For a useful conspectus see T. Normand, *Scottish Photography: A History* (Edinburgh: Luath Press, 2007).

89. C. Geertz, *Local Knowledge: Further Essays in Interpretive Anthropology* (New York: Basic Books, 1983),, p. 4.

90. MacDonald, 'Geographies', p. 3. Memories are thereby kaleidoscopic.

91. See Misztal, *Theories of Social Remembering*, p. 25: 'This decline of the credibility of photographic images . . . is a threat to the status of memory as it raises the question of whose vision of the past and whose memories should be trusted'.

92. P. Nora, 'Between Memory and History', *Representations*, 26 (1), 1989, pp. 7–25 (p. 7).

93. Misztal, *Theories of Social Remembering*, pp. 53, 46, 127. See also A. Huyssen, *Twilight Memories* (London: Routledge, 1995).

94. See H.-T. H. Tai, 'Remembered realms: Pierre Nora and French national memory', *American Historical Review*, 106 (3), 2001, pp. 906–22.

95. Schudson, 'How culture works', p. 58.

96. Ibid. pp. 160–9, 170.

97. On the connections between memory and imagination see P. Ricoeur, *Memory, History, Forgetting*, trans. K. Blamey and D. Pellauer (Chicago: University of Chicago Press, 2006), pp. 5–44.

98. For a helpful primer see P. Burke, *Eyewitnessing: The Uses of Images as Historical Evidence* (London: Reaktion Books, 2001).

99. I do not, however, consider art or cinema (with the exception of certain works associated with John Grierson), other than in passing.

100. As with indexicality, the terms emic and etic have roots in linguistic analysis and have been used within cultural anthropology. While an emic account describes beliefs or behaviours that are meaningful to the actors themselves, within a specific society, an etic perspective describes the views of observers external to that society and reflects concepts that can be judged according to shared 'scientific' categories by fellow-observers. It follows that, unlike emic accounts, which are unique to particular settings, etic perspectives are used to explain patterns among cultures, the misguided assumption being that the observers themselves thereby possess cultural detachment.

101. T. Nairn, 'Old nationalism and new nationalism', in G. Brown (ed.), *The Red Paper on Scotland* (Edinburgh: EUSPB, 1975), pp. 22–57 (p. 36).

Section I

Encountering Modernity

CHAPTER 2

Before and after modernity: the legacy of Adam Ferguson

INTRODUCTION

In 1766, James Boswell, having returned from a Grand Tour accompanied by Rousseau's mistress, left London for his native Edinburgh, where he took his final law examination and joined the Scottish bar. Meanwhile, ensconced in the Advocates Library, the Professor of Pneumatics and Moral Philosophy, Adam Ferguson, was completing his pioneering work, shortly to appear (despite David Hume's misgivings) as *An Essay on the History of Civil Society* (1767). These were heady days in the precincts of the Scottish Parliament Building, when cultural conversation in the Old Town was as high as the odours of its teeming streets. On 16 August 1773, Ferguson dined at Boswell's house, with Samuel Johnson who had just begun his Scottish journey. They debated the authenticity of Ossian's poetry, and their colleague Lord Monboddo's ideas about human evolution, Johnson ridiculing the latter's notion that men once had tails.[1]

In the second half of the eighteenth century Scotland's urbanisation and industrialisation were accompanied by a remarkable outpouring of moral and social philosophy. Treatises published in Edinburgh exerted a huge intellectual influence throughout Europe, yet the entanglement of social thought within the material and cultural forces of the period sometimes blinds us to its contemporary implications. Sociology's memory of Adam Ferguson is a case in point. Posterity has treated him 'rather decently', but his 'fame as the forgotten philosopher' suggests the somewhat hazy manner in which he has been remembered, or rather his legacy understood. It is telling that a twentieth century American philosopher finding Ferguson's fulsome epitaph (all 183 words) set in the wall of St Andrews cathedral should confess his ignorance of the existence of the great Enlightenment figure,[2] and then in his subsequent quest for understanding fail to appreciate that the inscription was itself composed by Sir Walter Scott. Some have argued that, contrary to being ignored or undiscovered, Ferguson is much renowned amongst political philosophers,[3] while, among other epithets, he has been identified as 'The Father of Modern Sociology'.[4] Yet, although the retrospective labelling of a Scottish Enlightenment suggests its successful insertion into the canon of philosophical historiography, and the profundity of Smith and Hume rests beyond doubt, the disciplinary mnemonic of Ferguson's imprint within sociology has been fainter than one might expect, its students by and large having been socialised into regarding him as something of a distant progenitor.[5] Countless references allude to Ferguson's part in the conception of sociology, but his presence during its early development seems indistinct, and although his influence is recognised the lineages remain obscure: Ferguson may have anticipated the development of sociology by Comte and Spencer, but neither appears actually to have read his works, although Marx certainly did.[6] Meanwhile Herman avers that 'Ferguson's closest reader would be Wilhelm Friedrich Hegel'.[7] Undoubtedly, Hegel, Marx and Spencer each drew on Ferguson in their exposition of guiding sociological ideas. Yet, it is also evident that he was 'forgotten for the duration of the century in which Anglo-American sociology began to emerge and define itself as a discrete discipline'.[8]

THE EMERGENCE OF CIVIL SOCIETY

Rather than attempt to revise the intellectual history of sociology, it is instructive to evaluate Ferguson's contribution in its own right and, in particular, to assess the significance of his major work, An Essay on the History of Civil Society (1767).[9] It is impossible to comprehend nationhood without understanding civil society. As McCrone points out, 'national identity is sustained by a complex set of social institutions and organisations which rear us, educate us, keep us on the legal straight and narrow, and govern us . . . If anything, feeling and being "national" is the outcome of the process of civil societalisation . . . the result mainly of the channels and mechanisms which shape us and make us feel that way'.[10] This 'civil societal' inflexion upon socialisation pure and simple marks the significance of a particular and modern conception of identity that connects individuals, institutions and nations. Herman's insistence that being Scottish is 'a way of viewing the world . . . so deeply rooted in the assumptions and institutions that govern our lives today that we often miss its significance, not to mention its origin [in] the Scottish Enlightenment'[11] is a bold, not to say highly contentious claim, especially when it is commonly acknowledged that the very idea of a Scottish Enlightenment was only 'born as a distinct subject of scholarship between thirty and forty years ago'.[12] Nevertheless, there are strong historiographical grounds for taking at least some of his rhetoric seriously. Brewer, for instance, argues that while the nineteenth-century discourse of sociology became saturated with references to the social structure, this was only possible because Scottish Enlightenment thinkers had severally developed the 'conjectural' method of history and applied a 'stadial' model of development to the analysis of civil society.[13] This conceptualisation has since been so influential as to be read as commonsense. For instance, it is conventional to regard the idea of the nation as a discrete and unified entity, 'an invention required by a specific phase of the development of the system of nation-states in the global development of modernity'.[14]

Among the characteristics Smith, Ferguson and John Millar shared in their writings was a vision of society as both a natural and moral order, the causation of which could be revealed by general laws, and a focus on the relationship between social change and moral development. In the quest to illuminate such laws and relationships they relied upon a 'conjectural' approach to history by which, in the absence of reliable documentation other than the fragmentary observations of travellers and missionaries, they were able to fashion grand narratives of social evolution by making plausible suppositions based upon 'the principles of [men's] nature and the circumstances of their external environment',[15] premises that 'simultaneously explained current circumstances and rendered the apparent chaos of history intelligible'.[16] In attempting thus to classify past societies, and indeed to conduct an comparative armchair anthropology of present ones, they drew upon a 'stadial', or stage-based, model first devised by Pufendorf,[17] and later adapted by Kames, whose *Sketches of the History of Man* [1778] expounds human progress from ubiquitous savagery to civilised society according to a 'four-stage theory of history', beginning with hunting, moving through 'the shepherd state', thence agriculture, to commerce. Robertson, meanwhile, used the theory as a template for 'organising the history of Western civilisation' since the fall of Rome, so as to present a vision of the emergence of the European system of nation states.[18] The secular impact of such a way of thinking was profound and lasting, the four-stage theory being, for instance, the overall schema that anticipated Marx's characterisation of historical materialism according to successive modes of production.[19]

Likewise, Ferguson's key contribution to the Scottish Enlightenment was to establish a framework for the comparative study of social change based upon stages of civilisation. However, he adopted neither the four-stage model, nor a concern with modes of subsistence; instead, his value to Marx, and to sociology more generally, lay in his anatomisation of social institutions and social processes, including private property, social class, exploitation, alienation, political subordination, and the division of labour.[20] In the *Essay*, he conceives history lineally via a three-stage ('tri-stadial') model of social structure – society moves from 'savage', through 'barbarous' to a 'polished' phase by means of what he regards as natural and inevitable progress, ambition being the primary generator of change as we become increasingly refined. On the basis of a broad range of secondary ethnographic sources from 'accounts collected from every quarter of the earth',[21] his schematisation followed a gradual social evolution from a simple, 'natural' state to a presently complicated and artificial condition. The aim was 'not to invoke an anthropology of difference but to achieve general explanation',[22] and the sequences he narrates are thus ideal-typical rather than unique and particular, as would have been revealed by documentary history: he refers, for instance, to the starting point as a 'savage' expression of 'man's primeval state' amongst 'rude and unpolished hordes'. Yet, even in this primitive state, people are already living in a *social* condition, in 'tribes', 'families' or 'clans'.[23]

Civil society, being the realm of everyday public participation, occupies an intermediate space between the family and the state. It represents 'the sphere of culture in the broadest sense. It is concerned with the manners and mores of society, with the way people live. It is where values and meanings are established, where they are debated, contested and change'.[24] In short, it is a conduit for practical consciousness. Ferguson delineates a two-tiered model of social order whereby the individual, by following such instincts as 'self-preservation' *inadvertently* secures social harmony. Thus the pursuit of private interests, he argues, often works to the public good. Insofar as the unit of explanation was the individual actor, Ferguson employed a moral psychology similar to Smith and Hume. At the same time, however, the origins of social order could not be found in individualistic accounts of Great Men. 'Nations', he says, 'stumble upon establishments which are indeed the results of human action but not the execution of any human design'.[25] This discovery of the law of unintended consequences eliminates from explanation the grand classical schemes of law-givers, preferring ordinary interests and motives. However, three assumptions underpin his logic: first, there are constant and universal principles of human nature driving individuals; secondly, these serve a divine plan; and, thirdly, the model of social development assumes we are evolving progressively towards greater sophistication, perfectibility and 'civilisation'.

Ferguson exemplifies the Scots Enlightenment, yet we would be mistaken to think that he typifies it, for his history and social philosophy are distinguishable from those of his contemporaries by their pervasive pessimism.[26] Unlike Smith and Hume, he denied that the pre-occupation with private interests was a universal human characteristic. It may have been typical of commercial societies, but he claimed that limited motives founded on self-love rather than altruism were 'alien to the mentality of rude and barbarous people'.[27] Whereas Smith felt that all individuals at all times lacked the imagination to extend good will and sympathy beyond a narrow range of fellow beings, Ferguson saw this as a problem induced by modernity. Specifically, the division of labour caused social inequality, while bureaucracy bred political indifference. While, of course, Marx and Durkheim were to develop similar notions, his was the first clear exposition of the idea of alienation; 'that in creating the complex structure of civilisation, man has created something, without anyone willing it, in which he can no longer recognize his humanity, which is no longer a society in which he shares, but something which stands over against him . . . and if he is divorced from his community he is divided against himself'.[28] Although it was conventional after Kant to regard the 'unsocial sociability' of savages as evidence of limited fellow-feeling, Ferguson contends that 'barbarians, while their societies are far from orderly or comfortable, practise virtues lost in polished societies, among them a devotion to . . . heroism . . . [and] ignorance of a self-interest distinct from the common [good] . . . which, while it makes regular government and subordination impossible, at the same time obviates tyranny and encourages civic virtues'. Indeed, he hints at the moral superiority of the savage over the civilised condition on grounds that the former did not suffer 'the vicious consequences of the division of labour'.[29] Since his categories are based on social structure, 'effective political condition' and 'civic spirit', not refinement in commerce or the arts, 'it is entirely possible for a nation to be 'polished' or 'civilised' without necessarily being commercial'.[30] On one matter he is implicitly optimistic: that, *contra* both Hobbes and Rousseau, humankind is naturally sociable and has always lived in some kind of civil society. Whether or not we have ever been modern, Ferguson avers that 'we have always been social'.[31] Herein lies a fundamental sociological insight that sets him apart from his contemporaries: 'Human behaviour can only be understood socially . . . Ferguson demonstrates the incoherence of the Enlightenment conception of individualism in its metaphysical variant by showing how all forms of existence are "necessarily forms of social existence"'.[32] Thus, as Brewer remarks, his insight 'marks the point where sociological discourse on the structure of society begins to emerge out of the discourse of civic humanism and conjectural history . . . sociological discourse originated partly in a special type of history and then developed independently because it focused on questions of social change'.[33]

A MYTH OF BIOGRAPHY?

One explanation of why Ferguson felt differently from his contemporaries lies in a myth about his supposed Highland roots. The *Essay* invokes a time-space substitution, whereby the absence of documentary evidence for historically remote peoples is 'repaired by reference to the characteristics of still extant rude societies'.[34] It was not, of course, unusual in the eighteenth century for supposedly 'barbarous' and polished societies to exist contemporaneously on different parts of the globe. But their apparent co-existence within the same society did require some explanation. If a linear transformation from rudeness to polish was historically inevitable, then the sufferings of 'barbarous' Highlanders after Culloden and in the ongoing Clearances were justifiable as progress toward civilisation. Against this, it is conventionally argued that because he was a loyal Highlander and Gaelic speaker, Ferguson regarded capitalist society as fundamentally flawed in that the interests of private property distorted values by rating men according to what they possessed rather than who they were. A standard sociological interpretation sees Ferguson, along with his Enlightenment colleagues, attempting to forge a conceptual apparatus to deal with the commercial modernisation of Scottish society:

> The background to the Scottish Enlightenment was the economic and commercial development of Scotland, which reinforced the traditional division between Catholic, feudal Highlands and Protestant, capitalist Lowlands. The contrast between 'civil society' in the Lowlands (with its new system of social ranks, urban conflicts and moral change) and 'barbaric' society in the Highlands (with its traditional hierarchies, stable agrarian structure and static morality) provided the original focus for the theory of civilisation.[35]

It is mistaken to regard Ferguson as basing his arguments purely and simply upon such a contrast. Aside from being a romanticised misreading of Highland society, which was anything but stable or static in the earlier eighteenth century and whose clan hierarchy had been feuding and fracturing for generations, this view misrepresents the *Essay* as 'a Highlander's journey to selfhood'.[36] While the contrast between his Highland origins and present situation is certainly recognised in his preference for small-scale social structures, and while he elsewhere caricatures the Highlands as an imagined social space of wild, uncouth clannishness, his own upbringing hardly fitted this picture. Born in 1723, Ferguson hailed from Logierait, a parish in the Highland border zone of south Atholl, in which his father, who was the Church of Scotland minister, busily evangelised. His had been a difficult task, and although by the close of the eighteenth century over 80 per cent of the parish population belonged to the Established Church and just 0.45 per cent were Roman Catholics, when he had died in 1754, and for some years after, matters were politically turbulent. As late as 1791, his successor was moved to remark of his parishioners that 'twenty years since they were universally Jacobites; they are now, however, well affected to the present government'.[37] Although educated at the English-speaking Perth Grammar School and St Andrews University, the young Ferguson was made deputy chaplain to the 43rd, later Black Watch regiment, a militia actively recruited within the Highlands to 'watch' against rebellion, because he could speak Gaelic, the everyday tongue prevalent in his home area. The year was 1745, and he had been appointed by special dispensation, having yet to complete his full term of theological study, such was the concern to communicate the Hanoverian message. Ferguson's own experience clearly reflects the complexity of social transition rather than any clean dichotomy rent between Highland and Lowland ways of life.

Nor was his own interpretation a case of his looking back to the time of his own childhood, and, indeed to the rural present – to a parish world, steeped in the Knoxian verities and local morality of face-to-face communities, familiar to us from Tönnies. It may seem logical to assume that he would contrast the rural *gemeinschaft* of Logierait and the nascent urban *gesellschaft* of cosmopolitan Edinburgh in which he lived and moved. Yet as Brewer indicates, 'Ferguson never mentions his Highland roots in the *Essay* and nowhere in the two volumes of his letters . . . does he engage in an autobiographical narrative'.[38] Arguably, since biographical reflexivity as we understand it today was not something in which he, or any contemporaneous philosopher, would have engaged, to suppose that he drew upon modern notions of self and identity would be anachronistic: 'the self had still not emerged as a social entity, in which people turn inward to become aware of their own activity in relation to a social world they share intersubjectively with others'.[39] Civil society was 'about sociability, not in the sense of intimate *gemeinschaft*, the essence of community, but as *gesellschaft*, the ordering of relations between people not intimately connected, not of kin, but of sociability among strangers'. This required 'a particular type of "self" – mutable, able to see interests as transient'.[40] Yet the reflexivity and interiority necessary to such a fluid awareness were not characteristic of the eighteenth-century individual. Instead, selfhood remained a moral concern. What Smith, in *The Theory of Moral Sentiments* (1759), and Ferguson, in the *Essay*, recognised anew was the significance of the social bond; that is, 'sentiments restricted to the private domestic sphere like love, concern, affection, cherishment and empathy, become projected onto public space' with the result that the individual's moral sense is seen to derive from social roots – an insight that focuses attention upon the underlying normative system of trust, benevolence, duty and sociability nowadays known as social capital.[41] Virtue was thus threatened by the modernisation project because the social bond was under stress. For Ferguson, citizenship arose through the individual's sense of civic obligation, while, in line with Calvinist doctrine, personal morality always had social consequences. Nonetheless, like the sociologists writing over a century later, in the deracination of social and geographical mobility that characterised urban-industrial growth he apprehended alienation and anomie.

THE AETIOLOGY OF CORRUPTION AND COMMUNITY

For Ferguson a 'polished' yet commercial stage produces communities in imminent danger of collapse in the same way that the Roman Empire fell owing to the weakening of civic spirit: people become 'servile', apathetic rather than politically conscious; the division of labour leads to specialisation which erodes social cohesion, dampens mental faculties and leads to a bureaucracy which constrains participation in public affairs and restricts citizens' interests to private business. Meanwhile, the hubris of imperialism results in nations becoming too large to support communal sentiments.

The paradox between optimism about human progress over time and pessimism concerning the present commercial age can only be resolved by rooting out the problems of emergent capitalism. Here he prefigures Marx's dialectic method. However, rather than focus on materialism, Ferguson sees the issue as one of theodicy: progress is part of the Providential design, therefore 'free will and the positive function of adversity in human progress are posited as key harmonising constructs'.[42] Suffering is all part of the pattern. Yet Ferguson rejects the standard interpretation of impending doom as punishment for luxury, immorality and apathy (de Tocqueville's great threat to democracy). He does not hold with a concept of sin and does not regard God as a distant First Cause – there is no lost paradise to be mourned, and no Noble Savage; he is not moved by eschatology. As Hill avers: 'Ferguson's fear is not of modernity itself, but of any of its aspects which might threaten public virtue, and these, in Britain's case, happened to have been brought on by industrialisation, commercialism and imperialism'.[43] Indeed, the increased wealth of nations, growth of cities and the advent of relative tranquillity are in some senses positive by-products of an ultimately progressive process. If God destines us for perfection, this can only be achieved eventually – we cannot go back. Ferguson's history has to be both open-ended and purposeful, so the pathologies of modernity are seen not as evils but as errors that must be corrected: some units, institutions and mechanisms are wrong, but 'mankind' at large will continue to progress except when citizens fail to cultivate civic virtues. It is crucial, therefore, that individuals remain voluntary *moral agents*, and since the only certain way to this is self-discovery through daily interaction with others, civil society remains the route to salvation. The interesting word here is voluntary, for it is the exercise of choice that is educative – we learn by making mistakes. In his *Principles of Moral and Political Science* (1792), Ferguson reasons that although the ends are prescribed and fixed by God, the means employed in realising them are a matter for individual choice. The perfect society is a learning curve, and poor choices can lead and have led to disastrous detours. Perfection is achieved by working through failures and agents are in a permanent state of emergent godliness. Put non-theologically, 'history [was], therefore, the gradual liberation of people from ignorance', a formulation that, for its time, was unusual in connecting individual moral improvement with the common good. He saw society as 'an intelligent structure which transcend[ed] the abilities of individuals', citing, for example, the invention of language as beyond the genius of any one person.[44] If we substitute social determinism for theodicy, then such thinking presages debates over methodological individualism and the social construction of reality. His style might indeed be characterised as 'methodological holism'.[45]

Far from being retrogressive in his approach, Ferguson provides an idealistic vision that involves the possibility of reworking real communities on the basis of a different dynamic from that which he sees surrounding him in urban-industrial Scotland. He is often cited as a creature of time and circumstance, in that mid-eighteenth century Scotland was 'a living sociological museum of stages or modes of existence', with Highland clans representing the shepherd stage, rural society the agricultural, and the Lowlands the rising commercial heart.[46] But his point here is a general one: real civility at any stage of social evolution depends on community, and people can only be fully human when exerting themselves in and for the group, albeit at the expense of a wider unity. We might regard the close-knit rural enclaves – parish society – with which he had been intimately familiar as similar (in mind, at least) to Anderson's imagined communities: created as a result of shared beliefs; 'limited' in that they were more or less antagonistic towards those outside; fellowships of equals as neighbourhoods characterised by 'a deep, horizontal comradeship'.[47] The nationally-binding cultural force of this perceived moral community is evident in its subsequent paradigmatic status within Scottish fiction, from Burns and Scott, through the Kailyard and after (see Chapter 4). Such is social construction. But the parish was also very much a present reality, a working unit. An interesting comparison might be made between what Ferguson foresaw as the natural unfolding and operation of social laws and deliberate attempts at social engineering in the decades following. One such example was that of Scotland's leading churchman, Rev. Thomas Chalmers (also educated at St Andrews and Edinburgh, Professor of Moral Philosophy in the former) to instil education, social care and charity on a self-help footing within *urban* Glasgow, in St John's parish, explicitly on the basis of how these things were done in Scottish rural districts at the time. While it has been claimed that Chalmers' treatise *The Christian and Civic Economy of Large Towns* (1821–3) is 'probably the most widely read Christian response to the problems of industrialisation ever published in English', in his parish Chalmers tried to apply Malthus by foisting principles of political economy onto practical Christianity through the re-organisation of poor relief, establishing schools and building district churches.[48] Or again, one might compare Ferguson's diagnosis with the quest for a co-operative spirit that drove Robert Owen to build New Lanark. Ferguson suggests in the *Essay* that (feudal) society will lose its communal and unified capacities, but 'once citizens have quit the villages and towns they will reform into smaller social units elsewhere and begin to re-establish their sense of community and eventually their civic virtue'.[49] This is precisely what many displaced Scots did during the nineteenth and early twentieth centuries – witness both Highland and Lowland emigrants to the New World. Equally, if the capitalist division of labour and possessive individualism resulted in relationships that dissolved the bonds between individuals and society, model experiments such as those of Chalmers or Owen were clearly not workable on a grander scale without revolutionary rather than evolutionary change, hence Marx and Engels's critique of Hegel.

Marx sets civil society apart from the state, in that he regards it not as a sphere where man behaves as 'a species-being in community with other men', but as 'the sphere of egoism', where religion, for instance, is 'no longer the essence of community, but the essence of differentiation', where the individual 'decomposes' into Protestant, Catholic or Jew and citizen.[50] If we pursue this logic, then both atomisation (separating individuals from their neighbours) and alienation (separating individuals from themselves) will follow. Yet there is also an argument for civil society as the means of liberation from what Gellner calls the 'tyranny of cousins'. If in the economic sphere the free market reflects the movement from relations of status to relations of contract, equally, in the social sphere relations of exchange need no longer be pervaded by interdependent ties of kinship. Indeed, the state, according to functionalist theories of nationhood, requires its subject to be capable of shifting allegiance or membership to facilitate flexible, instrumental ties. Such an agent, Gellner's 'modular man':

> can combine into effective associations and institutions, without these being total, many-stranded, under-written by ritual, and made stable through being linked to a whole set of relationships, all of these then being tied in with each other and so immobilized. He can combine into specific-purpose, ad hoc, limited associations, without binding himself by some blood ritual. He can leave an association when he comes to disagree with its policy without being open to the charge of treason. A properly terminated contract is not an act of treachery, and is not seen as such. A tenant who gives due notice and pays the recognized rent, acquires no stigma if he move to a new tenancy. Yet these highly specific, unsanctified, instrumental, revocable links or bonds are effective! This is civil society: the forging of links which are effective even though they are flexible, specific, instrumental.[51]

Within this recognisably modern civil society, Ferguson would argue that a 'species-being in community' could be maintained, but only if both vitalism and virtue remained active in the absence of their traditional, ascriptive underpinnings. That is to say, his rediscovered community was one animated not by reason, but by passion and 'a language of civic morality' which could help people to 'interpret their unique situation'.[52] He encourages us to look 'for means by which to psychologically and imaginatively reconstitute such virtue', a cultural solution which involves 'recovering and even reinventing a tradition . . . recreated from ancient history, a variety of contemporary "anthropological" sources as well as "relics of the local past"'.[53] In this, Ferguson's ideas were prototypical rather than nostalgic, but to what extent do they bear scrutiny in the context of contemporary society?

ENLIGHTENING MICHEL MAFFESOLI

It is instructive here to compare Ferguson with theorists of late- or post-modernity, such as Michel Maffesoli. Ferguson published the *Essay* nine years before Adam Smith's *Wealth of Nations* (1776) and in this regard it antedates modern capitalist thought; it was also pre-modern in that not only were urbanisation and capitalism still relatively recent phenomena, but mass literacy and mass media, the nation-state, representative democracy and, indeed, socialist republics were things of the future. By contrast, Maffesoli's influential work, *The Time of the Tribes* [1988](1996) is a reflection on the emergence of post-modern forms of sociality in an age of globalised digital communication, multiculturalism and the decline of grand narratives.[54]

The key word here is sociality, for this concept forms a bridge between Ferguson's pre- or proto-modern thinking and Maffesoli's theorisation of post-modernity. If, following Simmel, we regard the 'impulse to sociability'[55] as providing the '*glutinum mundi* and connecting tissues of everyday interaction', then sociality has characterised every known human society. However, it has taken many forms, from Tönnies' *gemeinschaft* to the 'friendship' of unstable groups identified by Schmalenbach (clearly part of *gesellschaft*), and Weber's sect-like *bünde*, which disrupted the civil order.[56] It has been mooted that the relationship between sociality and the social was formerly cohesive but that, 'under modernity, all forms of sociality were disciplined under a regime of rationality and utility. Sociality was banished into the realm of private life'. Meanwhile, the public sphere was 'purified' as the space of rational men.[57] Maffesoli follows Weber in arguing that during the process of modernisation 'elective affinity groups' emerge precisely because of alienation and the absence of sociability under capitalist labour relations.[58] Yet he contends that the social dynamic of post-modernity is one that sees not the contraction of the social into the individual, but rather the development of 'neo-tribalism': 'The ambience of an era . . . is built on a fundamental paradox: the constant interplay between the growing massification and the development of micro-groups, which I shall call tribes'.[59] These are groups whose values are essentially 'archaic' ones of community and belonging, albeit that they are helped to flourish by hyper-modern global media and communications technology. He advances the claim that despite the apparent triumph of individualism, separation and alienation under modernity, the post-modern self is becoming re-attuned to the force of collective identification. *Puissance*, the motivating life-force, is an immanent energy that characterises humankind generally, but one that finds expression in different ways according to the prevailing form of society. Thus, while pessimists have attributed the demise of the social to the rise of inward-looking soul-seekers, absorbed with their own 'minimal selves' at the expense of their duties as citizens,[60] we should instead consider the impact of our basic need for sociality – finding meaning through the company of others – albeit one that may be driven by fears of inner soullessness as much or instead of solidarity against some external threat.

Maffesoli's argument contributes critically to the growing body of treatises documenting the decline of civic engagement, of which Putnam's *Bowling Alone* (2000) is the most celebrated.[61] At the same time, in so far as sociability is about group 'ethos', he also asserts the pull of social bonds: 'the polyvocality and heteroglossia of individual opinions are wilfully suppressed or tempered by individuals anxious to belong above all else'.[62] The crucial distinction between the ethics of sociality and the morality of the social is one that depends upon the conditions through which persons identify collectively. Maffesoli contends that the social consists of imposed constructs such as political parties and the civil service that recognise persons only as functionaries, where morals are reduced to obligations and relations are contractual. By contrast, individual agents are increasingly capable of identifying with fluid social forms, such as temporary emotional communities, in which ethical rules develop. Such a diverse and relative civil society sees 'the end of universal morality and the flourishing of alternative lifestyles.'[63]

If anything, Ferguson's 1767 disquisition presents a more prescient analysis of the sociology of everyday life than does *The Time of the Tribes*. While Ferguson's mentor Montesquieu was concerned with complex social interdependencies, Ferguson himself was as much interested in the transformation of mores, or, to use Comte's term, social dynamics. And as the Sorbonne sociologist was to do some 220 years later, the Edinburgh philosopher relied a good deal on an innate 'vigour of the spirit' to explain the human impetus to form groups. Likewise he privileges 'instincts' over 'speculations', affective action over premeditated intervention. There, however, the similarity ends, for Ferguson's explanation of community is altogether more materialist and rationally inspired than Maffesoli's. People always join groups, he states, in order to oppose others, hence what he calls 'the habit of society'.[64] They do not need to be spiritually moved, or even emotionally predisposed, to 'bathe in the affectional ambience' identified by Maffesoli.[65] In this, he recognises that 'sociality accounts for the maintenance of an atmosphere of "normality" . . . one might interact politely (but coldly) with a rude stranger while suppressing the desire to hit him or her'. It may thus be duplicitous, or be reflected in 'the ironic, complicitous silence of the oppressed'.[66] But rather than acting out of a sense of alienation and disengagement from the social, Ferguson's ideal individuals behave out of rational self-interest. A human, he posits, is 'by nature a rational being'.[67] Thus the individual recognises that 'to preserve himself, is to preserve his reason, and to preserve the best feelings of his heart', the goal of civil society being the happiness of individuals. From this perspective, 'every desire is a personal enjoyment', whether the wish be selfish or benevolent towards others, and people will delight in acts of generosity rather than regarding these as obligations.[68]

Of course, Ferguson acknowledges the idealism of such statements, no more trusting the civil society of his day than Maffesoli has confidence in post-modernity to deliver harmony. He laments the ascendancy of commerce, with its attendant division of labour because: 'Nations of tradesmen come to consist of members who, beyond their own particular trade, are ignorant of all human affairs, and who may contribute to the preservation and enlargement of their commonwealth, without making its interest an object of their regard or attention'.[69] It follows that: 'If national institutions, calculated for the preservation of liberty, instead of calling upon the citizen to act for himself, and to maintain his rights, should give a security, requiring, on his part, no personal attention or effort; this seeming perfection of government might weaken the bands of society, and, upon maxims of independence, separate and estrange the different ranks it was meant to reconcile'.[70] Here we have a situation not dissimilar to that found both 'in simple or barbarous ages, when nations are weak' and, indeed, in Maffesoli's characterisation of post-modern society, where, 'the public is a knot of friends, and its enemies are the rest of mankind'.[71] But, crucially, from the perspective of late eighteenth-century Scotland, Ferguson suggests a very different route out of such decadence.

Instead of regarding disengagement from the social as the precondition for new forms of sociality that can apparently ensure ethical subsistence alongside and against some kind of ghostly bureaucracy – Maffesoli's sociality always being *opposed* to the social – he advances a plea for moral agency that sees the citizen as central to the salvation of the social order.[72] The resurgence of active citizenship does not occur by some extraneous sleight of hand, still less through Smith's 'hidden hand' of the market. Ironically, self-interest – the very soil in which corruption thrives – provides the bedrock for the continuance of community: 'The public interest is often secure, not because individuals are disposed to regard it as the end of their conduct, but because each, in his place, is determined to preserve his own. Liberty is maintained by the continued differences and oppositions of members, not by their concurring zeal in behalf of equitable government'.[73] So long as there are tensions between groups within the polity, civil society will persevere. This formulation may clearly be applied to pre-modern states and to the interpretation of the dialectics of capitalism under modernity. Yet Maffesoli would question its validity for understanding the contradictions of the post-modern where the polity is arguably no longer the arena in which cultural power is fought out. If fear of emptiness drives the post-modern self towards sociability, Ferguson's pre-modern 'primitives' were led by 'affection, the love of company, and the desire of safety'.[74] Nevertheless, both the primordial savage and the Georgian citizen share an innately 'amicable disposition' in which 'the foundations of a moral apprehension are sufficiently laid'.[75] Should vitalism pervade the human condition – as Maffesoli would aver – then there is no reason why public morality should remain distinct from popularly grounded ethics, unless, as both would also agree, capitalism forces social alienation.

An important point of difference thus concerns the link between power and the populace. For Maffesoli, popular disregard for the political process is a sign of the failure of bureaucratic reality, and it is gradually being replaced by the politics of lifestyle, hence the emergence of 'lifestyle enclaves', new social movements and other groupings drawn together by shared interests and providing both social support and outlets for expression.[76] Yet he does not render problematic the fact that power does still inhere in government and that, short of outright revolution, only a formally codified legislature can protect the rights of the many against the abuses of the few. It is here that Ferguson's warning of the dangers of political passivity, 'that remissness of the spirit . . . which is likely to end in political slavery',[77] still applies, for the danger of Maffesoli's position is in arguing that local vitalism and emotional engagement are enough, that the cultural swerve away from the old dualisms of modernist sociology will suffice to save our sociality.

Much hinges on the notion of proxemics, a term generally taken to mean the analysis of the effects of spatial distances between individuals and groups. Maffesoli invokes this idea to consider the relationship between the self, the distanced moral order of the social and the close 'being together-ness' of sociality: 'There are times when what matters is less a question of the individual than the community of which he or she is a member, or when the great history of events is less important than histories experienced every day . . . These two aspects seem to me to characterise what can be rendered by the term'.[78] Ferguson's proxemics are rather different, for although he clearly understands the disarming effect of the distance between the seat of government and the lives of a nation's subjects, he does not see any solution to the problem of alienation through sociality simply in and for itself. Without an ongoing sense of moral agency, by which the citizen engages with the institutions of the state, the individual and, indeed, all groups of which he or she is a part, risk becoming powerless: 'The dangers to liberty . . . can never be greater from any cause than they are from the supposed remissness of a people, to whose personal vigour every constitution, as it owed its establishment, so must continue to owe its preservation'.[79] To ignore that power which resides in the bureaucracy is simply folly, especially when it is plainly decadent, for 'in times of corruption, they flatter themselves, that they may continue to derive from the public that safety which, in former ages, they must have owed to their vigilance and spirit, to the warm attachment of their friends'.[80] Thus, the 'habits of a vigorous mind are formed in contending with difficulties', and 'the fortune of man is [only] entire while he remains possessed of himself' as a player in the polity.[81] Significantly, then, Ferguson's thinking predates the advent of the modern social imaginary where 'the people' see themselves as auto-constitutive and autonomous from officially established politics, where 'civil society emerges in a kind of performative speech act [and] what constitutes the public is nothing other than the common action of discussing itself'.[82] This vitalistic Durkheimian formulation, where 'the world of the will takes precedence over that of representation'[83] is one that Maffesoli adopts in his notion of the 'social divine', where the deity dissolves into the collectivity. Ferguson, in trusting to God's overarching providence, remains pre-modern.

Nevertheless, Ferguson and Maffesoli share a desire to re-enchant society through the invigorating spirit of community. In advocating a version of participative social democracy, Ferguson emphasises the connection between community and communication: civil society operates as the framework by which popular substantive ethics are merged with formal morality. In this sense his reasoning, though pre-Weberian, is similar to Habermas. Maffesoli, by contrast, claims that societies have moved beyond the crisis of legitimation and argues that this is partly because their formal morality has been forsaken by the people, who have developed fresh, oppositional and polyvocal codes of ethics, these being reflected through sociality. Ferguson wants to broker a civic polity which, although it may be riddled with tensions, is nonetheless coherent: citizens can exercise their moral agency to effect change. Like his contemporary, Adam Smith, he accepts the likelihood of private vices, but sees no difficulty in these being linked to public virtues. To re-iterate:'The public interest is often secure, not because individuals are disposed to regard it as the end of their conduct, but because each, in his place, is determined to preserve his own. Liberty is maintained by the continued differences and oppositions of members, not by their concurring zeal in behalf of equitable government'.[84] However, Maffesoli sets the polity versus the people, whose ethical disengagement arguably robs them of 'official' public agency.

Ferguson's proxemics are as much geographical as cultural:

> They who possess the interior districts, remote from the frontier, are unused to alarms from abroad. They who are placed on the extremities, remote from the seats of government, are unused to hear of political interests; and the public becomes an object perhaps too extensive, for the conceptions of either. They enjoy the protection of its laws, or of its armies; and they boast of its splendor, and its power; but the glowing sentiments of public affection, which, in small states, mingle with the tenderness of the parent and the lover, of the friend and companion, merely by having their object enlarged, lose great part of their force.[85]

Small nations, like small communities, are more likely to inspire citizenship and foster successful civil societies than larger nation-states. Yet there is a tension here, because if such polities are distant from the locus of power, they become disengaged. Ferguson's thinking may have lacked the biographical reflexivity of an 'epistolary' self.[86] Yet, writing in Scotland in the latter part of the eighteenth century, just twenty years after the clan system had been comprehensively dismantled by the British state, and hailing from a Calvinist and Hanoverian family living on the Highland border, his logic should not perhaps surprise us.

CONCLUSION: CIVIL SOCIETY AND THE PUBLIC SPHERE

In his plea for a sociology that regards cultural life as 'having relative autonomy from the social structural forces that surround it', Jeffrey Alexander contends that civil society ought to be understood as the 'civil sphere', 'a solidary community of autonomous individuals . . . a universalizing one . . . that transcends primordial ties of family, ethnicity, and race, hierarchies of class and divisions of religion, a community that sustains collective obligations and individual autonomy at the same time'.[87] Pace Ferguson's argument that motives of self-preservation can result fortuitously in social harmony, Alexander argues that self-interest and power are insufficient to bind persons in a secular faith. Since the state, family, religion and, indeed, community itself are regarded as 'particularistic and sectoral rather than universalistic and societal', 'the hierarchies of these spaces often conflict with the processes of building solidarity in this wider sphere of civil life'.[88] Thus civility and civic duty are qualities that go beyond not only the idea of the citizen as a member of a state, but also – at least, sometimes – the loyalty claims of home and hearth. While the non-state institutions of eighteenth-century Edinburgh marked a civilising contrast with the barbarous Highlands, capitalist social relations were to be corrosive of authentic personal or political ties. Such were the active alienation and nascent anomie of Scottish society in Ferguson's time. For Alexander in the twenty-first century, Habermas, Jean Cohen and others have 'failed to define the civil sphere as distinctive vis-à-vis such arenas as family life, and neglected entirely the relation between the civil sphere and such arenas as culture, religion, ethnicity, and race'. Because the particular interests of the socio-cultural enclaves we inhabit restrict the development of wider solidarities, social repair can only occur where these interests can be translated into broader, societal values via, for instance, the hegemony of social movements like feminism. Therefore, a prospective civil society should nowadays be conceived of as 'a solidary sphere, in which a certain kind of universalizing community comes to be culturally defined and to some degree institutionally enforced'.[89] Yet, as with Ferguson, so too with Maffesoli, it is collective vitalism 'from below' that must initially provide the impetus for change. States, concludes Alexander, 'must be compelled to moral action by an outraged civil sphere. As long as there remains some shred of democratic vitality, states can often be mediated in a civil way'.[90]

Thus the concept of civil society provides a hermeneutic key to the complexity of the public sphere. While the difficulties of renewing civil societies encountered by the free states of former Eastern Europe since the collapse of communism have been salutary, the public sphere will always require more than institutional guarantees, for a populace unaccustomed to open public debate will not know what to do with freedom when it achieves it.[91] As a Polish political scientist remarks, somewhat ruefully, 'civil society is not only a descriptive category but also a normative one for it presupposes a certain level of civic culture and civic conscious-ness'.[92] Meanwhile, devolution has presented Scotland with a new and different polity. Undoubtedly, the debate over constitutional change in the UK since the 1970s, 'evoked the distinctiveness of Scottish civil society, and its capacity to frame economic and political issues independ-ent of (central) state effects'.[93] But that distinctiveness was not something new; rather, it was, and is, a set of peculiarities traceable at least to the moment of Scottish modernity.[94] In so far as 'the New Scotland' exists, it is held to represent 'the historical consolidation of a coherent and distinc-tive national civic culture of progressive pluralism'. However, since social statistics indicate that 'plurality and community are eroding', as regional, religious and ethnic differences diminish while social divisions between deprived and affluent become more rigid, the Fergusonian dilemma remains urgent: 'how can a virtuous collective civil society be sustained in the midst of successful, amoral, fragmenting commercial society?'[95]

This question was to haunt Hegel, as it has haunted social theorists since. Indeed, the debate over Hegel's view of the purposes of civil society is one that applies more generally to discussions of the social and the public sphere: is civil society 'the realm of instrumental relations between atomized and isolated individuals . . . a realm devoid of moral qualities, which require[s] management by external principles: the corporations, and the "police"', or does it embody 'the space where the higher principle of modern subjectivity [can] emerge and flourish'?[96] It can, of course, be either, depending on the prevailing stimuli. Within liberal democracies, the autonomy of civil society from the state, the economy and the private realm of the home lends it a crucial mediating role. Whereas Smith sees free-market economics at its heart, and indeed as providing generative and enabling conditions for its existence, Ferguson's sociology stems from *cultural* roots. Here, as market fundamentalism violates public culture, the urgent need is to nurture civil society as the place of disputation. And as Shils pointed out, liberal democracy especially needs civility precisely because it permits the open pursuit of conflicts.[97]

In an age where communication may be simultaneously global yet highly differentiated, where the notion of 'a public sphere can only exist if it is imagined as such',[98] we need more than ever to ask questions of the idea of the nation as a common space of social and cultural conversation. It has been suggested that the relative neglect of civil society as an analytical framework reflects 'the implicitly statist assumptions and the curious intellectual history of [British] sociology'.[99] Ferguson's big idea draws attention away from the high politics of state and nation towards something more tangible, for if we are to develop an appropriate ethics to guide us in the public sphere, then it is to the relationship (or not) between culture, community and citizenship that we must turn. Yet, as McCrone puts it: 'Being and feeling Scottish is not the result of historic flights of fancy, of misplaced attachment to locality. Neither is it the outcome of political or constitutional affiliation'.[100] The civil self is more than merely the citizen, with rights conferred on him or her by the state, or the consumer. Perhaps what is most compelling about civil society is how the concept conveys ideas about collectivities that defy any simplistic equation of identity with the social. It prompts us to ask the question: Who is imagining what society and how?

NOTES

1. H. M. Milne (ed.), *Boswell's Edinburgh Journals, 1767–1786*, Edinburgh: Mercat Press, 2001), p. 107.

2. R. Sorensen, 'Fame as the forgotten philosopher: meditations on the headstone of Adam Ferguson', *Philosophy*, 77, 2002, pp. 109–14 (p. 110).

3. J. D. Brewer, 'Putting Adam Ferguson in his Place', *British Journal of Sociology*, 58 (1), 2007, pp. 105–22 (pp. 105–6).

4. L. Hill, *The Passionate Society: The Social, Political and Moral Thought of Adam Ferguson* (Dordrecht: Springer, 2006).

5. E. Zerubavel, *Social Mindscapes: An Invitation to Cognitive Sociology* (Cambridge, MA: Harvard University Press, 1999), p. 85, notes that 'when sociologists say, as many often do, that sociology was "born" in the 1830s with the work of Auguste Comte, they are implicitly also saying that their students need not read the work of Aristotle, Hobbes, or Rousseau, which is, after all, only "pre–sociological"'. Ferguson may be added to this august list.

6. K. Marx, *Capital*, vol. 1 (Harmondsworth: Penguin, 1976), p. 483, cites Ferguson's thinking as critical in the formation of the concept of division of labour.

7. A. Herman, *The Scottish Enlightenment: The Scots' Invention of the Modern World* (London: Harper Perennial, 2006), p. 213. He continues: 'Marxism owes its largest debt to Ferguson, not Rousseau, as the most trenchant critic of capitalism and as the great alternative to Adam Smith as the prophet of modernity'.

8. Hill, *Passionate Society*, p.6.

9. A. Ferguson, *An Essay on the History of Civil Society* [1767], edited with an introduction by D. Forbes (Edinburgh: Edinburgh University Press, 1966) is the definitive hard–copy text, while A. Ferguson, *An Essay on the History of Civil Society* [1767] (Kitchener, Ontario: Batoche Books, 2001) is also available as an on–line resource via ebrary [http://site.ebrary.com/lib/aberdeenuniv/Doc?id=5000128 Accessed June 2009]. All subsequent references are to the latter.

10. D. McCrone (2007), 'Recovering civil society: does sociology need it?', http://www.institute–of–governance.org/publications/working_papers/recovering_civil_society Accessed June 2009.

11. Herman, *Scottish Enlightenment*, p. vii.

12. J. Robertson, 'The Scottish contribution to the Enlightenment', in P. Wood (ed.), *The Scottish Enlightenment: Essays in Re-interpretation* (Rochester, NY: University of Rochester Press, 2000), pp. 37–62 (p. 37).

13. J. D. Brewer, 'Conjectural history, sociology and social change in eighteenth century Scotland: Adam Ferguson and the division of labour', in D. McCrone, S. Kendrick and P. Straw (eds), *The Making of Scotland: Nation, Culture and Social Change* (Edinburgh: Edinburgh University Press, 1989), pp. 13–30.

14. C. Craig, *The Modern Scottish Novel: Narrative and the National Imagination* (Edinburgh: Edinburgh University Press, 1999), p. 30.

15. H. M. Höpfl, 'From savage to Scotsman: conjectural history in the Scottish Enlightenment', *Journal of British Studies*, 17, 1978, pp. 19–40 (p. 20), quoting D. Stewart, *Account of the Life and Writings of Adam Smith*, prefixed to A. Smith, *The Theory of Moral Sentiments* (New York: Kelley, 1966), pp. xli–xlii.

16. Brewer, 'Conjectural history', p. 15. The term 'conjectural history' was coined retrospectively by Dugald Stewart, a pupil of Ferguson, in D. Stewart, *Account of the*

Life and Writings of Adam Smith [1793] (see above), which also introduces A. Smith, *Essays on Philosophical Subjects* (Dublin: Wogan et al., 1795), pp. ix–cviii (p. liii).

17. I. Hont, 'The language of sociability and commerce: Samuel Pufendorf and the theoretical foundations of the "four stages" theory', in A. Pagden (ed.), *The Languages of Political Theory in Early-Modern Europe* (Cambridge: Cambridge University Press, 1987), pp. 253–76.

18. Herman, *Scottish Enlightenment*, p. 96. Edward Gibbon was also indebted to the theory.

19. As Hill indicates (*Passionate Society*, p. 65), the emergence of private property was regarded as a key factor by all these theorists.

20. Brewer, 'Conjectural history'. Ferguson wrote the entry on history in the second edition of the *Encyclopaedia Britannica* (Edinburgh: Bell and Macfarquhar, 1780), an article that included the first published timeline diagram 'representing at one view the rise and progress of the principal states and empires of the known world'. His use of parallel timelines allowed the reader to compare civilisations visually, contributing to the development of the 'comparative method' in history 'whereby differences in, say, national destinies are related to distinctive features of peoples who otherwise share many properties and propensities. This enabled informed speculations about what would happen were a given people to encounter a specific condition – say, slavery, which animated many eighteenth- and nineteenth-century political discussions' (S. Fuller, 'The normative turn: counterfactuals and a philosophical historiography of science', *Isis*, 99, 2008, pp. 576–84 (p. 577).

21. Hill, *Passionate Society*, p. 63, citing Ferguson, *Essay*, p. 8, and several such sources.

22. Ibid. p. 63.

23. Höpfl, 'From savage to Scotsman', pp. 24, 27.

24. McCrone, 'Recovering civil society', citing K. Kumar, 'Civil society: an inquiry into the usefulness of an historical term', in *British Journal of Sociology*, 44 (3), 1993, pp. 375–95 (pp. 382–3), who refers to this conceptualisation as 'fundamentally Gramscian' (p. 389).

25. Ferguson, *Essay*, p. 143.

26. L. Hill, 'Adam Ferguson and the paradox of progress and decline', *History of Political Thought*, XVIII (4), 1997, pp. 677–706 (p. 677).

27. Höpfl, 'From savage to Scotsman', p. 35.

28. D. Forbes, 'Adam Ferguson and the idea of community: a commemoration', in D. Young, A. J. Youngson, G. E. Davie, D. Forbes, The Hon. Lord Cameron and A. Frazer, *Edinburgh in the Age of Reason* (Edinburgh: Edinburgh University Press, 1967), pp. 40–7 (p. 46).

29. Höpfl, 'From savage to Scotsman', p. 28.

30. Hill, 'Adam Ferguson', p. 679n.

31. Hill, *Passionate Society*, p. 62. On this he is at one with Aristotle and Grotius. Cf. B. Latour, *We Have Never Been Modern*, trans. C. Porter (Cambridge, MA: Harvard University Press, 1993).

32. Hill, *Passionate Society*, p. 63, citing T. Benton, 'How many sociologies?', *Sociological Review*, 26 (1978), pp. 217–36 (p. 226).

33. Brewer, 'Conjectural history', p. 26.

34. Höpfl, 'From Savage to Scotsman', p. 25.

35. N. Abercrombie, S. Hill and B. S. Turner, *The Penguin Dictionary of Sociology* (Harmondsworth: Penguin, 1994), p. 371.

36. Brewer, 'Putting Adam Ferguson', p. 106.
37. T. Bisset, 'Parish of Logierait', pp. 75–87 in J. Sinclair, *Statistical Account of Scotland, 1791–99, Vol. 5* (Edinburgh: William Creech, 1799), pp. 78–9, 82. The figures were: Established Church – 1800, Episcopal – 390, Roman Catholic – 10.
38. Brewer, 'Putting Adam Ferguson', p. 115.
39. Ibid. p. 118.
40. McCrone, 'Recovering'.
41. Brewer, 'Putting Adam Ferguson', pp. 118, 108. See A. MacIntyre, *After Virtue* (London: Duckworth, 1985), pp. 95–6.
42. Hill, 'Adam Ferguson', p. 683. My argument here effectively paraphrases Hill; 'aetiology of corruption' is her term (p. 689).
43. Ibid. p. 687.
44. Ibid. pp. 699, 678.
45. Hill, *Passionate Society*, p. 57.
46. B. Eriksson, 'The first formulation of sociology: a discursive innovation of the eighteenth century', *Archives Européennes de Sociologie*, 34 (2), 1993, pp. 251–76 (p. 272), cited in Hill, *Passionate Society*, p. 3.
47. B. Anderson, *Imagined Communities* (London: Verso, 1991), pp. 6–7.
48. M. A. Noll, 'Thomas Chalmers (1780–1847) in North America (c. 1830–1917)', *Church History*, 66 (4), 1997, p. 762–77 (p. 765).
49. Hill, 'Adam Ferguson', p. 705.
50. K. Marx, 'On the Jewish question', in R.C. Tucker (ed.), *The Marx-Engels Reader*, 2nd edn (New York: W. W. Norton & Company, 1978), pp. 26–52 (p. 35).
51. E. Gellner, 'The importance of being modular', in J. Hall (ed.), *Civil Society: Theory, History, Comparison* (Cambridge: Polity, 1995), pp. 32–55 (pp. 41–2).
52. Hill, *Passionate Society*, p. 10, citing N. Phillipson, 'The Scottish Enlightenment', in R. Porter and M. Teich (eds), *The Enlightenment in National Context* (Cambridge: Cambridge University Press, 1981), pp. 19–40 (pp. 21–6).
53. Hill, *Passionate Society*, p. 11.
54. M. Maffesoli, *The Time of the Tribes: The Decline of Individualism in Mass Society* [1988] (London: Sage, 1996).
55. G. Simmel, trans. E. Hughes, 'The sociology of sociability', *American Journal of Sociology*, 55 (3), 1949, pp. 254–61 (p. 255).
56. R. Shields, 'The individual, consumption cultures and the fate of community' in idem (ed.), *Lifestyle Shopping: The Subject of Consumption* (London: Routledge, 1992), pp. 99–113 (p. 105); E. Shils, 'Primordial, personal, sacred and civil ties: some particular observations on the relationships of sociological research and theory', *British Journal of Sociology*, 8 (2), 1957, pp. 130–45 (p. 134).
57. Shields, 'The individual', p. 106.
58. On Weber's diverse usage of this term (originally Goethe's) see R. H. Rowe, 'Max Weber's elective affinities: sociology within the bounds of pure reason', *American Journal of Sociology*, 84 (2), 1978, pp. 366–85.
59. Maffesoli, *The Time of the Tribes*, p. 6.
60. C. Lasch, *The Minimal Self: Psychic Survival in Troubled Times* (London: W.W. Norton & Company, 1985).
61. R. D. Putnam, *Bowling Alone: The Collapse and Revival of American Community* (New York: Simon & Schuster, 2000); see also R. D. Putman, 'The strange disappearance of civic America', *The American Prospect*, 7 (24), December 1995.

62. Shields, 'The individual', p. 106.
63. M. Evans, 'Michel Maffesoli's sociology of modernity and postmodernity: an introduction and critical assessment', *Sociological Review*, 45 (2), 1997, pp. 220–43 (p. 232).
64. Ferguson, *Essay*, p. 10.
65. M. Maffesoli, 'The ethic of aesthetics', *Theory, Culture and Society*, 8 (1), 1991, pp. 7–20 (p. 11).
66. Shields, 'The individual', p. 106.
67. Ferguson, *Essay*, p. 64.
68. Ibid. p. 64.
69. Ibid. p. 210.
70. Ibid. p. 221.
71. Ibid. p. 253.
72. See Maffesoli, *The Time of the Tribes*, Chapter 3 (pp. 56–71), which is entitled 'Sociality vs. the Social'.
73. Ferguson, *Essay*, p. 149.
74. Ibid. p. 13.
75. Ibid. p. 44.
76. R. N. Bellah, R. Madsen, W. M. Sullivan, A. Swidler, and S. M. Tipton, *Habits of the Heart* (Berkeley: University of California Press, 1985).
77. Ferguson, *Essay*, p. 301.
78. Maffesoli, *The Time of the Tribes*, p. 123.
79. Ferguson, *Essay*, p. 258.
80. Ibid. p. 256.
81. Ibid. pp. 295, 264.
82. S. Crocker, review of C. Taylor, *Modern Social Imaginaries* (Durham, NC and London: Duke University Press, 2004), *Canadian Journal of Sociology Online*, January–February 2005, p. 2.
83. Evans, 'Michel Maffesoli's sociology', p. 222.
84. Ferguson, *Essay*, p. 149.
85. Ibid. p. 253.
86. L. Stanley, 'The epistolarium: on theorizing letters and correspondences', *Auto/Biography*, 12, 2004, pp. 201–35, cited in Brewer, 'Putting Adam Ferguson', p. 116.
87. J. C. Alexander, 'The meaningful construction of inequality and the struggles against it: a "strong program" approach to how social boundaries change', *Cultural Sociology*, 1 (1), 2007, pp. 23–30 (pp. 24, 26).
88. B. S. Turner, 'Civility, civil sphere and citizenship: solidarity versus the enclave society', *Citizenship Studies*, 12 (2), 2008, pp. 177–84 (p. 178).
89. J. C. Alexander, *The Civil Sphere* (New York: Oxford University Press, 2006), pp. 30, 31, cited in Turner, 'Civility', pp. 178–9. See J. L. Cohen and A. Arato, *Civil Society: The Limits of Marxian Critical Theory* (Amherst: University of Massachusetts Press, 1992).
90. J. C. Alexander, 'Civil sphere, state, and citizenship: replying to Turner and the fear of enclavement', *Citizenship Studies*, 12 (2), 2008, pp. 185–94 (p. 183).
91. J. Habermas, 'Problems of legitimation in late capitalism, in P. Hammerton (ed.), *Critical Sociology* (Harmondsworth: Penguin, 1978), pp. 363–87.
92. D. Pietrzyk, 'Democracy or civil society?', *Politics*, 23 (10), 2003, pp. 38–45 (p. 38).
93. McCrone, 'Recovering civil society.

94. In Herman's view, the *Essay* 'coined the term *civil society* as synonymous with modernity itself' (*Scottish Enlightenment*, p. 212).
95. G. McLennan, review of L. Paterson, F. Bechhofer and D. McCrone, *Living in Scotland: Social and Economic Change since 1980* (Edinburgh: Edinburgh University Press, 2004), *Sociology*, 40 (3), 2006, pp. 592–3.
96. S. Khilnani, 'The development of civil society', in S. Kaviraj and S. Khilnani (eds), *Civil Society: History and Possibilities* (Cambridge: Cambridge University Press, 2001), pp. 11–32 (p. 23); see also M. Reidel, *Between Tradition and Revolution: The Hegelian Transformation of Political Philosophy* (Cambridge: Cambridge University Press, 1984).
97. E. Shils, *The Virtue of Civility: Selected Essays on Liberalism, Tradition and Civil Society* (Indianapolis: Liberty Fund, 1997), p. 76.
98. C. Taylor, *Modern Social Imaginaries*, *Public Culture*, 14 (1), 2002, p. 85; cf J. Habermas, *The Structural Transformation of the Public Sphere* (Cambridge, MA: MIT Press, 1989).
99. McCrone, 'Recovering'.
100. Ibid.

CHAPTER 3

The eyes of modernity: John Grierson's sociology

I am thinking of the problem indicated by Marx as well as by anyone in his *Poverty of Philosophy*: that with technological advance come changes in human relationships and therefore a different conception of the 'person'. I am thinking of the lag between technological progress and the patterns of thought and feeling which make it workable and therefore tolerable. I suggest, following better authority than mine, that the inevitable concomitant of the world technological revolution, which now makes us each one dependent on everyone else, must be a new way of looking at things, in which we become less object-minded and less person-minded and more relation-minded.[1]

INTRODUCTION

In embracing the need for a sociological vision as central to the interpretation of culture and place, a number of Scottish scholars may be cited in the early twentieth century, Patrick Geddes and Robert MacIver among them. But it was a film director, rather than an academic – and one who 'spent almost his entire adult life outwith Scotland'[2] – who was to have perhaps the most profound and lasting effect upon the nation's social imagination. John Grierson finds his place in the Scots Myth by dint of being a classic example of the Great Man: an individual who rose from a humble background to lead the world with a key innovation. It would indeed be difficult to imagine today's visual media without his intervention as 'the Father of Documentary'. A vast amount has been written on the early years of the British non-fiction film movement, particularly about his seminal role within it, and inevitably any account must furnish the reader with some biographical detail, repeating much of what has already been stated and debated. However, my concern is more specifically with Grierson's sociological ideas and how he brought these to bear in the perceptual encounter with industrial society. He does not in any explicitly theoretical sense follow any Scottish line of descent: while his thinking could be stretched to building upon Ferguson, his emphasis lay not with civil society but squarely with reworking the social. The influences of German romantic idealism are rather more obvious. What is important is how this most strident of propagandists sought to understand and communicate the 'drama of modernity' as it unfolded within Britain during the earlier-twentieth century. His big idea was that moving film could be used to create a new observational art form through which society might be interpreted; that the world could be better understood by picturing 'reality' than by inventing cinematic stories. He wanted to transform the public sphere by altering popular awareness of social problems and potentials, but his success or otherwise in this regard is a moot point. What matters is how he visualised contemporary social relations. In grasping at this social imaginary, we are forced to conclude that his vision was arrived at by a logic peculiarly affected by his Scottish experience of education.

POLITICS AND EDUCATION

Grierson exemplifies that curious breed of Scots intellectual who saw no contradiction in fervently supporting democratic socialism while simultaneously believing in the Calvinist doctrine that 'the elect have their duty' to impart their superior knowledge in making the world better for the unenlightened masses. As with the lad o'pairts myth, the two were held in close tension by a commitment to education, yet rather than bemoaning the ethical dilemma of individual success deriving from egalitarian principles, it was the unfeasibility of the Scottish tradition in education in coming to terms with the modern 'new order' that exercised him.

The trauma of radical social change ran very close to home. In an autobiographical essay, he recounts growing up in Cambusbarron near Stirling, where his father's philosophy as a schoolteacher was 'strictly individualist. Education gave men a chance in the world . . . Behind it all was the dream of the nineteenth century – the false dream – that if only everyone had the individualist ideals that education taught – free men in a free society, each in independent and educated judgement – [they] would create a civilization such as the world had never seen before'.[3] However, as 'the life of the village became more and more affected by strikes and lock-outs', he began to see that liberal education led to understanding but that this, in turn, only spawned conflict: 'the prevailing idea was as always that the individual might be more enlightened . . . The smashing of that idyllic viewpoint has been probably the greatest educational fact of our time; and I saw it smashed right there in my village and I saw the deep doubt creep into the mind of that schoolmaster [his father] that everything he stood for and strove for was somehow wrong.' Having argued that in the 'great drive for a socialist Britain', 'the miners themselves and the economists among them' were supplanting his father as an educational force, Grierson concluded, first, that 'education can only, at its peril, detach itself from the economic processes and what is happening in the world', and, second, that 'the individualist dream in education is over and done with in a world which operates in terms of large integrated forces. There is nothing I can think of so cynical today as to teach a boy that the world is his personal oyster'.[4] Victorian and Edwardian ideas no longer fit progressive modern times.

Although a Fabian during his time at Glasgow University, Grierson found the party-political process futile, and the voters lacking in knowledge and public-spiritedness. He nonetheless maintained strong socialist views.[5] While still a student he preached at two Highland kirks 'until he gave a radical sermon and was defrocked'.[6] He reflected disparagingly on his spell in adult education in Newcastle upon Tyne, shortly after, as consisting of 'teaching Plato to a lot of old clerks and spinsters . . . who evidently wanted to know about Plato, but would have been better occupied raising hell about the slums of the city, the malnutrition of its children and its horrible schools'. While education and social involvement were crucial goals, he was dissatisfied about the routes – the media of communication – used to engage people. Yet the resolution of this problem came not through traditional education, nor commitment to politics, but via his interest in the arts, and more particularly in his development of the documentary idea. In this, however, the logic and impetus was to be, as he himself said, 'social not aesthetic'.[7] Ironically, it was also coloured by a fair dose of Platonic thinking about how and by whom the state should be run. If Ferguson had 'fretted about the increasingly important role of bureaucratic rationality and centralised planning in the running of societies and, in particular, their effects upon the moral strength of nations',[8] Grierson, as we shall see, had few such qualms.

SOCIAL SCIENCE AND THE MEDIA

From the 1920s, the origins of documentary film-making can be discerned amongst a range of otherwise unconnected initiatives – Soviet newsreels and epics, Robert Flaherty's *Nanook of the North*, the European avant-gardist city symphonies and Hollywood Westerns.[9] The role of Grierson in fusing ideas and techniques from each of these disparate ventures was massive, and, yet, as he was to point out, 'the idea of documentary . . . came originally not from film at all, but from the Political Science school in Chicago round about the early twenties'. In 1924, having won a Rockefeller Fellowship, Grierson began graduate research at the University of Chicago. Ellis and McLane consider that he opted for Chicago 'because of its distinguished social science faculty'.[10] Crucially, for our understanding of his sociological approach, however, he enrolled in Political Science, not Sociology. His developing concern lay with public policy rather than the urban ecology associated with the then pre-eminent Chicago School of Sociology, and his ideas about culture leant therefore to matters of citizenship and statecraft rather than to ethnographic observation. Important later differences with Flaherty were to turn on this distinction. Meanwhile, although his interests in the moulding of social attitudes were doubtless influenced by his supervisor, Charles Edward Merriam, an advocate of centralised state planning,[11] the effect of journalist Walter Lippmann's *Public Opinion* (New York: Macmillan, 1922) on his thinking about the power of mass media and the nature of communication was profound.

Although he did not seem aware of his contemporaries Mead and Cooley, Lippmann's treatment fell squarely within the social construction of reality.[12] He argued that 'if democracy is to be spontaneous, the interests of democracy must remain simple, intelligible, and easily managed. Conditions must approximate those of the isolated rural township if the supply of information is to be left to casual experience. The environment must be confined within the range of every man's direct and certain knowledge'.[13] With the transformations of modernity, it follows that 'in any society that is not completely self-contained in its interests and so small that everyone can know all about everything that happens, ideas deal with events that are out of sight and hard to grasp . . . The only feeling that anyone can have about an event he does not experience is the feeling aroused by his mental image of that event.' Thus, 'at the level of social life, what is called the adjustment of man to his environment takes place through the medium of fictions . . . [that is] *representation* of the environment' (*my italics*).[14] Rather than make judgements based on experience, we will believe the 'pictures in our heads', effectively the 'pseudo environment' created by the media.[15] This notion has a clear parallel with Hegel's concept of *Vorstellung*, whereby religious images act to simplify ideas but in doing so mislead by omitting key elements or introducing extraneous ones. The press thus create problems of knowledge, in that while 'the function of news is to signal an event; the function of truth is to bring to light the hidden facts, to set them in relation with each other, and to make a picture of reality on which people can act'.[16] Two highly contentious conclusions ensue: first, democratic theory does not work since it relies upon informed citizens making rational decisions on public issues, which they cannot since they no longer inhabit self-contained village communities and the facts available to them are distorted by the media; second, 'truth' becomes a matter of experts 'making the unseen facts intelligible to those who have to make the decisions'. In other words, representative government needs to be advised by experts, while public opinion should be organised *for* the press, not by it. For Lippmann, the task of such organisation lay with political science 'as formulator'.[17] Because of the scale and complexity of global information, he contended, 'we have to summarize and generalize. We have to pick out samples, and treat them as typical.'[18] Such sampling requires the expertise of statisticians; otherwise, we end up with misinformed stereotypes.[19] The way is thus paved for the 'manufacture of consent'[20] by a supervised knowledge class based on analysis rather than on rule of thumb.

This advocacy of collective comprehension patrolled by an elite was redolent of Presbyterianism, while Grierson, like Lippmann, followed Plato in regarding the public as herd-like and in need of governing by a specialised class with far wider interests. His classicism placed the state logically prior to the individual. And, in an echo of his despair over his father's ideas about education, he recognised that, in the industrialised world of the 1920s, 'the collective complexity of the problems being faced seemed . . . to demand a kind of democratic education that went beyond the individual stuffing himself with knowledge'.[21] As he put it: 'For three hundred years we have had our focus on the individual. We have distinguished him from the objective world as the Middle Ages did not think of doing . . . In fact, the individual outlook becomes less and less valuable and more and more harmful unless it is transmitted into the corporate outlook'.[22] In this interpretation of modernisation – as transition from pre-industrial ascription, via individualism, to high-modern statism – Grierson's sociology offers a solution to the anomie caused by the demise of local community ties in a larger social setting. Or, to use the Marxian term, 'for him, public relations and propaganda were overlapping notions that offered a solution to the threat of alienation and possible breakdown of society'[23], for through them the hidden connections between individuals, materials, processes and institutions could be revealed, re-acquainting the worker with his product, the citizen with his part in the social organisation of the industrial whole. By contrast, in its sensationalising of news the press failed to make these connections. It was necessary, he felt, to get 'away from the servile accumulation of fact and [strike] for the story which [holds] the facts in living organic relationship together'.[24] In this quest, Grierson began to consider film at the suggestion of Lippmann whom he first met in 1925. It was the start of a process that led to the birth of documentary cinema as a means of articulating this directive social model. Documentary cinema would work because it was the appropriate medium for the newly globalised social order:

> Invention, industry, fast communication, international commerce have turned the problem of the individual from a village problem into a city problem and the affairs of a nation into affairs of the whole world . . . [cinema can] let an individual into the new and more sophisticated relationships of modern life. It can not only set man against a real horizon; but it can also set him against what really counts – the horizon of the city, of the crowd, of the class – the horizon of world affairs. If you consider this individual as standing no longer on a stage as big as the family – or the village, or the country, but on a stage as big as international finances, you will appreciate that cinema might have been created for the occasion, to take the place of the stage drama, to carry human appreciation from one stage of development to another. It might do much to bring us that contact with the newer reality which we lack. It might do much to give us an imaginative grasp of events that have become too complicated for our apprehension.[25]

Transforming the Social

To understand the role of documentary film in lending this 'imaginative grasp', we must first appreciate the importance of Grierson's view of the social as the proper domain for political regulation, for this is where his way of seeing was truly innovative. Rob Aitken argues thus: 'For Grierson, the key object of cultural governance – and the key space animated by the work of documentary film – was the 'social' figured as cohesive and systematic space within which individuals and individual action were to be enmeshed and governed. Grierson sought a new order – an order in which culture would be deeply implicated – which both prefigured an active individual citizenship and, drawing on notions of social security, located those individuals within a broader unified "social" field'.[26] A Foucauldian interpretation of governmentality, as the techniques and mentalities through which states aim to nurture citizens so as to fulfil their policies, conceives a privileged place for the social. Here, 'problems are not conceived in terms of individual pathology or moral weakness but in a language of society as a whole'.[27] For example, it is argued that the welfare capitalism characteristic of Western European and other welfare states between 1945 and the 1970s developed inclusive forms of social citizenship through full employment, the provision of public services and social security.[28] The development of this social model required individual agents to perceive themselves as its citizens, and for this to occur there had first to be shifts in the means of perception. It is here that Grierson performed a vanguard role during the 1930s: 'This new social order requires a new form of culture, and film . . . can help instrumentalize the active bonds of the social world'.[29] By making visible the threads by which individuals connected to one another, documentary would '"bridge the gap" between the citizen and his community',[30] this community being understood as 'a world which is organically related to their own interests and their own functions within the nation', and indeed the wider world.[31] We need to examine therefore how through his revelation of the social fabric Grierson brought culture to act on the 'working surfaces of the social' so as to transform the public understanding of citizenship.[32] However, prior to this it is important to explore the manner in which his particular form of visual culture was itself produced.

CORPORATE CREATIVITY

Most readings of the development of 'documentary cinema' give the impression of a single movement with a unitary purpose. This was a myth that Grierson needed to promote and, and in many ways he was successful. While there were artistic schisms and the diverse ownership of production significantly influenced output, he succeeded extraordinarily well in establishing that 'corporate outlook' that was so central to his vision. And he did so precisely through a corporate organisation of production. He was able to persuade both commercial and public sector corporations to sponsor films 'in the national interest', while the films he produced presented a consistent image of the state being 'run as though it were a large corporation with a board of directors . . . a technocratic elite'.[33]

In 1927, Grierson returned to Britain on a personal mission to develop the documentary idea as a means of promoting national morale in the face of looming economic depression. Joining the newly-formed Empire Marketing Board [hereafter EMB], a government agency set up to encourage trade and circulation of foodstuffs within the British dominions, he recognised in its slogan, 'to bring the Empire alive', common ground between the government and himself: both were in the business of 'simplifying and dramatizing the concerns of citizenship'[34]. After struggles to convince the EMB of the educative value of film, and aided by the success of his film *Drifters* (1929) which it eventually funded, in 1930 he persuaded the Board to create a Film Unit with him as director.[35] Yet of the thousands of films that Grierson produced or contributed to creatively, *Drifters* was the only one that he himself wholly scripted, produced, filmed, directed and edited (he also worked as cameraman on *Granton Trawler* (1934)). Thereafter, as 'creative organizer'[36] he concentrated on developing the EMB Film Unit and its successors by recruiting budding film-makers of high intellectual calibre who became the mainstay of the British documentary tradition.[37] This team remained with him after the Unit folded in 1933 and he joined the General Post Office [GPO], forming, in turn, the GPO Film Unit, which after 1939 – and after Grierson had departed for Canada – became the Crown Film Unit of the Ministry of Information. The documentary 'movement's' boundaries were permeable and stretched at points to include the Shell Film Unit, Films of Scotland, and independent units working for a range of sponsors, such as the Realist Film Unit and Strand Film Company.

By drawing together a range of artistic styles and strategies, Grierson effectively created the myth of a movement.[38] But he also had an extraordinarily synthetic capacity to move, in Bourdieusian terms, between the cultural field of film-making, the economic one of his sponsors and the social/political field of government. By imposing rules of permissibility, he enabled directors to develop their aesthetic techniques while adhering to sponsors' requirements and, crucially, making films that promulgated his corporatist vision. As his colleague Basil Wright said: 'What he was getting was people who wanted to use film for purposes of aesthetic experiment, avant garde and whatnot. And he said, "Okay, I'll let you do this within a discipline. The discipline is that you are spending public money and you are working towards a sociological purpose".'[39] In the GPO period, for example, while *Pett and Pott: A Fairy Story of the Suburbs* (1934) was ostensibly made to advertise the telephone, it provided a vehicle for Cavalcanti's experiment in novel uses of sound and vision. More famously, the modernist *Night Mail* (1936) commissioned a poem by W. H. Auden, set to the rhythms of the post-train and music written by Benjamin Britten. *The Face of Britain* (1935), funded by the Central Electricity Board, depicted the dire effects of industrialisation upon the living and working conditions of working people.

Arguably, Grierson's democratic social philosophy was compromised by this furtherance of a corporatist model to deliver the state's message to its people, although he saw no inconsistency here, since in his Hegelian view both capitalism and the citizenry should serve the state. Indeed, his genius as a cultural intermediary lay in the brokerage of relationships between the creative personnel with whom he made films and his sponsors.[40] For

Grierson, these films were fruits of 'the original documentary thesis – that people needed a sense and understanding of their participation in the total activities of the state'.[41] He was thus in the business of attempting to transform the public sphere: in a Habermasian sense, documentary film was an aesthetic form of communicative action designed to shape public knowledge of social issues.[42] Here lie striking similarities with John Reith, pioneering Director-General of the BBC during the same era. Reith also hailed from a Scottish Presbyterian background, blazing an evangelical trail in the institutionalisation of a visual medium, in his case television broadcasting. Both men succeeded in incorporating non-commercial production and output within public service organisations, such that 'independence came to mean dependence on the state as a way of ensuring independence from commerce'.[43] Documentary cinema and broadcast news were lifted above the level of 'mere' entertainment and given an authoritative morality, but at the price of losing their autonomy from government. Such were the contradictions of 'independent' public-service media. The representation of national identity, its history and its potential, was accordingly shaped by the projection of an overly optimistic, yet gradualist vision in which consensus prevailed.[44] For some critics this has seriously devalued his work:

> Grierson continued to depend on an unrealistic utopian model of the relationship between documentary and the State, which he had derived from philosophical idealism, and which was incompatible with existing political circumstances . . . [and] led to the production of documentary films which were of minimal critical value . . . His theory of documentary film also implied a centralized hierarchical practice of social ideology production, in which social communication was passed down . . . to the public, and never vice-versa . . . Beneath the rhetoric of 'democracy' there was an underlying rhetoric, of a self-perpetuating bureaucratic elite.[45]

At worst, this has led to claims of 'right-wing money, left-wing kudos and films of dubious social worth in the middle'.[46]

Were these films simply public information shorts, we might leave matters there. But documentary was emphatically more than this, not just because of its arguably privileged 'independent' locus, but also because of how it interwove Grierson's sociological objectives with a particular communicative style. 'Social worth' is not the issue, albeit that it was Grierson's avowed aim. Indeed, to focus on the political impact of documentary, whether in terms of ideology, audience effect or social policy, is to miss the critical point that, at best, Grierson created a wholly new way of seeing society. It is proper that his output be seen in a production-of-culture context, but a fuller sociological evaluation requires investigation of his pioneering approach to documentary as a medium.

'THE CREATIVE TREATMENT OF ACTUALITY'

Grierson's dramatic method positioned itself fervently against popular theatrical tradition. This was in part because of a Calvinist aversion: 'Sin still, somehow, attached to play-acting . . . I was confirmed in cinema at six because it had nothing to do with the theatre.'[47] His vitriol was more specifically directed against the London West End stage, which he regarded as 'so effetely inbred and stupidly provincial that it can do our national publicity nothing but the greatest harm so long as we allow it to emasculate the method and manner of our films.'[48] The 'ordinary' that he wished to dramatise was very clearly not this: 'English literature, the English countryside, and the gentlemanly English life should be considered a gold mine for kinema exploitation. *I mean no such nonsense.*'[49] Hollywood entertainment films were similarly derided, although not so much for purveying a fantasy of life as for their individualist focus: 'we think of a world . . . in which the private problems and not the public problems of their lives are sorted out and solved . . . If the hero was a steel worker, did he ever make any steel? No, he was much too busy making love to the manager's daughter.'[50] Equally, documentary needed to provide more than factual information, what Grierson referred to as 'interest films of the old wheezy Cook's Tour variety'.[51] Crucially, it was to be about inserting drama into its portrayal of social life in order to convey the 'truth' hidden behind the facts.[52]

Grierson famously defined documentary as 'the creative treatment of actuality'.[53] Ever since the authenticity of documentary has been much debated. Clearly, his films were heavily constructionist, to the extent that there could be little, if any, 'actuality' remaining after 'creative treatment'.[54] It was never his aim to let the pictures tell their own story. Documentary film was not based on naïve realism, as were the interest films; rather, the dramatised narrative acted as a means of interpretation. While some critics regard this as duping his audience for the sake of getting a message across,[55] Grierson consistently pursued his Kantian line – the real was 'abstract and general', the phenomenal 'empirical and particular' – arguing that 'there is no such thing as truth until you have made it into a form. Truth is an interpretation, a perception'.[56] The specific role of the documentarian was to access the underlying meaning behind superficial appearances, albeit that this would mean using the phenomenal to understand it.[57] Images were thus used in a formalist, symbolic style to convey key themes.

It is possible to contend that Grierson was doing something more 'organic' than the fabrication implied by many. In his philosophy of rhetoric, Kenneth Burke develops the concept of the 'terministic screen' to explain the concatenation of symbols that together provide a lens via which the world makes sense.[58] Applied to film-making, Grierson's documentary method works with a similar representational steer. If 'actuality' is the raw footage from which a story is realised, it already carries within it the potential to become meaningful, that is, to be actualised. Doing this requires that the director have not just aesthetic, but also sociological insight in developing an holistic, gestalt-like 'treatment', one which forms a plausible grid of intelligibility 'that directs our attention and through which one sees reality'.[59] In this, Grierson followed Vertov's notion of 'film truth', the idea that by placing elements of actuality in a particular pattern, a deeper truth might be revealed than that initially visible to the observer. Through editing, Grierson felt enabled to deconstruct and rebuild reality: 'You are freed from the natural continuities of space and time and may build your images into any shape you please. You are only limited by the power of the spectator's mind to follow the inner significance of the continuity you choose [through] references which consciously or subconsciously build an attitude to the scene'.[60] He also adopted the Soviet use of montage to ensure dramatic tension in *Drifters*, a film first screened together with the British première of Eisenstein's *Battleship Potemkin* in 1929.[61]

Drifters was a prototype, designed to reveal 'the ardour and bravery of common labour'.[62] Through it, 'the ordinary person was made to realise, probably for the first time, that a herring on his plate was no mere accepted thing but the result of other men's physical toil and possibly courage'.[63] It was a pioneering attempt to use film to dramatise the workings of modern industry – in this case the Scottish East Coast herring fleet – in modernist fashion. In the first place, it sharply opposed Flaherty's 'obsession with the remote and primitive',[64] as in the pioneering salvage ethnography of *Nanook of the North* (1922), the Pacific Island docufiction *Moana: A Romance of the Golden Age* (1926) and the revelation of continuing hardships of traditional island life in *Man of Aran* (1934). The North Sea fishing was not that of Arctic Canada or Western Ireland, still less Samoa, and it differed precisely because of the technologies of modernity. The introductory sub-titles in the film read: 'The Herring fishing industry has changed. Its story was once an idyll of brown sails and village harbours – its story now is an epic of steel and steam. Fishermen still have their homes in the old time village, but they go down for each season to the labour of a modern industry'.[65]

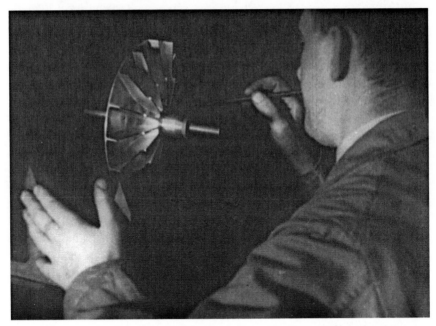

Fig. 3.1 Romance of the craftsman. Still from *Industrial Britain* (1931), directed by Robert Flaherty, produced and edited by John Grierson for the Empire Marketing Board.
© Post Office. Licensor www.scran.ac.uk

This said, Grierson borrowed several devices from Flaherty, for instance the use of non-professional actors to give a sense of authenticity and shooting on location.

By using narrative to structure 'actuality' Flaherty had provided a stylistic template.[66] However, while his stories purported simply to describe, Grierson's expository remarks – in this early, silent film subtitles rather than spoken word – always guided the viewer.[67] And whereas Flaherty's narrative method 'employed individual protagonists around whom to spin a web of episodic accounts of the struggle to survive, often in harsh environments',[68] Grierson felt that 'the really great use of cinema is in its capacity to tell the world in indirect propaganda the story of industrial organisations and communities', something best done by illustrating the processes involved.[69]

He was accordingly 'dismissive of what he described as Flaherty's emphasis on "man against the sky" in favour of films "of industrial and social function"'.[70] Grierson wanted to depict the epic of industry while acquainting people with their human role within it. Stylistically, this meant adopting the style of Soviet newsreels based on the rhythm of

Fig. 3.2 The epic of industry. Still from *Aero Engine* (1932), directed by Arthur Elton. Again made by the Empire Marketing Board when Grierson was head of the film unit. © Post Office. Licensor www.scran.ac.uk

machines to 'bring creative joy to all mechanical labour'.[71] Achieving a *sense* of the authentic was more important than replicating reality, thus by editing and synecdoche he used images of turbines, furnaces and workshops to represent the energy and vigour of the modern. Both epistemologically and substantively, it meant doing sociology rather than anthropology. On one level, this was about where one sought stories: 'Beware the ends of the earth and the exotic: the drama is on your doorstep wherever the slums are; wherever there is malnutrition, wherever there is exploitation and cruelty'.[72] More fundamentally, such direction reflected a political desire for informed citizenship:

> The basic force behind it was social not aesthetic. It was a desire to make a drama from the ordinary to set against the prevailing drama of the extraordinary: a desire to bring the citizen's eye in from the ends of the earth to the story, his own story, of what was happening under his nose. From this came our insistence on the drama of the doorstep. We were, I confess, sociologists, a little worried about the way the world was going . . . We were interested in all instruments which would crystallise sentiments in a muddled world and create a will toward civic participation.[73]

In the context of the Depression and given who his sponsors were it is no surprise that the documentaries of the 1930s should reflect a plea for national propaganda conjoined with a celebration of the machine age:

> We are the industrial pioneers of the world, we are the makers of steel, the builders of bridges, the shipwrights of the world' [but] 'We leave size to the Chicago and North-Western and the Santa Fé when we have a Cape to Cairo. We leave power to the United States Steel Trust when we have Beardmore's [biggest employer in the west of Scotland] and Dorman Long's and Vickers . . . We cannot be big for nothing, and it is for the English [sic] kinema to get down to the job of proclaiming our national show for what it is – and would be . . . nothing less will serve us at this very fateful period in our economic history.[74]

But, more profoundly, Grierson discerned a fractured sociological vision – he wanted to close the gap in understanding between man [sic] and modernity so that in place of alienation people would find self-awareness. Hence the observation that 'our imaginations are out of touch with the world we live in. My suggestion has been that we have lost contact with the actual, and because we have lost touch with the actual, we have lost the power of interpreting it'.[75] Yet, in rectifying this, it was one thing to claim that through 'films of man and his work . . . the vital interests of community are . . . marshalled and manoeuvred'[76], but quite another to regard such creative manipulation as somehow connecting with the class interests of his subjects.[77] On this disjunction would hang manifold subsequent critiques. While these recognise the constraining influence of the conditions under which the films were produced, arguably they underplay the *potential* unlocked through Grierson's insightful progression. In retrospect, he saw a clear trajectory:

> I always think of documentary as having certain fundamental chapters. The first chapter is of course the travelogue, that is, the discovery that the camera can go about: it's peripatetic. The second chapter is the discovery by Flaherty that you can make a film of people on the spot, that is, you can get an insight of a dramatic sort, a dramatic pattern, on the spot with living people. But of course he did that in respect of faraway peoples, and he was romantic in that sense. The third chapter is our chapter, which is the discovery of the working people, that is, the drama on the doorstep, the drama of the ordinary. But there is a fourth chapter . . . in which people began to talk not about making films *about* people but films *with* people. That was the beginning of *cinéma-vérité*, when people started going down and getting close to people . . . Flaherty didn't really know what was going on among the Aran Islanders; he was too distant from them. But when the people went down and made *Housing Problems* in Stepney, they knew the people, and you could recognize right away that this was a new relationship.[78]

And in this odyssey, Grierson saw himself as engaged in a 'battle for authenticity':

> Not so long ago, the materials of steel and smoke were not considered 'romantic' enough for pictures . . . Today, people find industry and the skills that reside within it, magical and exciting. But it was relatively easy to find beauty in the lives of fishermen and steel workers. Their dramatic atmosphere was ready-made. Documentary moved on to more difficult work when it proceeded to dramatize the daily activities of great organizations [and social problems] . . . describing not only industrial and commercial spectacle but social truth as well . . . These simple films went deeper . . . They showed the common man, not in the romance of his calling, but in the more complex and intimate drama of his citizenship.[79]

His vision was one where:

> It [cinema] would go down into the slums, to listen to the personal experiences of Mr Smith and Mrs Jones. They would talk about bugs and rats, about children and their illnesses, about cooking and living in one room, about washing in the backyard. They would talk in their vernacular straight to the microphone. It would be a revelation that would affect public judgment . . . direct, unedited use of camera and microphone . . . I would like to see the cinema describing people as well as machines: living conditions as well as production achievements. I want these unknown neighbours and lost communities about us to be given their voice.[80]

Here lies recognition that realism was insufficient and that films 'must *involve* the individual in the process of creating solidarity, in the interdependence of his society, in the "drama" of his citizenship'.[81] All of which sounded very noble, but most of which was not actually achieved, either because 'direct, unedited' footage was itself selective or because in its descriptive nature it failed to connect the threads of any such drama. In *Coal Face*, for example, we see 'close-up images of men's hands working with machinery, not [over] footage of the results. Pneumoconiosis is not mentioned'.[82] The working class may have been the heroes, but audiences rarely glimpsed 'the concrete facts of their lives – what they earn, how they live, or what they eat'.[83]

A Retreat from Meaning?

The claim that such work romanticised the worker, as Flaherty had made marginality sentimental, is difficult to dispute. Yet Grierson's motives in doing so are disputed. His more ardent critics argue that if the impetus was 'social not aesthetic', aesthetics nevertheless played the major role in shifting the viewer's attention from hard analysis of social problems to a superficial rhetorical gaze that *looked* revolutionary but ultimately justified reformist solutions. Brian Winston, for instance, contends that 'extending film's potential from imperial propaganda tool to instrument of domestic social engineering required nothing more than the provision of an aesthetic theory'.[84] That theory was a 'documentary realism' that enabled Grierson to retain his leftist credentials while promoting paternalism, and its associated method was one of concentrating on visible surfaces 'while managing to run from the social meaning of those surfaces'.[85]

To a degree, this conflicts with the views of Raymond Williams who saw in documentary the novel elicitation of 'structures of feeling' – not formal ideologies, but 'meanings and values as they are actively lived and felt'.[86] To the extent that the sociological imagination aims to develop 'the capacity to range from the most impersonal and remote transformations to the most intimate features of the human self – and to see the relations between the two',[87] Grierson formulates a dialectic by attempting to clarify 'the elements of contemporary uneasiness and indifference', but he does this by imputation, rather than by developing awareness directly *from* his subjects. He termed the documentary movement 'an adventure in public observation'. For Stuart Hall, it certainly heralded 'an innovatory "way of seeing"' in that:

> The documentary style was . . . an emergent form of social consciousness: it registered, in the formation of a social rhetoric, the emergent structure of feeling . . . Here we encounter that fateful nexus where there is a striking rendezvous between the subject-matter and content of historical experience, the revolutionary development of the means of production, and – in response – the evolving forms and styles of collective social perception.[88]

Yet, as with the innovatory style of its sibling, *Picture Post*, 'it pinpointed exploitation, misery and social abuse, but always in a language which defined these as "problems"'. Consequently, 'there is a rhetoric of change and improvement there, of people capable of resilience and courage. However, there isn't anywhere a language of dissent, opposition or revolt'.[89] Critics have focused on *Housing Problems* (1935), 'a typical product of the Grierson School in that its central concern is to inform the citizenry of their duties and to reassure them that their betters are aware of their needs'. As they continue, 'the film employs the Problem-Solution paradigm. In this instance, the problem is that of slum clearance and the solution is to demolish the old houses and to resettle the displaced communities in high rise flats'.[90]

Similarly, in *The Face of Britain* and *Industrial Britain*, Winston argues:

the slums are [thus]sandwiched between a wonderful past and a beautiful future . . . but [at] a moment . . . in the unfolding history of the nation, a moment that will pass – thanks to the electricity generating industry. This 'problem moment' structure allows for a social ill to be covered (permitting a radical reading of the final film) while at the same time denying that the ill has real causes and effects (permitting conservative funding for the film).[91]

Since sponsorship conditioned an optimistic view of social change that would have conflicted with informed social analysis, such analysis was elided. Nevertheless, Grierson's vision was all about imagined community. As Sir Stephen Tallents, a key enabler of the Griersonian project and leading establishment propagandist, recalled:

He was shocked at the meagre content of community life everywhere. Its enrichment depended, he thought, on a better understanding of the stuff of which it was compounded . . . 'Education', he was to say of the public . . . 'has given them facts but has not sufficiently given them faith.' It was necessary to touch the imaginations of the people . . . and their imaginations could best be touched by eliciting and presenting to them in dramatized form the exciting material which he found in the real life around him.[92]

And faith, of course, lay in the evidence of things unseen.

There is elegant plausibility in Winston's critique, and much may be true, but the conclusion that so much 1930s documentary was thereby 'impotent social observation' misses a crucial point.[93] Winston contends that because the slums were photographed to make them appear 'exotic and strange', and 'industry became a site of high-contrast drama between light and shade, not a place of hazard and alienation . . . the dehumanising quality of industrial life was never captured'.[94] We are at cross-purposes here about who is alienated from what. In Grierson's repudiation of individualism in cinema, personal alienation through the workplace and social conditions of industrial society may not have been portrayed; indeed, he was later to remark that he had been interested in 'making industry not ugly for people, but a matter of beauty, so that people would accept their industrial selves'.[95] Instead, his aim was to remedy the estrangement between the generically conceived individual and government, hence the 'drama of his citizenship'. This was where he saw agency mattering.

Grierson certainly acknowledged that his director would edit a sequence by using 'every trick he knows to sensationalise it . . . the best cue is tattoo or organised spectacle'.[96] But his objective was not to dramatise for its own sake; rather, he sought a *relational* perspective whereby the connections between people and machines, people and people, even – if nebulously – people and politics, could be elaborated so as to reveal the sensibility of the modern age. Like Picasso, whose work he admired and which he saw as broadly misunderstood, he was fragmenting images and repositioning the elements to suggest different ways of looking. The resultant picture suggested a logic 'in which we become less object-minded and less person-minded and more relation-minded'.[97] It was not so much about understanding where people stood now, but where they might otherwise be if only his utopian ideals of government could be realised so they would fit dutifully into place in the 'new order'. With hindsight this perspective has produced some startling contradictions, as, for instance, in *Housing Problems* where 'the deep communality of working class life' is very briefly glimpsed as people relax and play in alleyways. Since the sociologist would now recognise that it is precisely such informal bonds that the planners subsequently destroyed, MacLennan and Hookham contend that this disjunction exposes just how 'the working class subjects in the film are by and large deprived of any sense of agency. Their historical fate is to be acted on by experts following a period of surveillance. Their task is to be grateful'. And, more generally: 'There was a place for everyone and everyone was to be in their place. The role of film was to explain both to the postal worker, etc. and the rest of the nation how she fitted into the grand scheme of things'.[98] Yet, in advance of the solutions adopted in pursuit of a welfarist Postwar state, these ameliorist conceptions of British society must have appeared visionary. Whether this somewhat paternalist trait condemns Grierson as propagandist ideologue of the knowledge class (Hartley) or, conversely, provides evidence of his 'superb demotic style' (Williams), we are back to the inherent idealism of his sociological imagination.[99]

Because Grierson embraced a Hegelian concept of the state, his picture of society is especially suited to being characterised as a social imaginary. Certainly, a broad-brush, emblematic approach to social interpretation and integration at the level of the nation was eminently suited to the task that befell Grierson and his colleagues at the end of the Thirties. After 'ten years of government service', Grierson left the GPO Film Unit in 1937, having set up Film Centre, a consultancy which, 'made investigations and prepared reports for any group interested in the use of documentary films'.[100] Here his key project was the Films of Scotland series.

FILMS OF SCOTLAND

As Scotland began to recover from the Depression and war loomed large in Europe, plans to promote economic resurgence with a symbolic show of national enterprise came to fruition with the international

Empire Exhibition held at Bellahouston Park, Glasgow between May and December 1938. Attracting over 12 million visitors to its hundred-plus sites, palaces and pavilions, the Exhibition sits chronologically mid-way between Glasgow's two other grand expositions, the International Exhibition of Science, Art and Industry of 1888 and the Glasgow Garden Festival of 1988.[101] In promoting the nation its role was educational; and most significantly, it was Scots themselves who were to be educated. In a Foucauldian sense, 'the public not only bec[a]me subjects of knowledge but [were] themselves part of the spectacle'.[102] Here was 'a model lesson in civics in which a public regulated itself through self-observation'.[103] Such internalisation of the national story, recognising the social as the canvas for its governmentality, was certainly an objective of the films screened at the Empire Exhibition, the documentaries comprising the first Films of Scotland series.

The conventional understanding of how these films came to be part of the Exhibition is characterised by a late-dawning discovery:

> though a fine film theater had been built as a national showcase, suddenly it was realized [in 1937] that there was a dearth of Scottish material on film, apart from what Grierson had done at the EMB and GPO and the romanticisms of English and American feature studios. To compensate for this lack, a Films of Scotland Committee was hurriedly formed by the Scottish Development Council . . . Grierson drew up a programme of seven films which were to describe 'in vivid summary,' as Hardy wrote of them, 'the country's character and traditions.'[104]

While the matter may have been urgent, the Secretary of State for Scotland, Walter Elliot, had already been active in developing the EMB's use of film, sitting in on the making of scripts and bringing 'his dashing imagination to the service of the producer'.[105] Films of Scotland was thus part of a corporate, statist initiative to make films in the national interest, and, though he liked to think of himself as something of a socialist rebel, Grierson's collaboration with the Tory Secretary of State was as pro-establishment as it was propagandist. This is not to say, however, that his endeavour was not revolutionary. The seven films have been rightfully applauded as, 'constituting the first attempt in the history of film to give a coherent account of a nation' and giving 'a unique and remarkably comprehensive record of a country's achievement and outlook'[106]. For this alone they commend themselves to our analysis, not least as creative constructs imbued with definite ideological and stylistic aims.

Since contemporary audience research does not exist, the impact of these films upon the national consciousness remains unknown. After the Empire Exhibition, the Films of Scotland series was taken to the New

York World Fair (1939), where, however, the British Council halted its showing, claiming that the films did not provide 'a sufficiently ceremonial or picturesque presentation of life in Britain'.[107] Grierson eschewed such spectacle, condemning this as characteristic of Nazi cinema's 'highfalutin parades against the skyline'.[108] His was a different style of propaganda, with – as we have seen – another prospect in mind: neither Riefenstahl's glorification, nor Flaherty's exotic 'man against the sky', but 'a real horizon . . . of world affairs'.[109] Meanwhile, according to Hardy, altogether these seven films had 4,725 showings to an estimated total British audience of 22,491,000 between 1938 and 1954.[110] This, however, was largely attributable to the fact that they were regularly screened as 'quota quickies' – shown because cinemas were then obliged by law to project a percentage of home-made films. Winston asserts that 'despite the rhetoric, the public effect of documentaries was largely insignificant'.[111] Furthermore, since the media only construct what Habermas calls a 'pseudo-public sphere' they allow scant latitude for audience disagreement or response.[112] Nevertheless, there was much commentary on radio and in the press about these films, and, perhaps more importantly, there was what Grierson termed 'the "hang-over" effect' or lingering impression.[113]

In one sense, popular reception is immaterial. My contention here is that while media and cultural studies hold a place for Grierson as massively influential in the development of documentary cinema and by extension television, and he is remembered particularly for *Drifters* and *Night Mail*, these little-known Scottish films produced at the end of his most significant decade are worthy of analysis because they demonstrate how, for the first time in the history of the genre, a team of producers, directors and scriptwriters attempted to construct a plausible account of nationhood. In their realisation of Grierson's sociological understanding of the role of film in projecting a vision of the social, the Films of Scotland series was remarkably 'the fullest documented account of a country's life and achievement then in evidence'.[114]

Grierson quickly conceived a timely rhetoric to support the venture:

> The problem seemed especially important to the Scot in 1938. Never before had he so needed to summon up his strength of character and remember his traditions. No country was more badly hit by the economic changes between the wars . . . The shipping of men was our speciality, and for the first time probably in Scotland's history the younger generation had of necessity to look at its own country and see what could be done about it . . . A first duty was the articulation of Scottish problems to the Scot and the firing of his mind and heart to the need of his generation . . . to interpret, and, where possible, dramatize the growing points in Scottish life . . . using the cinema to maintain the national will.[115]

At last, by means of 'a powerful medium which can give a country an imaginative sense of itself', popular representation could move beyond the Kailyard: 'the music-hall tradition of kilties and comics ha[d] been all too eagerly served'; now 'the intention was to make Scotland's very problems – which stemmed mainly from the legacy of nineteenth-century industrialism – exciting'.[116] 'Realist' in manner, yet utopian in perspective, Grierson felt that as well as celebrating Scottish life and achievement these films should work 'so that Scotsmen themselves might learn a little more of what was happening under the surface of national life'.[117] Their titles give some sense of common thematic coverage: *The Face of Scotland* contemplated the role played in national affairs by the character of the Scots people from the Roman invasion to the present day; *Wealth of a Nation* contrasted the heavy industrial past based on the country's rich resources with a clean, planned future; *They Made the Land*, while stressing the historic struggle to bring the land into agricultural use, also considered new scientific techniques in animal breeding; likewise, *Sea Food* was about traditional resources yoked to modern methods, this time in the fisheries; *The Children's Story* proudly addressed Scottish educational traditions but also showed applied training for young adults in typing and printing; *Scotland for Fitness* was a campaigning health promotion film focused on outdoor activities for all; and *Sport in Scotland*, while emphasising the significance of sport to the country by ranging from grouse moors to Hampden Park, featured how facilities were being developed to 'span the qualities of hardihood and skill, tempered with toughness' that, again, exemplified the Scots' character. In each, the historical combination of natural resources and human ingenuity is revered while a strong message of continuity shapes the development of a brighter future. This was the mission of 'the documentary men, whose vision has sought to go beyond party politics to a deeper sort of national story . . . passing from the negative to the positive'.[118]

These films were, of course, fundamentally concerned with interpreting and moulding the social. In the only detailed study to date, Richard Butt provides a persuasive analysis of the work of Films of Scotland as part of a formative educational strategy.[119] He argues that the mediated public sphere was one that informed people about national problems and how to manage them by getting beneath the surface of events to the 'growing points' of 'what was going on'. But, of course, this required an interpretative steer: these documentaries did not just aim to represent the nation, they tried to expand the public sphere through an enhanced conception of citizenship, while, at the same time extending the reach of government. In *Wealth of a Nation*, for example, during a sequence that shifts from exteriors of factories to 'Sir Henry (?) and others [a professor and a civil servant] at meeting concerning the economy', then to the Offices of the Scottish Development Council, the viewer is granted access to the private speech of politicians and technocrats, before the film cuts to general views of typists, then to plans for the site of an industrial estate. As in any modern democracy, education is central to the production of a shared national culture,[120] and the voiceover of *The Children's Story* expresses the clear connection to citizenship:

> a revolution is taking place, teachers are discovering new ways to prepare their children for citizenship in the modern world . . . This is the Scotland of the future, a Scotland that is turning from the academic brains of the past, a Scotland bent on exploring to the full all the possibilities of life . . . looking to the needs of their own country, to the needs of citizens who will take part in the government of modern Scotland.

In these films, education is also 'explicitly concerned with transforming public cultural practice'. In *Scotland for Fitness* one sequence focuses on Mr Barr the hill walker, who, notes Butt, 'is no Romantic':

> His solitary hill walking belongs to a middle class aesthetic that is both rational and reflexive. His engagement with the landscape lacks the idealisation of the experience of involvement that . . . lay at the heart of . . . the theory of the Sublime . . . Hill walking produces rational knowledge about Scotland . . . Sir Ian [Colquhoun, Chairman of the Fitness Council] states this explicitly: 'In this room is a map of Scotland, mountain, loch and glen, we want to get you to know that country, and what is equally important, get to know the people who dwell there, and understand their point of view'.[121]

As Butt avers, a key function of the 1938 documentaries was to inculcate ideas of community, belonging and participation. Yet this was membership of a selective version of the nation, a collectivity whose coherence could only be assured by the imaginative re-working of memory and tradition to fit the purposes of the present. This particular 'creative treatment of actuality' becomes most evident in *The Face of Scotland*.

THE NATION IN FILM

The Face of Scotland was directed by Basil Wright, who also wrote the commentary, and produced by John Grierson, who narrated a brief section of the film.[122] In thirteen short minutes it distils what Grierson, in Hegelian mode, would regard as the spirit of the nation. As Schlesinger avers, it exhibits 'the special role of cultural producers as active constructors of national identity'. By focusing on 'the role of cultural institutions and practices through which the chain of identity between past and present is forged', a mythical national identity, 'mediated by the continual, selective reconstitution of "traditions" and of "social memory"', is portrayed.[123] The following analysis reveals how visual and spoken narratives are woven together to develop this identification:

Shotlist[124]: Credits (.56 [minutes]) gvs [general views of] Borders landscape, Cheviot Hills and shot of a Roman [Hadrian's] wall (1.49).

Narrator[125]: [Voice of Roman soldier] "'Our advanced guards were met with a widespread and desolate silence" . . . It stands there to this day, a confession that there was one land, at least, they were not to conquer'.

Comment: the silent desolation at the border suggests an unyielding place of unknown character. For Butt, the wall remains as 'both testimony to the threat of invasion and as evidence of its repulsion'.[126] It is a symbolic boundary, but one that also reflects continuity between past and present.

Shotlist: Highland scenery (2.25) shot of stones weighing down heather roof thatch. Peat turf (2.34). A farmer feeding a lamb, cattle grazing, general views of men cutting and stacking peat (3.32).

Narrator: 'It offered to its inhabitants only a meagre living . . . The land that bred a stern and hardy race, toughened by the struggle for existence on its ungrateful soil'.

Comment: the tenacity and stoicism of the Scots is portayed as arising organically from the grim, centuries-long struggle to eke out an existence from this unyielding, hostile landscape.[127] Interestingly, there is no suggestion that much of the Scottish 'wilderness' was man-made as a result of overexploitation, population clearance and non-sustainable land use policies; rather, the present-day condition of the remoter fastnesses is assumed have been a pre-existing habitat.

Shotlist: shots of Stirling and Edinburgh castles (4.08).

Narrator: 'Across its landscape rose many castles and keeps . . . They stand there still today, [ruins] which yet bear manifestations of having been places of strength and terror'.

Comment: such strength of character is seen as having been necessary to the defence of their 'wee bit hill and glen' as feuds raged, particularly with the English. Like Hadrian's Wall, these monuments again testify to continuity between past and present; they represent symbolic lieux de mémoire.

Shotlist: blackhouses and a new house (4.30) gvs [general views of] crofters at work, ploughing, etc (4.49) village church as people enter yard (5.08) statue of John Knox (5.19) ext[erior of] village school (5.39).

Fig. 3.3 Self-sustaining communities who 'made their own culture'. Still from *The Face of Scotland* (1938), produced by Grierson's Film Centre. © Post Office. Licensor www.scran.ac.uk

Narrator: 'the people of this land made for themselves a simple but individual civilization. Their communities were very small, for they were limited by the fertility of the land. The binding factor in these communities was the family . . . they made their own . . . culture. From these people came Robert Burns, and it was their life that he celebrated: "To make a happy fireside chime/ To weans and wife/ That's the pathos and sublime/ Of human life".'

Comment: more ecological determinism. The egalitarianism necessary for survival in small, self-sustaining communities predisposes them to a domestic, familial form of culture, hence the celebration, when transposed to the wider imagined community, of Burns as the people's poet *qua* national bard.

Shotlist: brief shot of fishing village, shots of church (5.45) city church steeple (5.50) int. church, congregation sing hymns. Woman playing the organ as boy works bellows (6.35).

Narrator: 'Their forthright nature demanded a religion which allowed for a personal relationship between God and man . . . This Calvinist creed became famous for its strictness' but also gave us the 'grace and simplicity of the metrical psalms'.

Comment: the Reformation is read as a necessity, as though only Presbyterianism could satisfy the Scottish character. The disciplinary rule of the kirk sessions is considered firm but ubiquitous.

Shotlist: Boy doing his homework (6.45) Landscape (6.55) shot inside classroom during lesson. Gvs [general views of] streets in Ecclefechan, birthplace of Thomas Carlyle (7.11) St. Salvator's College in St. Andrews [Error: Marischal College, Aberdeen] and Edinburgh Old College (7.26) inside lecture hall during a lecture.

Narrator: 'Perhaps Scotland's most important debt to the Church is her educational system. John Knox's *Book of Discipline*, codified in 1560, and the constant energy and initiative of the kirk sessions, instituted a nationwide system of parish and grammar schools . . . These schools gave equal instruction to the children of rich and poor alike . . . from the smallest and the most obscure villages came the constant stream of young men to the great Scots universities.'

Comment: The historical treatment is specific here, lending factual and scholarly weight in support of the defining myths of Scottish egalitarianism and the 'democratic intellect'.

Shotlist: Student in candlelit attic room studying.

Narrator: 'The tradition here, like that of the crofts from which they came, was one of hard and ceaseless toil. Many starved their bodies to feed their minds. They studied through long winter nights in fireless, unfurnished, dimly-lit garrets.'

Comment: The dialectic between communitarian ethos and individual determination finds personification in the lad o' pairts, whose character serves him well in the struggle against hardship. This gritty aptitude is seen to have emerged ancestrally and organically from the battle to tame the land.

Shotlist: Back to lecture room (7.45) student at window overlooking the Old Quad, Edinburgh (7.50) statue of Sir Walter Scott at the base of his monument in Edinburgh (7.54) shots inside operating theatre (8.02).

Narrator: 'The qualifications for success were not means and money, but brains and industry. Thus Scotland bred great philosophers, like Reid and Hume, poets like Dunbar, writers like Scott and Stevenson, Lister, who established the principles of antisepsis, and a legion of others.'

Comment: In turn, the lad o'pairts becomes the enterprising Scot, intellect and application reflected in great thoughts, writing and invention. The pivotal connection between pre-modern and modern Scotland lies in the use of the word 'industry' to capture both the diligence and drive of these individuals and – as we are about to see – the mushrooming transformation of the industrial revolution.

Shotlist: model of Watt's rotary steam engine, followed by shots of various liners built on the Clyde. Int. steel workshop and steel works (8.53) drawing of an old village, a factory chimney (9.08) shipyard workers leave yard. Long shot over rooftops to industrial landscape (9.17).

Narrator: 'At the end of the eighteenth century, James Watt of Greenock perfected the rotary steam engine, and so released the mineral wealth of the central area of Scotland . . . Round the Clyde thundered the new industries . . . the face of the country was utterly changed'.

Comment: the arrow of causation points directly at Scots inventors, particularly Watt, as catalysts. Thus, although the shift, both factually and visually, is abrupt, there is again continuity in the determining characteristics.

Shotlist: shot of a ruined blackhouse (9.23).

Narrator: 'But these people, crowded together in the smoke and sound of the drumming factories, were of the same stock as the crofters . . . Behind every Glasgow family, they say, you will find a croft, a farm or a fishing village. The Scottish industrial workers still had the best qualities of the peasants – the same hardihood, the same ability. They were inventors, they made new things . . . In engineering shop and shipyard they bred great craftsmen.'

Comment: the people may have migrated from rural self-sufficient communities to the urban central belt, and in so doing become wage slaves, but they have passed down through generations their age-old peasant qualities. And it remains these to which Scotland's success may be attributed. Despite Grierson's fear of modernity begetting alienation, the social transformation of Scottish society appears not to have restricted the outlets for communally-built resourcefulness. In this reading, people had never lost touch with 'the actual'.

Shotlist: East end of Princes Street, Edinburgh (9.25) shots inside St. Vincent Bar, Edinburgh, as men drink, discuss football and play dominoes, i/c [intercut] with shots of ruined crofts and blackhouses (9.57).

Comment: Butt remarks that 'while the contrast between rural past and urban present seems absolute, the narration argues otherwise'. Moreover, 'the effect of dissolving, rather than cutting, between the images of the croft ruins and the men in the pub is to assert a continuity between the two sets of images'.[128] Repetition of the ruined blackhouse image, juxtaposed, sometimes simultaneously, with shots of contemporary urban sociability (the pub), then work scenes (the factory), is used both to accentuate the pastness of a lost way of life and to enfold the memory of such within the sensibility of the present. The silenced, remote but foundational stone voices of belonging persist in the chatter and smoke of the busy here-and-now.

Shotlist: riveters at work (10.05) int. steel works (10.28) half-moon battery, Edinburgh Castle, as the one o'clock gun salute is fired. Long shot across Princes

Fig. 3.4 'The character of the Scottish race.' Still from *The Face of Scotland* (1938). © Post Office. Licensor www.scran.ac.uk

Street from Castle (10.40) pipes and drums (11.00) Lone piper, dressed in rags, marches along the top of the trenches in World War I. Brief shot of men in trenches and of artillery fire (11.10) memorial and shrine at Edinburgh Castle (11.45) Scottish lion rampant flying from flagpole (11.52).

Narrator: 'many of the soldiers who marched away behind the pipes and drums were the engineers, the riveters, the puddlers, the miners. They carried with them . . . the fighting traditions of Bruce and Wallace.'

Comment: an interesting return to the military trope in order to connect the apparent ordinariness of the workplace to a more heroic sense of patriotic masculinity. Again, this is regarded as historically inbred.

Shotlist: United Airways aircraft [G-ACAN] as it takes off from airport (11.59) hydro-electric power station (12.07) shots of a football crowd, c/u [close-up] and crowd scenes (12.55) pan over rooftops of Edinburgh and up to the castle (13.12) ecs [end credits] (13.19).

Narrator: 'Whatever the future holds, Scotland may face it boldly, for her greatest asset is to be reckoned not in terms of money and banks or capital investments in plant and machinery but in the character of her people. So today, in the roar of a Glasgow football crowd, you may well observe the vigour and the enthusiasm, the ambition and the unconquerable determination of the Scottish race. Today they are the same race of whom, nearly 500 years ago, the historian Hollinshed spoke: "Thereunto we find them to be courageous and hardy, offering themselves often unto the uttermost perils with great assurance, so that a man may pronounce nothing to be over-hard, or past their power to perform.'"

Comment: As Butt notes, in the 23 shots of the football match only four show the action on the pitch:

the focus of the camera's interest is not the match itself . . . and only local knowledge allows identification of the teams as they are not specified in the narration. The focus of the camera is the crowd, shot the majority of the time in close up, because, as the narration explicitly states, in the crowd can be seen the 'character' 'of the Scottish race'. This, finally, is 'The Face of Scotland'.[129]

The film concludes with the key point, given the Empire Exhibition context, that Scotland's wealth lies not with capital but with her people (intriguingly, there is no mention here of abundant natural resources). It is not the means of production, nor simply labour that matters, but the applied qualities – resourcefulness – of the labour force. The visual shift from football crowd, to houses, to castle reiterates the continuity between popular pastime, domestic life and proud patriotism.

Throughout, the message is carried by singularly masculine imagery, beginning and ending with shots of military defences, interlaced with stories of battle, toil on the land, science and engineering, industrial muscle, football. While it needs to be remembered that the film was made in 1938, in the run-up to war when patriotism was being rallied for the coming military struggle, and in a largely pre-feminist era when popular appeals to common identity stressed the bonds of the 'common man', nevertheless the specific qualities of the 'Scottish race' – dourness, determination, strength in adversity – are also those associated with male rather than female stereotypes. This nationalism, where 'stock' 'repeats elision of the difference between race, nationality and culture', is firmly of the ethnic variety, its blood-and-soil patriotism serving the 'national interest' of the period rather than attempting to deal with the complicating fact that 'by the time Scotland could be classed as a nation it was composed of five distinct ethnic groups'.[130] As with the reticence to broach internal boundaries of class, region or religion, the script authoritatively occludes such difference. Meanwhile, the emphasis on external boundaries, emphasised by the opening scenes of Hadrian's Wall, sets up Scotland as 'an object of knowledge approached from the outside'.[131] The contemporary traveller, like the Roman legionary, is initially 'met with a widespread, desolate silence', a mysterious country that is subsequently made explicable but which always remains apart in its home-grown distinctiveness.[132]

While Butt's analysis is closely perceptive, particularly in its interpretation of how continuity of 'character' is maintained, this racial nationalism, based not on pre-ordained ascription but upon an achieved identity arising from the functional interaction between human beings and the landscape, underpins a conception of social identity that is simultaneously broader than itself, in that it applies to Scottish institutions and an understanding of the origins of modernity, and narrower, since it embraces only a handful of ingredients. Thus the struggle with the land conditions the domestic democracy of an idealised egalitarian community, which in turn enables the distinctive features of the Presbyterian kirk and educational systems, from which emerge the lad o' pairts and the enterprising Scot. Needless to say, this organicist background is used to explain the social democratic vision of Great Men – inventors, missionaries, philosophers, writers, industrialists, politicians, broadcasters; Carnegie, Keir Hardie, Reith and, of course, by extension Grierson. In this sense, it is downright patrician too. Yet this summary figuration of Scottish national identity does not map neatly onto Grierson's personal rationale, for although he may be regarded as a quintessential lad o'pairts, he held, as we have seen, fundamental reservations about the idea. More significantly, the whole logic of the film appears to contradict the basis of the Lippmannite position he so fully espoused, for here perduring local community and its familial values are the very microcosm of an imagined national community, the fulcrum of continuity rather than the displaced traditional antithesis of effective modern communication. *The Face of Scotland* reveals the function of historical representation: signs of nationhood emerge from the encounter with landscape; meaning is somehow wrought from contingency, legend supplants history.[133]

This is the route back from alienation, but it leaves us a long way yet from the ideal speech of a participatory democracy. Compared to Flaherty's 'close-up portrait of a group of people, remotely located but familiar in their humanity', Griersonian documentary 'dealt with impersonal social processes'.[134] In adopting the view that 'it is only through the State that the person and the will of the person can be greatly expressed',[135] Grierson pursued a formalist approach in which narrative, being empirical and 'phenomenal', was simply a vehicle for signalling abstract, general meaning. In his films, it was the narrator or the 'commentary' that spoke, with occasional subtitles and 'types' rather than ordinary people glimpsed in cameos. The rare footage of everyday conversation, for example the scenes in the pub in *The Face of Scotland* where men discuss football, convey only that 'stilted camaraderie [which] was to become an important trope in the wartime propaganda output – a way for a class-ridden and historically divided society to be portrayed as "one nation"'.[136]

By 1939, 'the British documentary movement had reached the climax of its development as an influence on the British cultural and political scene'.[137] The previous year, Grierson had sailed for Canada where he had been appointed Consultant to the government, and where he was to create the National Film Board. He later returned to Britain, remaining actively influential until his death in 1972. The original Films of Scotland series was still showing in cinemas in 1954, while the next year a second Films of Scotland Committee was set up ostensibly 'to sell a big story about a small country in a new and exciting way'.[138] Together, the two Commmittees produced 168 films on Scottish life between 1938 and 1982. However, though an independent public relations machine promoting Scotland abroad and to its own people, the second Committee essentially existed to advertise those industries, local authorities and national organisations that sponsored individual films.[139] On occasion Grierson himself was involved, as in the early 1960s when he wrote treatments for *The Heart of Scotland*, a documentary about the history and industries of his home area, sponsored by Stirlingshire County Council, and *Seawards the Great Ships*, a tribute to shipbuilding on the Clyde and the first Scottish film to win an Oscar.[140] Films of Scotland forms a link in the chain of visualisation that was to become 'Scotland the Brand', but that is for the most part another story from a different era, as indeed is the history of Scottish film during the second half of the twentieth century.

CONCLUSION

As Tudor avers, John Grierson was 'the first major exponent of a socially derived theory of film . . . centring his aesthetic on a morality of social responsibility'[141]. That aesthetic was primarily one of symbolic expression,[142] a poetic perspective designed to reveal the interdependence of social relationships, albeit in impressionistic ways that caught the imputed spirit of the age rather than its precise mechanics.

Griersonian documentary drew on many influences. Because of the 'profound, if unacknowledged, effect on his rhetorical positions' of nineteenth-century French realism – 'from working methods (the flight from the studio) to subject matter (the working class); from purpose (public education and social agitation) to justification (the artist as a political actor)' – Grierson has been styled a 'latter-day Courbet'.[143] French impressionism, then Flaherty, Strand and German expressionist cinema, taught his group that documentary could not be journalistic but must seek ways to penetrate beneath the surface of things.[144] The stylistic innovations of Soviet cinema, particularly Eisenstein's use of montage and Vertov's notion that fragments of actuality which, 'when organized together, have a deeper truth that cannot be seen with the naked eye', but also Pudovkin's assertion of the resilience of the individual, and Dovzhenko's portrayal of the modernisation of rural life, were seminal. There was also a 'sociological purpose' shared with British writers Orwell and Priestley and expressed in 'the desire to break through the crust of tradition and inherited social-sightlessness which had kept the greater half of Britain such a well-guarded secret from the other, lesser but more powerful half'.[145] Nevertheless, Grierson was never backward in singing the praises of his own group. In a review of an exhibition of Picasso's works, he remarked that the artist was 'part of the revolution in expression . . . [however] In my own documentary medium, I have seen the old-time conception of the object and the person broken up much more drastically in time and space, and I confess I do not think Picasso's aesthetic is as new or far-reaching as Paul Rotha's or Stuart Legg's'.[146]

While the Griersonian development of documentary film was profound, it owed most to Grierson's own intellectual formation in striving to connect philosophical idealism with a sense of social duty. In this, his progenitors were Kant, Hegel and Calvin. He was certainly no naïve realist, for his vision depended not upon observation but interpretation. Firstly, following Kant's critical distinction between how things are in and of themselves (noumena) and how they appear to us (phenomena), Grierson argued that 'the only reality which counts in the end is the interpretation which is profound',[147] that 'truth', being about perception, does not inhere in concrete, everyday experience but in an abstract, all-encompassing understanding.[148] 'We affirm the right,' he said, 'to a transcendental view point in which *attitudes to the real* determine its continuity.'[149] Thus, to re-iterate: documentary required the 'creative treatment of actuality', in part through the 'subordination of naturalistic verisimilitude to symbolic expression'.[150] Secondly, such expression codified a set of historically determined, and determining, ethics. Here Grierson was straightforwardly Hegelian, while himself a product of his time, following the Glasgow University school of Edward Caird and A.D. Lindsay, both in their idealist metaphysics and in their politics, Caird being a Victorian progressive liberal and Lindsay a Christian socialist. He wanted to express the industrial essence of the age, an aim that meant acknowledging that 'our knowledge of objects will be imperfect except when we recognize that they are only partial aspects of the ideal whole',[151] and most significantly that personal character could only be meaningfully realised as an embodiment of the state (or, in Scotland, the nation). In this, he clearly rejected the Victorian individualist sensibility in favour of 'an approach that emphasised social purpose and the political role of the artist'.[152] And, it was here, thirdly, that his Presbyterian upbringing facilitated acceptance of the seemingly extreme: 'You can be "totalitarian" for evil and you can also be "totalitarian" for good. Some of us came out of a highly disciplined religion and see no reason to fear discipline and self-denial . . . learned in a school of philosophy which taught us that all was for the common good and nothing for oneself'.[153] This last influence was as much stylistic as ethical for a man who, having been a lay preacher during his university years, was to use film self-consciously as a form of propaganda, famously quipping: 'I look on the cinema as a pulpit.'[154]

What Grierson preached, therefore, was how an immutable set of values could be realised as a result of their engagement with the forces of historical change. In this he was at pains to accentuate the positive by managing and re-arranging observations so that the 'real' was simplified and revealed in film. All was interpretation, but the illusion of documentary lay in convincing his audience that it simply and transparently recorded what existed on the ground.[155] Analysing the enduring contrast between the country and the city, Raymond Williams writes that 'the novelist offers to show people and their relationships in essentially knowable and communicable ways', but since these 'could not be simply known or simply communicated' they had 'to be revealed, to be forced into consciousness' by the writer.[156] In the same way, Grierson's trawlermen, miners, mail crews, slum dwellers, 'industrial Britain', 'Scotland' and the rest become 'knowable communities'. However, there is one important difference. Williams' thesis hinges on the contention that, '[A] valuing society, the common condition of a knowable community, belongs ideally in the past . . . But the real step that has been taken is withdrawal from any response to an existing society. Value is in the past, as a general retrospective condition'.[157] Clearly, this is applicable to much Scottish literature – Scott, the Kailyard – as it is to the English novel. Yet the argument does not hold for Grierson and documentary film precisely because his ethical sense, albeit bound to values with a strong historical pedigree, is one that pervades his sense of the present and guides society forward. To this extent, his achievement lay in attempting to provide a social anatomy of the contemporary. The political edge of his approach was blunted because he described problems rather than offered solutions, but the sociological legacy of his work lies in his development of a new way of seeing the social which, while apprehending the novelty of the present and near-future, nevertheless regards this as part of a continuing unfolding of enduring virtues. In this somewhat idealist encounter with modernity we find his documentary social imaginary.

NOTES

1. J. Grierson, 'Picasso – a postscript', *Tribune*, 25 January 1946 (Grierson Archive, University of Stirling, reference G5.21.1. Hereafter, notes to material in the Archive begin with the reference number).

2. F. Hardy, 'Introduction', in F. Hardy (ed.), *John Grierson's Scotland* (Edinburgh: Ramsay Head Press, 1979), pp. 9–16 (p. 9).

3. J. Grierson, *Education and the New Order* (Democracy and Citizenship Series, pamphlet no. 7, Canadian Association for Adult Education, 1941), reprinted in F. Hardy (ed.), Grierson on documentary (London: Faber & Faber, 1966), pp. 261–71 (p. 263); J. Ellis, *John Grierson: Life, Contributions, Influence* (Carbondale and Edwardsville, IL: Southern Illinois University Press, 2000), p.7, notes that Grierson accounted for himself according to three combined influences: educational drive from his father; an attraction to politics and public service from his mother; and an interest in the arts, which was not a family characteristic.

4. J. Grierson, *Education and the New Order*, (pp. 264–5).

5. Ellis, *John Grierson*, p. 6, cites F. Hardy's radio broadcast, *Scottish Life and Letters* (Scottish Home Service, BBC, 15 May 1966): 'the Scotland he knows in his heart . . . is the Scotland of fifty years ago, when the Church was still strong and the Calvinistic disciplines still counted for something. On the other hand, Clydeside was wild with the new Socialism. It was a stirring period in which the old self-disciplined, sensible Scottish tradition was lit up with wild new hopes and new rhetoric and new poetry of expectation.'

6. Ellis, *John Grierson*, p. 14.

7. E. Sussex, 'The golden years of Grierson', *Sight and Sound*, 41 (3), 1972, pp. 149–53.

8. L. Hill, *The Passionate Society: The Social, Political and Moral Thought of Adam Ferguson* (Dordrecht: Springer, 2006), p. 11

9. Grierson commented: 'What I know of cinema I have learned partly from the Russians, partly from the American westerns, and partly from Flaherty' (Hardy, *Grierson on Documentary*, p. 136). See also I. Aitken, *The Documentary Film Movement: An Anthology* (Edinburgh: Edinburgh Unversity Press, 1998), p. iii.

10. J. Ellis and B. McLane, A New History of Documentary Film (London and New York: Continuum International, 2005), p. 57.

11. P. Morris, 'Re-thinking Grierson: the ideology of John Grierson', in T. O'Regan and B. Shoesmith (eds). *History on/and/in Film* (Perth: History and Film Association of Australia, 1987), pp. 20–30 (p. 22).

12. M. Curtis, 'Introduction to the Transaction Edition', in W. Lippmann, *Public Opinion* (Edison, NJ: Transaction Publishers, 1997), pp. xi–xxxvi (p. xvii).

13. W. Lippmann, *Public Opinion* (Sioux Falls, SD: NuVision Publications, 2007), p. 154. (Subsequent references are to this edition).

14. Ibid. pp. 14–15.

15. Lipmann entitles the first chapter of *Public Opinion* 'The world outside and the pictures in our heads' (pp. 9–24).

16. Curtis, 'Introduction', p. xviii

17. Lippmann, *Public Opinion*, pp. 23–4.

18. Ibid. p.88.

19. Indeed, Lippmann brought the term stereotype (in its commonly understood metaphorical sense) to our vocabulary – see his chapters on 'Stereotypes as defense' (pp. 59–64) and 'The detection of stereotypes' (pp. 79–94).

20. An idea later much developed by Noam Chomsky.

21. Ellis, *John Grierson*, p. 22.

22. Quoted in Morris, 'Re-thinking Grierson', p. 24.

23. J. L'Etang, 'Grierson and the public relations industry in Britain', in J. Izod and R. Kilborn, with M. Hibberd (eds), *From Grierson to the Docu-Soap* (Luton: University of Luton Press, 2000), p. 91.

24. J. Grierson, 'Propaganda and education', address delivered to the Winnipeg Canadian Club, 19 October 1943, reprinted in Hardy, *Grierson on Documentary*, pp. 280–94 (p. 290).

25. G3.11.3 (Typescript of lecture on 'The theatrical tradition in cinema', from series 'The art of the cinema and its social relationships', University College Leicester, Department of Adult Education, Spring Term 1934). The reference to 'a real horizon' relates to Flaherty.

26. R. Aitken, 'Geopolitical order, social security and visuality: the National Film Board's Japanese internment project', http://www.cpsa-acsp.ca/papers.2006/Aitken. dpf, p. 20. Accessed June 2009.

27. Ibid. p. 20.

28. Subsequent shifts in forms of government, both national and local, were accordingly linked to the decline of 'the social', or, at least, of its definition as collectivist and universal. See N. Rose, 'The death of the social? Refiguring the territory of government', *Economy and Society*, 25, 1966, pp. 327–56; K. Stenson and P. Watt, 'Governmentality and the "death of the social"? A discourse analysis of local government texts in South-east England', *Urban Studies*, 36, 1, 1999, pp. 189–201.

29. R. Aitken, 'Geopolitical order', p. 20.

30. Grierson, 'Propaganda and education', p. 289.

31. J. Grierson, 'Films and the ILO', Philadelphia, public address, 26 April 1944, Speeches file. Montreal: Archives National Film Board of Canada, cited in R. Aitken, 'Geopolitical order', p. 21.

32. For a critical analysis of the varieties of 'work' that culture does in this regard, see T. Bennett, 'The work of culture', *Cultural Sociology*, 1 (1), pp. 31–47.

33. Morris, 'Re-thinking Grierson', p. 35.

34. J. Grierson, 'The Course of Realism', in C. Davy (ed.), *Footnotes to the Film* (London: Lovat Dickson/Peter Davies, 1937), pp. 137–61, quoted in Ellis, *John Grierson*, p. 35.

35. See Ellis, *John Grierson*, pp. 31–109 for a detailed history of Grierson's years at the EMB and GPO Film Units.

36. E. Barnouw, *Documentary: A History of the Non-Fiction Film* (Oxford: Oxford University Press, 1983), p. 89. B. Ryan, *Making Capital from Culture: The Corporate Form of Capitalist Cultural Production* (New York: de Gruyter, 1992), p. 124, uses the term 'creative managers' to refer to those who act as mediators between 'creative personnel' and 'owners and executives'.

37. They included: Basil Wright, Stuart Legg, Arthur Elton, Humphrey Jennings (all Cambridge graduates), Edgar Anstey, Paul Rotha, Alberto Cavalcanti, Len Lye,

John Taylor, Norman McLaren, Pat Jackson, and Grierson's sisters Ruby and Marion.

38. Despite the tendency to talk of a 'British documentary film movement', Grierson fell into dispute with several directors, including Paul Rotha and Edgar Anstey, largely over political differences. See R. Low, *History of British Film, Vol. 5, The History of British Film, 1929–1939: Documentary and Educational Films of the 1930s* (Routledge, 1996), pp. 50–1.

39. J. Beveridge, *John Grierson, Film Master* (New York: Macmillan, 1978), p. 69, quoted in B. Winston, *Claiming the Real: The Griersonian Documentary and Its Legitimations* (London: BFI Publishing, 1995), p. 59.

40. Morris, 'Re-thinking Grierson', p. 25, notes that 'corporativism' and 'corporate' were 'two of Grierson's favourite terms'.

41. G5.16.1. Article on the British Government's attitude to public information (author unknown).

42. M. Chanan, 'Documentary and the public sphere', in Izod et al. (eds), *From Grierson to the Docu-Soap*, pp. 221–30 (p. 221).

43. 'British documentary movement', http://www.britmovie.co.uk/history/bdm.html Accessed June 2009. See also Chanan, 'Documentary and the public sphere', p. 224: 'The rationale which Grierson constructed to obtain official backing is cousin to the more formal and orthodox arguments for public service broadcasting elaborated by Reith in the process of the transformation of the BBC from a private company to a public corporation'.

44. I. Aitken, *Film and Reform: John Grierson and the Documentary Film Movement* (London: Routledge, 1990), p. 168: 'he did not believe in the need for a social-ist transformation of society. Similarly, although he believed that the State was the most important agent of reform, he did not believe that it should become too powerful.'

45. Ibid. p. 194.

46. Winston, *Claiming the Real*, p. 60.

47. Grierson, 'The course of realism', reprinted in Hardy, *Grierson on Documentary*, pp. 199–211 (p. 199).

48. G2.17.12 ('Teach the world what we have to sell', unknown periodical source, n.d.): 'We are, in spirit, too near the somewhat tired and somewhat shabby sophistication of Piccadilly, too close to the English stage and its traditions. We are, dramatically speaking, rather provincial and parochial'.

49. Ibid. As if to counter one national stereotype with another, the magazine's editor wrote in his preamble: 'The writer of the following article is a Scot who has an almost unique talent for bringing imagination into the world of practical work'.

50. G2.16.5 (Lecture on film making as a career).

51. G2.17.12.

52. As he put it: 'The dramatic level of apprehension is the only one that relates man to his Maker, his neighbor or himself. I set it over against the informational level on which the poor liberal theory of education had been humourlessly insisting for half a century'(G3.14.5 (J. Grierson, 'The story of the documentary film', *Fortnightly Review*, 152 (146), 1939, pp. 121–30)). Ellis's remark (*John Grierson*, p. 358), that 'he was simply asking that documentaries be about social matters that were part of the public life (rather than fictions about individuals), that they be shot in the locale in which those matters were important (rather than in studios and on back lots), and

that the people who experienced those matters and who lived and worked in those locales be shown (rather than professional actors pretending to be them while living and working somewhere else)' is insufficient. Film critic Philip French writes: 'There was a time in the 1930s when documentary film-makers considered themselves servants of purity and truth, and looked down on fiction films. There was a certain hypocrisy in their position, as documentaries then were infinitely more contrived than they are today' (Philip French, 'The death of innocents', *The Observer Review*, 3 February 2008). This more nearly captures Grierson's stance, although it misses the key point that 'truth' for Grierson was not about facts but interpretation.

53. Hardy, *Grierson on Documentary*, p. 13.
54. Winston, *Claiming the Real*, p. 11.
55. Aitken, *Film and Reform*, p. 70: 'Although he recognised that film interpreted reality, he did not believe that the average spectator should share that recognition and believed that a convincing illusion of reality was essential in order to make the narrative as powerful as possible.'
56. Winston, *Claiming the Real*, p. 12.
57. J. C. Ellis, *The Documentary Idea* (Englewood Cliffs, NJ: Prentice Hall, 1989), p. 7 (citing Paul Rotha).
58. A. Kiewe, 'The crisis tool in American political discourse', in O. Feldman and C. De Landtsheer, *Politically Speaking: A Worldwide Examination of Language Used in the Political Sphere* (New York: Praeger, 1998), pp. 79–90 (p. 81).
59. Ibid. p. 81.
60. G3.9.6 (lecture on 'The Cutting Bench' from series 'The art of the cinema and its social relationships', University College Leicester, Department of Adult Education, Spring Term 1934).
61. For some the idea of 'film truth' created by manipulation of images is unconvincing. Regarding *Drifters*, one critic talks of its 'complicated untruths': 'The cabin scenes were shot on the shore. The fish were in a tank at the Plymouth Marine Biological Station and, anyway, were roach not herring. The Lerwick trawler failed to catch a thing when Grierson was aboard and so more footage was picked up on a Lowestoft trawler' (B. Winston, Review of Ellis, *John Grierson*, *Visual Anthropology Review*, 16 (2), 2000–1, pp. 92–6 (p. 93)). Montage was later used to emphasise societal contrasts – between country and city, old and new, agricultural and industrial, and so on.
62. 'And', he continued 'simple themes of the same sociological bearing have served us ever since' (Grierson, 'The course of realism' (Hardy reprint), p. 205).
63. P. Rotha, *Documentary Film* (New York: Hastings House, 1952), pp. 97–8. Ever the opportunist, Grierson was guided in his choice of topic by the knowledge that the Financial Secretary to the Treasury was obsessed with the herring fisheries.
64. Barnouw, *Documentary*, p. 85.
65. *Drifters* (1929); cf. Barnouw, *Documentary*, p. 98, notes how, when *Man of Aran* won first prize at the Venice film festival, 'dissenters – especially Grierson and his group – asked how Flaherty could possibly have ignored, amid a world of economic crisis, the social context in which Aran islanders carried on their bitter struggles. Was he aware of the evils of absentee landlordism?' Rotha, *Documentary Film*, pp. 106–7, referred to Flaherty's characters as 'waxwork figures acting the lives of their grandfathers'.
66. Winston, *Claiming the Real*, p. 19.

67. Barnouw, *Documentary*, p. 99: 'A Flaherty documentary had been a feature-length, close-up portrait of a group of people' whereas Grierson specialised in 'a short film fused by a "commentary" that articulated a point of view – an intrusion that was anathema to Flaherty.'

68. D. Williams, 'Crossing the cattle drive: Grierson and Australia', in Izod et al. (eds), *From Grierson to the Docu-Soap*, pp. 35–45 (p. 39).

69. G2.17.9 ('Films and industry, *Marketing*, March 1932, p. 12). He continues: 'Beyond each product are the origins of its materials, and the functions across the world of its finished forms; and lighting up every process are the men who perform it, with their services and loyalties and intricacies and ambitions . . . to humanise and make significant each product . . . The large scale dramatising of our industries is at hand'.

70. Winston, *Claiming the Real*, p. 51.

71. See Dziga Vertov's essay, 'The Factory of Facts'. Soviet cinema likewise celebrates modernity, as in Dovzhenko's *Earth* (1930) where the revolutionary struggle to establish farming collective reflects 'the penetration of a new life with its new social relations and machinery into the patriarchal patterns of a Ukrainian village' (O. Bobrova, 'Cinematic poetry of Alexander Dovzhenko', 25 June 2007, http:// www.vor.ru/culture/cultarch86_eng.html Accessed June 2009).

72. As he said to Flaherty: 'You keep your savages in the far place Bob; we are going after the savages of Birmingham' (P. Rotha, ed. J. Ruby, *Robert J. Flaherty: A Biography* (Philadelphia: University of Pennsylvania Press, 1983), p. 319).

73. Sussex, 'The golden years', pp. 149–53.

74. G2.17.8 ('A big movie idea', *John Bull*, 21 March 1931, p. 7).

75. G2.16.3 (Lecture on documentary as treatment of reality).

76. G2.17.7 ('Propaganda film technique: suitable subjects and their treatment', *Kinematograph Weekly*, 18 December 1930, pp. 38–40).

77. This view betrays a Hegelian preference in Grierson's interpretation of alienation, in that the conflict is one between 'objective' nature – or industrial environment – and human consciousness. By contrast, in Marx's critique feelings of estrangement are produced through social relations (in the act of the enforced production by workers of objects that do not belong to them).

78. E. Sussex, 'Grierson on documentary: the last interview', *Film Quarterly*, 26 (1), 1972, pp. 24–30 (p. 30). *Housing Problems* (1935) was sponsored by the British Commercial Gas Association.

79. J. Grierson, 'Battle for authenticity', *Documentary* Newsletter, 1939, reprinted in Hardy, *Grierson on Documentary*, pp. 215–17 (pp. 215–16).

80. G3.14.1 ('As the cinema sees us', *Daily Herald*, 29 October 1935).

81. A. Tudor, *Theories of Film* (London: Secker & Warburg, 1974), p. 69.

82. Winston, *Claiming the Real*, p. 51.

83. R. Barsam, *Nonfiction Film* (Bloomington: Indiana University Press, 1992), p. 99.

84. Winston, *Claiming the Real*, p. 35.

85. Ibid. p. 38.

86. R. Williams, *Marxism and Literature* (Oxford: Oxford University Press, 1977), p. 132.

87. C. Wright Mills, *The Sociological Imagination* (Oxford: Oxford University Press, 1967), p. 7.

88. S. Hall, 'The social eye of *Picture Post*' [1972], in G. Jordan (ed.), *'Down the Bay': Picture Post, Humanist Photography and Images of 1950s Cardiff* (Cardiff: Butetown History & Arts Centre, 2001), pp. 67–72 (p. 71).

89. Ibid. pp. 71–2.
90. G. MacLennan and J. Hookham, 'Documentary theory and the dialectic: a dialectic critical realist approach', paper prepared for IACR conference *Debating Realisms*, Roskilde University, 17–19 August 2001, p. 5. See also J. Hartley, 'Housing television: textual studies in TV and cultural studies', in C. Geraghty and D. Lusted (eds), *The Television Studies Book* (London: Arnold, 1988), pp. 33–50.
91. Winston, *Claiming the Real*, p. 42.
92. S. Tallents, 'The first days of documentary', *Documentary News Letter*, 9 (55), 1947, pp. 76–7, quoted in Ellis, *John Grierson*, p. 34. As Secretary of the EMB, Tallents first employed Grierson to make documentaries. The relationship continued when both moved to the GPO. Tallents later joined Reith's BBC as its first Controller of Public Relations and Deputy Director General.
93. Winston, *Claiming the Real*, p. 96.
94. Winston, *Claiming the Real*, p. 38. There are interesting parallels with photo-journalism here – see the discussion in Chapter 6 concerning Brandt's images of the Gorbals.
95. John Grierson, *Take One*, January–February 1970, cited in Barnouw, *Documentary*, p. 91.
96. G2.17.7. Winston, *Claiming the Real*, p. 25, refers to Grierson's 'belief that nothing photographed, or recorded on to celluloid, has meaning until it comes to the cutting bench'.
97. G5.21.1.
98. MacLennan and Hookham, 'Documentary theory', p. 5.
99. Hartley, Housing Television'; S. Aspinall, 'A sadder recognition: Sue Aspinall talks To Raymond Williams about *'So That You Can Live'*, *Screen*, 23 (3–4),1982, pp. 144–52 (p. 148).
100. Ellis, *John Grierson*, pp. 108, 111.
101. See P. Kinchin, J. Kinchin and N. Baxter, *Glasgow's Great Exhibitions, 1888, 1901, 1911, 1938, 1988* (Dorchester: White Cockade Publishing, 1988).
102. R. Butt, 'Citizenship', http://sites.scran.ac.uk/films_of_scotland/Citizenship/index. htm Accessed June 2009.
103. T. Bennett, 'The exhibitionary complex', *New Formations*, 4, 1988, pp. 75–102 (p. 82).
104. Ellis, *John Grierson*, pp. 112–13.
105. J. Grierson, 'A Scottish experiment', Spectator, 6 May 1938. Reprinted in Hardy, *Grierson on Documentary*, pp. 212–14 (p. 214).
106. Ellis, *John Grierson*, p. 113, citing F. Hardy, *Grierson on Documentary*, p. 23. Despite this, few critics mention the Films of Scotland series. Hardy presents a somewhat hagiographic exception, while Ellis himself – Grierson's most comprehensive biographer – devotes a meagre 1½ pages (from 365).
107. Following Grierson's intervention, they were eventually shown in an American social science pavilion (R. Butt, 'History', http://sites.scran.ac.uk/films_of_scotland/History/chapter02.htm, citing J. Caughie and C. McArthur, 'An interview with Forsyth Hardy', in C. McArthur (ed.) *Scotch Reels* (London: British Film Institute, 1982), p. 82. Accessed June 2009.
108. J. Grierson, 'Battle for authenticity', in Hardy, *Grierson on Documentary*, pp. 215–17 (p. 216).
109. G3.11.3.

110. F. Hardy, *Scotland in Film* (Edinburgh: Edinburgh University Press, 1990), p. 235.
111. Winston, *Claiming the Real*, p. 59.
112. Chanan, 'Documentary and the public sphere', p. 225; cf. T. Adorno, T. and M. Horkheimer, 'The culture industry: enlightenment as mass deception', in J. Curran, M. Gurevitch and J. Woolacott (eds), *Mass Communication and Society* (London: Edward Arnold, 1977), p. 354: 'The sound film, far surpassing the theatre of illusion, leaves no room for imagination . . . hence the film forces its victims [its audience] to equate it directly with reality.'
113. J. Grierson, 'The E. M. B. Film Unit', *Cinema* Quarterly, Summer 1933, reprinted in Hardy, *Grierson on Documentary*, pp. 164–8 (p. 165): 'To command, and cumulatively command, the mind of a generation is more important than by novelty or sensation to knock a Saturday night audience cold; and the "hang-over" effect of a film is everything'. Many documentaries, including these, were distributed widely through a non-theatrical network of film societies, schools and libraries.
114. Hardy, 'Introduction', pp. 10–11.
115. Grierson, 'A Scottish Experiment', pp. 213–14.
116. Ibid. pp. 212–13; G7.2.6 (King) – Films of Scotland Cttee, 'A running account with history'.
117. G3A.4.1 and 2 ('Men and matters: film making in Scotland', script for BBC radio broadcast, 31 March 1938).
118. Hardy, *Grierson on Documentary* ('Battle for authenticity'), p. 217. One further film, *Dundee* (a history of jute, jam and journalism set against the contemporary city), was made by the first Committee, but never released owing to the outbreak of World War II.
119. R. Butt, 'History, ethnography, and the nation: the Films of Scotland documentaries', unpublished PhD thesis, Open University, 1996. A detailed synopsis is provided on-line at http://sites.scran.ac.uk/films_of_scotland/Scotland/index.htm. Subsequent quotations in this section are from the latter (Butt, 'Films of Scotland documentaries'). Accessed June 2009.
120. Butt, 'Films of Scotland documentaries', cites E. Gellner, *Nations and Nationalism* (Oxford: Blackwell, 1983), p. 63.
121. Butt, 'Films of Scotland documentaries'. Grierson himself talked of 'romanticism as a reflection of suburban inaction, lack of participation in affairs, lack of realisation of a role in a constructive world' (3.10.1).
122. Tellingly, his was the voice of John Knox.
123. P. Schlesinger, *Media, State and Nation: Political Violence and Collective Identities* (London: Sage, 1991), p. 174, cited in Butt, 'Films of Scotland documentaries'.
124. The full shotlist runs as follows: Credits (.56) gvs [general views of] Borders landscape, Cheviot Hills and shot of a Roman wall (1.49) Highland scenery (2.25) shot of stones weighing down heather roof thatch. Peat turf (2.34) A farmer feeding a lamb, cattle grazing, gvs men cutting and stacking peat (3.32) shots of Stirling and Edinburgh castles (4.08) blackhouses and a new house (4.30) gvs crofters at work, ploughing, etc (4.49) village church as people enter yard (5.08) statue of John Knox (5.19) ext [error] village school (5.39) brief shot of fishing village, shots of church (5.45) city church steeple (5.50) int. church, congregation sing hymns. Woman playing the organ as boy works bellows (6.35) Boy doing his homework (6.45) Landscape (6.55) shot inside classroom during lesson. gvs streets in Ecclefechan, birthplace of Thomas Carlyle (7.11) St. Salvator's College in St. Andrews and

Edinburgh Old College [Error: Marischal College, Aberdeen](7.26) inside lecture hall during a lecture. Student in candlelit attic room studying. Back to lecture room (7.45) student at window overlooking the Old Quad, Edinburgh (7.50) statue of Sir Walter Scott at the base of his monument in Edinburgh (7.54) shots inside operating theatre (8.02) model of Watt's rotary steam engine, followed by shots of various liners built on the Clyde, Int. steel workshop and steel works (8.53) drawing of an old village, a factory chimney (9.08) shipyard workers leave yard. Long shot over rooftops to industrial landscape (9.17) shot of a ruined blackhouse (9.23) East end of Princes Street, Edinburgh (9.25) shots inside St. Vincent Bar, Edinburgh, as men drink, discuss football and play dominoes, i/c [intercut] with shots of ruined crofts and blackhouses (9.57) riveters at work (10.05) int. steel works (10.28) half-moon battery, Edinburgh Castle, as the one o'clock gun salute is fired. Long shot across Princes Street from Castle (10.40) pipes and drums (11.00) Lone piper, dressed in rags, marches along the top of the trenches in World War I. Brief shot of men in trenches and of artillery fire (11.10) memorial and shrine at Edinburgh Castle (11.45) Scottish lion rampant flying from flagpole (11.52) United Airways aircraft [G-ACAN] as it takes off from airport (11.59) hydro-electric power station (12.07) shots of a football crowd, c/u [close-up] and crowd scenes (12.55) pan over rooftops of Edinburgh and up to the castle (13.12) ecs [end credits](13.19) (Scottish Screen Archive – http://ssa.nls.uk/film.cfm?fid=0034 Accessed June 2009).

125. These are selected sentences from the narrative. No full-text transcript appears to exist, although the film may be viewed (and listened to) in full at http://www.best-laidschemes.com/moviezone/the-face-of-scotland Accessed June 2009.
126. Butt, 'Films of Scotland documentaries'.
127. Butt, 'Films of Scotland documentaries', also comments on how a characteristic melancholy, best captured by the word 'dour', is evoked as something arising organically from inhabiting a harsh landscape, in that it 'suggests both the grimness of the land and the obstinate and stoical persistence of the Scots in forging a living from it'.
128. Butt, 'Films of Scotland documentaries'. This use of dissolves contrasts markedly with the Soviet editing techniques with which Grierson, Wright and others were so familiar, and where cutting was frequently used not to smooth the transition between images but deliberately to emphasise disharmony and collision. The latter, of course, served well documentaries that dramatised the shock arrival of the new social order.
129. Butt, 'Films of Scotland documentaries'.
130. Ibid.
131. Ibid.
132. This distance is emphasised by Grierson's unionist, almost internal-colonialist self-image: 'In my years of work I have travelled in many countries. My side arms have been Scots and very plainly so for I have neither concealed the accent nor the sense of walking before the Lord . . . the flag that has provided me the greatest comfort is English. When they say "Your great and illustrious country" they mean the thing that is strictly not Scotland but England. My Scottish origin gives me, but however undeservedly, a reputation in the moralities . . . But this other gives me size. I am a big shot and, whatever else they say of me, I, unlike the Scots, am a leader.' (G4.21.20 ('Article on internationalism and JG's Scottishness'). In similarly patronising mode, Donald Alexander, Scots director of *Wealth of a Nation*, recalls in picaresque vein reminiscent of Boswell: 'Once we took Legg [who was responsible

for the film's treatment] on a ceremonial drive round Scotland, with Grierson and Wright acting as official cicerones to the country he had written up but never seen' (D. Alexander, 'Stuart Legg: a close-up', *Documentary Film News*, 7, 1948, p. 68, cited in Ellis, *John Grierson*, p. 114). The comparison is not entirely apt, for while Dr Johnson states: 'The noblest prospect which a Scotchman ever sees, is the high road that leads him to England!', Hardy rightly notes that 'significantly [Grierson] pointed his night mail train northwards: an Englishman would undoubtedly have filmed the southward journey, ending in the metropolis' (Hardy, 'Introduction', p.10). Basil Wright, Englishman and Cambridge classicist, scripted and directed *The Face of Scotland*.

133. See M. de Certeau, *The Writing of History* (New York: Columbia Press, 1988), p. 205, and B. Anderson, *Imagined Communities* (London: Verso, 1991), p. 19, both cited in Butt, 'Films of Scotland documentaries'.
134. Barnouw, *Documentary*, p. 99.
135. Quoted in Morris, 'Re-thinking Grierson', p. 21.
136. Winston, *Claiming the Real*, p. 43.
137. Barsam, *Nonfiction Film*, p. 77. By this point EMB, GPO and associated units had produced around 300 films, 'all of them in some degree owing their existence to Grierson's leadership.'
138. G7.2.6 (A. B. King, 'A running account with history', n.d.). Sir Alex King was Chairman of the Films of Scotland Cttee from 1955 until 1973.
139. J. Sherington, *To Speak its Pride: The Work of the Films of Scotland Committee, 1938–1982* (Glasgow: Scottish Film Council, 1996).
140. Perhaps his most significant work, as executive producer, during this period was *The Brave Don't Cry* (1952) a dramatisation of the Knockshinnoch mine disaster made for Group 3, a state-funded co-operative that he was instrumental in establishing.
141. Ellis, *John Grierson*, p. 344.
142. Winston, *Claiming the Real*, p. 12.
143. Ibid. pp. 26, 29.
144. M. Cousins, 'Making history: the aesthetics of documentary', *Tate Etc.*, 6 (2006).
145. Hall, 'The social eye', p. 71; G3.11.3: 'the contact with common reality which cinema gives is . . . a very precious and salutary thing . . . this essential sociological reference . . . [cinema] is a magical instrument . . . because it fulfils a purpose . . . That purpose is a sociological purpose. The camera permits us to see the world and see it widely, it permits us to see our neighbours and see them intimately. It permits us to see how the other half lives; and that is only to say that it permits us to see a little more clearly the factors which condition our existence'. For Tudor (Ellis, *John Grierson*, p. 334), 'the problem lies in providing a cultural basis . . . a system of beliefs which will make modern, democratic, industrialised societies work . . . It assumes that a consensus achieved by increasing knowledge of the 'real' world will bind society together. Knowing how the other half lives will enable us to recognize and hold on to our common humanity' (A. Tudor, *Theories*, p. 74). Barsam, *Nonfiction Film*, p. 82, suggests that Grierson was more concerned with presenting this cross-sectional view of society than with awakening the viewer's sense of political possibilities. See also Aitken, *Film and Reform*.
146. G5.21.1.
147. G2.16.3.
148. See M. Bernstein, Review of I. Aitken, *Film and Reform*, *Film Quarterly*, 47 (2), 1993/4, pp. 51–2.

149. G3.9.6, *my italics*.

150. Aitken, *Film and Reform*, p. 109.

151. Morris, 'Re-thinking Grierson', p. 21.

152. Ibid. p. 20.

153. Grierson, *Education and the New Order* (Hardy reprint), p. 269. Lovell notes: 'It is not, perhaps, surprising that a mixture of Calvinism and neo-Hegelianism should produce such an emphasis' (A. Lovell, 'The documentary film movement: John Grierson, in A. Lovell and J. Hillier (eds), *Studies in Documentary* (New York; Viking, 1972), pp. 9–61 (pp. 22–3).

154. J. Grierson, 'Propaganda: a problem for educational theory and for cinema', *Sight and Sound*, Winter 1933–4, pp. 119–21 (p. 119) (G3A.5.1).

155. See Aitken, *Film and Reform*, p. 70: 'Although he recognised that film interpreted reality, he did not believe that the average spectator should share that recognition and believed that a convincing illusion of reality was essential in order to make the narrative as powerful as possible.'

156. R. Williams, *The Country and the City* (St Albans: Paladin, 1975), p. 202.

157. Ibid. p. 220.

Section II

Placing Identities

CHAPTER 4

Among the wee Nazareths: myths of moral community

INTRODUCTION

Both Ferguson's image of an ideal civil society and the Griersonian figure of the industrious citizen celebrate social participation. Yet the 'spaces' in which virtuous behaviour can flourish are rather different. For Ferguson, civil society constitutes an intermediate realm between the family and the state that in the modern context requires communication among strangers; for Grierson, model citizens effectively become *träger* of a top-down discourse of statist democracy. In each case, the cultural validity of the moral sphere of local – that is, place-bound – society is diminished, relegated to being the vestige of a past social order. Recently, scholars have argued that between 1707 and the mid-twentieth century an unquestioning 'banal unionism' prevailed, 'a structure that defined the comfortable if more limited *Gemeinschaft* of the Scots – dialect, locality and so on'. By contrast, the British *Gesellschaft* 'stood for a wider reality, and appealed more to intellectuals, as well as those inclined towards emigration'. For Nairn, the resistance to this broader world, 'the one the Scottish Enlightenment had so successfully involved itself with', condemned Scottish popular culture to an involuted parochialism, at least until such unionism was questioned, somewhat recently, by the post-devolution agenda.[1] The Western engagement with modernity does little to alter this perception, yet arguably an abiding notion of community as relations between people living in particular places sustains the very possibility of Scottishness as a credible vision. Arguably, indeed, contemporary Scotland works because the country has a long history of internal devolution, with political decision-making and social mediation reflecting pride in the continuing strengths of a collective civil realm (religion, education, trades unions, health and welfare) that has long been sustained by local, often neighbourhood traditions.[2] The idea of local community as microcosm of the nation is the obverse of the nation as imagined community. It is a way of seeing that suffuses our literature: both Burns' advocacy of egalitarianism and the counter-thesis so vividly evinced in the republican, but elitist writings of Hugh MacDiarmid share an emphasis on the significance of local self-determination in the genesis of national identity.

However, rather than this relation being seen as a cultural benefit, it has been roundly regarded as a disadvantage. In the seminal treatise upon Scottish literature of the early twentieth century, Gregory Smith writes disparagingly of a 'provincial' trait: 'There is no denying the fact that the Scot seldom strays from the village-pump and the familiar gable ends'.[3] Comprehending why the local should have acquired such hegemonic force and, indeed, why this should have been regarded so negatively in comparison with 'great national literature', requires evaluation not so much of the nature of social relations as of the way in which these have been portrayed. Contrary to the apparent ease with which the nation is envisaged as an imagined community, there is a difficulty in placing local-ity coherently within the national imaginary because particular types of place have come to signify the presence of 'community' while others are defined by its absence. As Chapters 5 and 7 respectively indicate, modern memory invokes longings for the solitude of the 'wild', depopu-lated Highland landscape or, conversely, the neighbourly values of the bustling city tenement. Between these iconic extremes, it is important not to underplay the significance of a specific milieu – lowland, rural or small-town, parochial and democratic – in capturing the ethical imagi-nation, by which I mean visualising how we should live. Arguably, this fictive space held paradigmatic status in the cultural morality of belong-ing and national identity in the century or so after 1850. And yet its very force betrays a paradox since Lowland rural communities and small towns provided the prodigious bulk of Scotland's emigrants during this period. Meanwhile, as industrialisation eradicated cottage industry and agricul-tural depression followed by mechanisation and amalgamation obliterated tenant farming, many left the land for the burgeoning towns and cities of the Central Belt. It was an unprecedented exodus, but what summoned critical enquiry, at least until the 1970s, was the apparent absence of con-temporary cultural output reflecting the brute facts of rural depopulation or industrial depression. Instead, Scotland became a country imagined in literature as 'out of history'. As Craig avers: 'this place of historical change – the industrial revolution – is also a place of no-history . . . it becomes a backwater of historical processes that happen elsewhere'.[4] Unwillingness amongst contemporary writers to confront the realities of change is seen as a denial borne of social trauma. This argument is very well worn, and Craig is at pains to contrast it with an alternative vision:

> By identifying Scotland with its popular literary successes, from J. M. Barrie and Annie S. Swan to A. J. Cronin and Compton MacKenzie, and ignoring its contributions to the development of modern consciousness through its contributions to such emergent disciplines as psychology and anthropology, Scottish culture as a whole has been represented as retarded and parochial.[5]

While this critique has recently been developed and extended, providing an important revision to the nation's intellectual history, much research remains to be done before the putative split between 'an "insane" subculture and its failed high culture' may be laid to rest.[6] My contention here is that in finding a legacy of escapism in the debased offerings of mediated mass culture, those latter-day critics who point to the Kailyard School and its offspring as the basis of a culturally deformed 'sub-nationalism', reify a misplaced historiography while underestimating the self-awareness of the consuming public.

THE PARISH PARADIGM

Amongst the perdurable qualities of Scottishness, according to socio-political observers, lies a certain communitarian spirit; to whit, being conscious of a greater sense of democracy than elsewhere, particularly England. As McCrone puts it: 'In the Scottish Myth, the central motif is the inherent egalitarianism of the Scots'.[7] Its roots, when not simply essentialised as a racial characteristic, are adjudged to lie in the impact of religious history. For example, Neal Ascherson argues that 'if Presbyterianism had failed, Scotland today would be little more than an item of British regional geography'. His claim is that the Covenanters, in 'their long struggle against Episcopacy and against the right of local landowners to impose their own nominees as parish ministers invented a new sense of plebeian Scottish identity . . . Authentic "Scottishness" acquired a democratic component, as the fight to defend the right of individual kirk sessions (parish elders) to choose their own ministers continued down the generations', culminating in the Disruption of 1843.[8] While this pattern of 'defying forces of hereditary privilege which sought to enforce a more submissive social order imported from England'[9] signals a specific understanding of the relationship between doctrinal belief and popular politics, another religiously inflected interpretation concerns the organisational effect of the Reformation whereby the instigation of a school in every parish laid the foundations for equality of opportunity in education, bringing forth many a lad o' pairts and heralding Davie's 'democratic intellect' as the basis for a nationally distinctive worldview of higher education.[10]

There is another, rather less sanguine view. Hart comments that 'a noteworthy feature of Scottish fiction is the moral primacy of community', a factor attributable to the 'strong sense of communal commitment' instilled by Presbyterianism.[11] But if religion has played a large part in developing national consciousness, it has nevertheless been regarded as culturally detrimental. For Craig, 'the iconoclasm of the Scottish Reformation . . . inscribes into Scottish culture a conception . . . of the imagination as fundamentally evil'; and it is evil because it questions the 'deep Calvinist desire for a world of absolute certainty'.[12] The picture here is less one of harmony, than of suffocating repression, where 'the Scottish community, and the Scottish imagination, was ruled in large measure by fear', against which the only antagonist had to be the individual accepting 'a terrible – a fearful – isolation'.[13] In this characterisation, the observer either capitulates to an underlying domination by doctrine and reifies a superficially harmonious society while failing to confront its underlying schisms, or he/she accepts a marginal stance, thereby consigning their insights to non-recognition by its deluded citizens. The local element of Scottish cultural development is thus derided, by taking parochial to mean confined to a narrow area of affairs and opinion. However, the coalescence of social values and relationships within the setting of the parish community has been central to the development and maintenance of an idea of nationhood. Consequently, the task for the historical sociologist, if not the literary critic, is one of unpicking the threads of popular engagement with cultural production that connect parish, peasant and proletarian across the transformations of society since 1750.

DEMOCRACY AND DECLINE

The parish has been the microcosm for the nation, the prism through which ways of belonging have been understood and may be interpreted. Its literary realisation has involved a symbolism that has by turns been cloyingly romantic or politically egalitarian, and while the Kirk has undoubtedly played a part, its heroes have been the ordinary folk. Ian Carter traces a trajectory, beginning in the late-eighteenth century, of popular writing that evidences 'two attitudes to the lowland peasantry, one sentimentally patronising and the other democratically supportive'.[14] Thus in Burns we have poems like *The Cotter's Saturday Night* in which the weary peasant sits by the fire with his family at prayer, humble yet holy, salt of the earth – 'From scenes like these all Scotia's grandeur springs'; but he also gives us *Is There for Honesty Poverty*, a rallying cry that foresees a future in which 'Man to man shall brithers be for a' that'. Arguably, this mixture of sentiment and democracy infuses, in varying degrees, the great mass of fiction about rural and small-town Scotland over the next two centuries – from John Galt's aptly titled novel of Ayrshire local life, *Annals of the Parish* (1821), right through to the popular television series *Dr Finlay's Casebook*, *High Road*, and, in more Highland garb, *Monarch of the Glen*.

Two pivotal elements in this development were the romanticisation of the Highlands – largely at the hands of Walter Scott – and the Disruption of the Church of Scotland in 1843. Scott's Tory sentimentalism pervades novels like *The Heart of Midlothian* (1818), in which peasant virtues 'can only be saved through aristocratic patronage'.[15] But fifty years later, the democratic mode of representing country life is exemplified in the writing of the radical Liberal William Alexander, whose work emphasises three themes: the peasant as hero; the importance of land and place; and 'kindly relations' between employers, servants and fellow beings. Like Charles Dickens, Alexander was a Victorian 'realist' writer who published his material in weekly serialised form, evoking his native Aberdeenshire, most famously in the novel *Johnny Gibb of Gushetneuk* (1871). He was born a peasant son in the heart of rural Grampian, and rose to become an Aberdeen worthy and editor of the city's major newspaper, the *Free Press*. In a series of articles about 'Aberdeenshire character and characteristics: old and new', he draws a vivid image of integrity formed in the relentless struggle with nature:

> I have fully in my mind's eye both him and those 60 acres of bleak looking 'reisk' [waste], with only a dozen or so acres brought under the plough in an indiffer- ently workman-like way when he took possession, and a steading, the erection of which . . . had not cost over £30. His money capital at the outset, in addition to a wife and a couple of young bairns, a half-worn animal of the horse species, a cow, and a few of the more indispensable farm implements, was less than £10 sterling. For years . . . he and his wife did every bit of work, out and in, upon the place, summer and winter, springtime and harvest . . . Every succeeding year saw several acres of that forbidding 'reisk' 'riven in' by that 'fersell' [diligent] little man's own unaided efforts . . . until a good slate-roofed new steading had come to supply the place of the old 'rape-thackit' [rope-thatched] one.[16]

The toiling, obsessive worker, enslaved by his own determination, gains his independence of spirit, his 'innate vigour' from 'the very strenuousness of the struggle'. Tenacity, enterprise and endurance, 'determination to push their way in the world', these are the traits of the self-made individual.[17]

In the process the peasant becomes inseparable from the land, while the land itself is eulogised, its beauty less that of arresting geological formations than one that has been moulded by generations of plough-teams.[18] It is the small tenant farmer who makes the land a fertile place, not the aristocratic 'improver'. This is the 'poor man's country', not so much a landscape on which to gaze as a land made fit for stock to graze.[19] And this sense of rightful possession is crystallised by what Alexander terms 'kindly relations', the moral economy of the parish community, motivated not by greed and capitalism, but by collective rituals of harmony between master and servant, peer and ploughman. Identity springs from locale, a place where the kirk focuses attention, and where a sense of vernacular authenticity is conveyed by use of dialect words and idiom. However, in Alexander's fiction local society is characterised not by abiding consensus but by conflicting communities of interest.

The full title of *Johnny Gibb* is *Johnny Gibb of Gushetneuk in the Parish of Pyketillim with Glimpses of the Parish Politics about A.D. 1843* and it is the Disruption of the Church of Scotland in that year – 'perhaps the most significant single event in the social history of Scotland in the nineteenth century' – that catalyses the action.[20] At first sight then, this is a story about doctrinal bickering in a rural backwater. Like so many Scots novels it was written a generation after the events it discusses and one anticipates a nostalgic tone. But *Johnny Gibb* uses the Disruption as a vehicle for plotting a powerful political tract.[21] In 1843 two-fifths of ministers and around half of their parishioners across Scotland renounced the (Established) Church of Scotland to form the Free Kirk. The catalyst for secession lay in a handful of attempts by the kirk to impose ministers against the democratic wishes of local congregations led by their elected elders. In their heartland rural districts, the social base of what was to become the Free Kirk consisted of small tenant farmers, crofters and farm servants whose interests clashed with those of an Established Church dominated by lairds and large capitalist farmers. Accordingly, they attacked landowners' policies of throwing down and demolishing crofts and cottar houses in order to avoid heavy Poor Law rates, while berating large farmers for trying to set themselves apart both socially, through upward social mobility, and physically, by consigning their servants to barrack-like accommodation and taking no interest in their moral or physical welfare. As a counter-image of ideal social relations they posited a society where lairds provided small leasehold farms that would allow ambitious and thrifty servants to gain a toehold on the farming ladder. The tensions between these two are played out in the action of *Johnny Gibb* – the tenant farmer of the title – and his friends exemplifying peasant virtue while other characters inhabit the 'caul' morality o' a deid moderatism', at once also the uncaring aloofness of capitalist agriculture.[22] An apparently religious dispute thus becomes the vehicle not simply for the emergence of class-based attitudes (which could have signalled the reduction of agrarian relations of production to the economic nexus) but for a broader politics of community, the ecclesiastical schism now appearing as the external face of a deeper moral dilemma concerning how people ought to co-exist.

Johnny Gibb lends force to Ascherson's point linking religiosity with egalitarianism, but its politics are about social solidarities as much as faith. The work inhabits a European realist tradition, prefiguring Grassic Gibbon's great novel of peasant crisis, *Sunset Song* (1932) some sixty years later.[23] However, the conditions of its production were markedly different. Donaldson ventures the challenging thesis that 'the significant part of the literary market in Scotland during most of the nineteenth century was not the middle class with its subscription libraries and imported English novels, but the Scots-speaking working class and the native writers who catered for it through the medium of the popular press'. Serialised weekly in the *Aberdeen Free Press* from September 1869 to December 1870, *Johnny Gibb* is certainly part of this indigenous tradition, as were several of Alexander's novels, including *The Authentic History of Peter Grundie* (1855) and *My Uncle the Baillie* (1876–7), both of which articulated urban social themes. His style was also typical in using speech-based vernacular prose. Donaldson estimates that at least five thousand full-length Scottish novels were published in serial newspaper instalments as part of this 'communications revolution' in the popular Scottish press, 'the main vehicle of popular culture during the period and the major locus of the creative life of the nation'.[24] However, with fewer and fewer such newspapers able to maintain local control and syndicated mass production increasing, their cultural autonomy waned and by 1900 'the long trivialisation of the Scottish press had begun'.[25] The way was clear for an emphatic shift from the realist to the sentimental, with the Kailyard (cabbage patch) rural romances of Barrie, Crockett and Maclaren between the 1880s and 1914.

The Kailyard style was one of sugary sentimentality, variously described as 'licorice schtick', 'wistfully nostalgic' and 'sentimental slop', the 'hospital romances' of their day, while the ideology was most certainly one of community, being set in rural parishes where 'harmony pervades every page', a factor rendering the product all the more fictional since the era when they were written was not a time of idyll at all, but the very period when the peasantry was in its final crisis before the death-blow of the First World War. As Carter remarks: 'This emphasis on community is revealing; like the divine right of kings two centuries before it asserts the value of a social arrangement at the precise moment in which that arrangement is under irresistable pressure.' [26] Such escapism extends the 'urbane silence' of the nineteenth-century Scottish novel, which according to Noble, 'scarcely deals with the chronic problem of the age, the new industrial city' but instead develops a structure of retrospect 'suffused with nostalgia for a lost green world . . . of pietistic peasants.' 'No culture', he continues, 'achieved such a repression of representation of urban life by promulgating such mythical rural alternatives'.[27]

It would be easy to regard Kailyard as representing no more than the nostalgia of an upwardly mobile group of authors pre-occupied with achieving their own social status by extolling the virtues of a lost rural innocence against the sins of the contemporary city.[28] Under the patronage of William Robertson Nicoll, a Free Kirk minister turned London editor, the novels sold in their hundreds of thousands, both at home and abroad. Kailyard both benefited from and contributed to the development of mass tourism linked to Balmoral and the extension of cheap rail travel. In this sense, it was a further phase in the invention of tradition begun by Walter Scott. Unlike those writers published in the Scottish popular press in the later-nineteenth century, Kailyarders 'related to their audience through the bourgeois book market'.[29] However, their material rapidly diffused to a broader base of consumers.

George Blake, writing in 1951, argues that readers enjoyed Kailyard because through its portrayal of rural characters as simple folk they could bask at a safe distance in their superiority.[30] The implication is that the market consisted of a generation which could recall with a contemptuous humour, relief even, the (fictionalised version of) life they had left behind, in much the same way that the townsfolk in Littlejohn's empirical parish study regarded the 'country bumpkins' still living in the countryside from which they had moved.[31] Kailyard simply canalised their thoughts and facilitated positive biographical reflection. Yet simultaneously theirs was a forgetting of the trauma of agrarian crisis – the real reasons why they had been forced to leave. For Blake, popular novelists were all the more contemptible for deliberately ignoring the brute facts of their country's transformation from a rural society to an urban-industrial one, a point reiterated by later Marxist critics.[32]

Carter takes a different tack, noting amongst Kailyard writers the recognition of decline: for Crockett, of religious sects; and Maclaren, both of religion and of social relations in agriculture.[33] With Barrie, the title of *A Window in Thrums* (1889) is significant, since the novel fictionalises the demise of handloom weaving in his birthplace of Kirriemuir, and thrums are the loose ends of warp threads remaining on a loom once cloth has been cut off. While such 'arcadian sadness' does nothing to mitigate the sins of evasion, it might help in locating the reasons why they wrote as they did. The fact that Kailyard stories are suffused with the tribulations of ministers highlights two elements: first, the parish is regarded as a central and binding force with the kirk at its centre; second, the kirk is the conduit through which all affairs filter and are evaluated. It is taken for granted that the egalitarian moral economy hinges around religion. But when this is threatened to the point of final extinction, the Kailyard triumvirate write 'of the virtues of peasant life as if by writing about them [they] could preserve them'.[34] The authors were aware of social change, but in clinging to the imputed remnants of a vanishing moral framework, Kailyard fiction was an attempted repudiation of spiritual disjuncture. In this they were quite open, Ian Maclaren noting 'it must be remembered that idylls do not pretend to give a full chronicle of life. They try to seize the moments at which the hidden beauty of the soul leaps into vision . . . to detect the divine in the carnal . . . to slake the eternal thirst of our nature for those waters of the ideal'.[35] For the consumers, a great many of whom were the city-dwellers and emigrants who had been dispersed by economic decline in the countryside, the attractions of harmony and security were doubtless considerable: readers seeking threads of continuity between the past mores of their grandparents and their own worldview as rural Scots by lineage need look no further. In this sense, the Kailyard mentality could inform aspirations as much as shore up wistful regrets – what is relevant about thrums is not that they are wasted remains, but that they may still be gathered up and woven into the social fabric, but in another time and place. Possibly. Yet, like Kailyard itself, this view seems unwarrantedly sentimental, and we can only speculate.

Of perhaps greater account than the reasons why people read the material at the time is the continuing ideological significance of the subsequent Kailyard Myth. Here the story of Nicoll's success in marketing the novels of Barrie, Crockett and Maclaren provides salutary guidance. Appearing from the late 1880s, these works coincided with a heated public debate, stimulated by the massive expansion of print culture alongside the spread of compulsory mass education, as to what constituted 'high' and 'low' literature. As periodicals packed with trivia began to flourish, this 'new journalism' was derided as down-market. Meanwhile – importantly for the direction Scottish parochial fiction would take – they came to supplant the local press which had been so significant as an outlet for vernacular realism. Nicoll was attuned to the expansion of the book-buying public and marketed his authors to great effect: Maclaren's *Beside the Bonnie*

Brier Bush (1894) was the highest-selling novel in America in 1895, while Crockett made the bestseller lists more often than any other author between 1891 and 1901.[36] While Nicoll's operation was ostensibly geared to 'the prosperous middle-class middlebrow Nonconformist market in England',[37] both authors sold huge numbers in North America, enjoying particular appeal among Scots emigrants. They were each read 'as widely in Scotland as they were in England and more widely than contemporary English novelists'.[38] Such success would in itself alarm later modernist critics, but it was Nicoll's promotion of Crockett and Maclaren as high culture, and the strategy adopted to effect this, that rendered the Kailyard School notorious among contemporary critics.[39] Although many highly-regarded authors contributed material in the periodical press, Nash shows that modernist writers were largely responsible for planting 'the idea that there was an unbridgeable chasm between journalism and literature'.[40] As literary editor with Hodder and Stoughton, Nicoll made a huge impact with his reviews in the *British Weekly*, a penny weekly with a six-figure circulation, and the *Bookman*, both his own innovations. He was thus able to claim literary prestige for his own authors, asserting, for example, that Maclaren was 'unsurpassed by any living writer in the gift of pathos', while being attacked for the 'unblushing effrontery' with which he set Crockett 'on a level with Sir Walter'.[41] In 1897, one perspicacious Glasgow critic vented his fear that through such high-profile puffery, 'a lot of second-rate material might become indelibly marked upon tradition'. He was right to be concerned, for as Nash concludes, Nicoll's commercially-driven placement of Scotland 'at the centre of British literary culture' elevated the Kailyard School to a position within the nation's cultural heritage altogether disproportionate to its literary standing. Nash comments that 'to many writers and critics of the time, good sales necessarily indicated artistic compromise, and this inverse relation between popularity and literary value became a fundamental part of Modernism'.[42] As he demonstrates, however, the really lasting damage was wrought by the presumption of Kailyard fiction to standards of 'high' culture.

For the sardonic or sceptical, contemporary reaction against Kailyard was definitively realised in George Douglas Brown's *The House with the Green Shutters* (1901). Brown had struggled against social stigma as an illegitimate child in Ayrshire to become a classics scholar at Oxford, where he felt the need to convey the falsity of what passed as contemporary Scots literature to his fellow undergraduates by penning the great anti-Kailyard novel.[43] The local gossips ('the bodies') in Brown's fictional community of 'Barbie' were a Kailyard staple, but, in their spiteful rumour-mongering, deliberately antithetical.[44] Likewise the singularly malicious actions and horrible fate of the novel's protagonist John Gourlay: 'The worst possible motives were ascribed to any action, as a comfortable and self-satisfied merchant was humbled through external pressure and the collapse of his family's internal stratification. The novel ends with patricide and a welter of gore that is positively Wagnerian' as Gourlay's son, an alcoholic, murders his father in a rage of resentment, spurred on by 'the bodies'.[45] There is no church in Barbie, nor any Christian redemption; instead, the novel opens outside the other great institution of popular culture: 'The frowsy chambermaid of the "Red Lion" had just finished washing the front door steps. She rose from her stooping posture and, being of slovenly habit, flung the water from her pail straight out'.[46] The petty insecurities of Barbie, brought on by greed for money, are symptomatic of a spiritual decay that could be attributed to industrial capitalism. However, one recent critic regards the novel as 'less a response to the Kailyard's neglect of social realities as a reaction against its vision of human nature. What makes Barbie "rotten to the core" is not its exposure to social and economic pressures but the attitudes and personalities of its inhabitants'. The community exists within a common literary space, and by inverting the Kailyard order of things yet retaining a focus on moral vocabulary, *The House with the Green Shutters* occupies the same paradigm, part of what Nash refers to as 'the anxiety over provincialism'.[47]

In grappling with this concern, no figure was more influential than the poet Christopher Murray Grieve, more familiar to many by his pen-name of Hugh MacDiarmid, who in his voluminous political criticism raised the status of Kailyard from a minor literary genre to a framework through which an entire culture saw itself. For MacDiarmid, Kailyard sat beside the Burns cult in popularising 'a fetish of reactionary provincialism in the heart of London'.[48] Barrie, Crockett and Maclaren were regarded as émigrés responsible for Anglicising Scottish culture. Thus, while Kailyard became the 'other' against which the Scottish Renaissance movement of the 1920s and thirties sought to define itself, popular representations of Scottish culture came to be regarded as foreign misrepresentations that required authentic remedy from within Scotland. Fundamental here was outright rejection of the parish paradigm. As Neil Gunn wrote in 1927: 'The Renascent Scot is – must be – intolerant of the Kailyairder, that is of the parochial, sentimental, local-associative way of treating Scotland and the Scots'.[49] Yet precisely because this version of the local was believed to be deeply embedded in the social psyche, considerable ingenuity was required to displace it.

The Brae was the favourite stance of the bodies.

Fig. 4.1 Spiteful gossip characterises the anti-Kailyard. Frontispiece from
The House with the Green Shutters.
All reasonable attempts have been made to trace the copyright holder.

MacDiarmid's lonely Republic

Anthony Cohen argues that since community is about symbolising ourselves and others 'people become aware of their culture when they stand
at its boundaries'.[50] Nowhere is this truer than in the rhetoric of Lewis
Grassic Gibbon (James Leslie Mitchell) and Hugh MacDiarmid who,
writing respectively from Welwyn Garden City and Shetland, argued
that 'distance from the Scottish Scene would lend them some clarity
in viewing it'.[51] While Grassic Gibbon's diffusionism positions him
somewhat tangentially in relation to nationalism, with which he had a
rather contradictory relationship,[52] MacDiarmid's poetry and political
writings everywhere espouse a 'crucial correspondence between the local
and the universal' in the development of a specifically Scottish vision.[53]
Strikingly, he also insists upon rural rather than urban settings.

Although a modernist (and by the same token a cultural elitist),

MacDiarmid repudiates metropolitanism as morally bankrupt. He distrusts the imperial core as in itself provincial but universalising in its drive to subsume difference, and foments instead a reverse discourse by foregrounding the cultural significance of the periphery.[54] Hence, for example, his conviction that 'the cultural "treasures" of humanity can still come "frae the lanely places,/No' the croodit centres o' mankind yet"'.[55] Politically, he 'promotes a modern Scottish Renaissance that speaks with the historically silenced voice of the uniquely local . . . [against] the obliteration of difference constituted by imperial expansion'.[56] On a sociological level this is a recognition of fragmentation, but ideologically it is a catalysing celebration of the virtues of small town, rural localism derived from personal engagement:

> Inspired by Langholm, MacDiarmid's best creative work was written in Montrose and Whalsay. It is by living and working in these peripheral places that MacDiarmid developed a political strategy through which to resist the symbiotic assault of anglification and capitalism and so suggest a radically nationalist Scotland.[57]

As Lyall demonstrates, the poetics of place found throughout MacDiarmid's work are those of a uniquely 'vernacular modernism', underpinned by the maxim that 'there is nothing more universal than the local'.[58] So, 'wishing to ensure Scotland's eternal future, he perceives that there can be no nation without the unending imagination of the community . . . "Until I saw a timeless flame/Take Auchtermuchty for a name,/And kent that Ecclefechan stood/As part o' an eternal mood"'. These places are microcosmic 'wee Nazareths', like Langholm, Montrose and Whalsay, in which the poet sees himself as the saviour Christ.[59] By contrast, he contends that 'a malign embodiment of modern capitalism is "the urbanisation of the mind" . . . the paralysis of internal colonisation and the detritus of industrialism defile Edinburgh and Glasgow', the 'alienation and anomie of living in big cities both augurs and augments the destructive malaise of modernity'.[60] Thus we revisit the phobic anti-urban-industrial invective of fellow advocate of the Scottish Renaissance, Edwin Muir, with whom MacDiarmid was indeed close, until they parted company over the latter's insistence on writing in braid Scots.

But for all its rootedness in the rural vernacular, MacDiarmid's vision breaks distinctively with the parish paradigm in the important respect that for him the virtues of small places most definitely do not inhere in their existing egalitarianism. His monumental poem, A Drunk Man Looks at the Thistle (1926) caricatures both the modernist Eliot and the democratic Burns; more generally Scotland, too, 'is defined as a parody of a culture'.[61] The parochial Scotland denounced here is exactly that 'damned democracy' whose 'egalitarian attitude of ordinary chumminess' the poet deplores.[62] While Empire capitalism has produced the alienated metropolitanism and proletarian decay of the cities, so a provincial culture, borne of the Reformation and carried forth by the Union, created a legacy of canny lads o'pairts, couthy Kailyard ministers and populist music hall characters, all 'fostered by a capitalist education system grounded in Calvinist self-repression'. For him, such philistinism cannot be overcome through a hegemonic consciousness of class-for-itself but only via the Nietzschian self-realisation of an intellectual vanguard: it is the cultural producers, not the consuming public, who will transform the nation. This is not without irony, of course, in that his elect elitism is itself a very Calvinist trait. MacDiarmid also exemplifies the very lad o'pairts learning that he excoriates: as a boy he lived below the Langholm library and boasted using it obsessively in garnering his own auto-didactic knowledge.[63] On one level, his conversion may simply be read as a case of international communism replacing provincial Scots Presbyterianism, yet the contradictions of MacDiarmid do not allow of easy resolution; they are deliberate challenges, in his words 'aye whaur extremes meet'.[64] His embrace of the defining cultural condition of the Scots, the Jekyll-and-Hyde syndrome known as 'Caledonian antisyzgy', prompts a medieval tendency in his thinking that is calculated by its very contrariness to undermine.[65] And this is in keeping with a desire to reinvigorate the nation by recourse to recovering a pre-Reformation, pre-Union sensibility. Craig contends that he 'annuls the past except as a series of precedents for himself'.[66] But in so far as all history is imbued with imagined mentalities – and we are talking here of identifications of the spirit – MacDiarmid's world we have lost becomes an ambivalent blueprint for a post-colonial future. The strategic maintenance of ontological integrity requires a concept of national anteriority, while rendering England as 'the Other'. This implies an essentialist working definition of a singular Scotland, albeit understood as irrational in the light of the primacy of a localised heterogeneity.[67]

There is nonetheless a sense in which cultural difference is underlain by a common set of concepts. Firstly, in opposition to the centralising tendencies of British internal colonialism that threaten to extinguish place-bound heterogeneity, MacDiarmid wants to create an autochthonous culture unified in its refusal to adapt to capitalist modernity.[68] Each different community is regarded, in its ideal incarnation, as culturally organic, thus 'Our ideal ethnological method/ May be fairly called the ecological one'.[69] Secondly, this rootedness is imaginatively consolidated by myths of racial origin, although these need not be national. For instance, MacDiarmid alludes to the Lerwick Viking festival of Up Helly Aa as 'a really marvellous spectacle [that] links past and present and reveals the distinctive and timeless background against which the generations come and go'.[70] Thirdly, it has been argued that during his brief sojourn in London and Liverpool, 'a sense of geographic and emotional displacement prompted the need for his creative vision to refocus around memories of home'– of Langholm as a 'secret reservoir', 'touchstone' and solace.[71] This comes despite his bitter critique of many of the town's community values, particularly its religiosity and its constraining notions of family. Having lost his first wife and children and on the verge of breakdown, a spiritual rather than social feeling of belonging provides a signal emotional resource. However, writing again from Shetland, he departs from the literary tradition of conceiving home from exile, because living on the Scottish margin, among the places of the periphery, he can claim there to be at least culturally at one, while it is mainstream Scotland that has become detached from its roots. Ultimately, however, the consequences can only be counter-productive. By trying to conjure up an image of the nation in his own image, MacDiarmid only set himself further apart from the populace:

> Radical individualism may represent a morally challenging position but it is also an invitation to radical isolationism, leaving writer and audience confronting each other in mutual denial: the audience will always fail to match the imagination of the writer and the writer's imagination will fail to participate in any process of communal self-imagining.[72]

NAIRN AND SUB-NATIONALISM

In like vain, Tom Nairn makes the point that MacDiarmid's 'nostalgic literary nationalism' was insufficiently comprehensive to affect the country's political consciousness.[73] Given the poet's elitism this is something of an understatement. Meanwhile, Nairn's own view of 'cultural subnationalism' in Scottish society, although Marxist, may itself be construed as very much a from-above analysis. Since, he argues, 'an intellectual class able to express the particular realities of a country, in a romantic manner accessible to growing members of the reading public – a class operating actively in the zone of general and literary culture' had failed to develop within Scotland during the nineteenth century, its national culture was, and is, at best a caricature. This political weakness rendered Scottishness 'merely' cultural, its putatively nationalist content finding vent in the form of two – deforming, thus sub-national – neuroses, the Kailyard and cultural emigration, each underpinned by vulgar tartanry. Those figures of Scots extraction who might have led an organic national culture – Mill, Macaulay, Ruskin, Carlyle, Gladstone – found themselves 'unemployable in their own country' and took the high road for England, leaving behind the backyard, or cabbage patch, that we know as Kailyard.[74] This lack of an intellectual vanguard is used to explain why Victorian Scotland had no great contemporary novels about class conflict, its burgeoning urban society or, indeed, the continuing social upheavals being rent in the countryside, Highland and Lowland, that gave rise to urbanisation, migration and emigration rather more generally. Exceptional writers, like Stevenson – who himself moved overseas – were not enough to sustain any sense of a national intelligentsia.

What Nairn fails to appreciate (he was not alone) was the voluminous and socially diffused basis of Victorian popular fiction in the local press, where the national imagination was alive and well. The country was 'a completely and lovingly imagined place, and a very different one from that visible through the narrow and distorting perspective of the printed book'. As Donaldson indicates, such fiction is 'not overwhelmingly backward-looking; it is not obsessed by rural themes; it does not shrink from urbanisation or its problems; it is not idyllic in approach; it does not treat the common people as comic or quaint'.[75] Either Nairn is unaware of this contribution to the national heritage, or it is conveniently forgotten since all that is geographically provincial must also be considered parochial in the pejorative sense. He proceeds to rant against Kailyard and its latter-day progeny as 'a sort of national infantilism', a 'sub-romanticism of villages peopled by morons', leaving Scots, as George Blake earlier put it: 'inveterately backwards in literary culture – bewildered and sentimental children bleating for the old securities of the parish life', all 'recognisably intertwined with that prodigious array of *kitsch* symbols, slogans, ornaments, banners, war-cries, knick-knacks, music hall heroes, icons, conventional sayings, and sentiments . . . to the point of forming a huge, virtually self-contained universe' of everyday popular culture.[76] So speaks the disparaging, if not despairing, modernist intellectual. He might have added postcards, calendars, food-product labels and much else in everyday material culture. Nairn acknowledges the robustness of the 'tartan monster': it 'will not wither away, if only because it possesses the force of its own vulgarity – immunity from doubt and higher culture'.[77] Politics aside, if indeed the Kailyard legacy remains, then it behoves us to consider its cultural impact upon the national mythscape, where the apparent absence of an urban dimension and the romanticisation of the rural are particularly striking elements.

So too, the link to cultural emigration whereby 'Scotland' was produced outwith its own geography. Except for Crockett, the Kailyard writers were themselves émigrés who wrote mostly for a public outside Scotland itself, albeit that diasporic Scots were prominent consumers. Thus the communities of 'Drumtochty' and 'Thrums', like Cronin's later 'Tannochbrae', while created and consumed externally, nonetheless found themselves central to the reified domestic imagination: 'Whether as the pawky simplicities of village life, or as swaggering through the heather claymore in hand, "Scotland" in the sub-romantic sense was largely defined by émigrés'.[78] This is also the land of *Kidnapped* (1886) and *Weir of Hermiston* (1896), of Stevenson's continuing contribution to the romantic spirit of adventure begun by Scott, written not from a mock-baronial pile in the Borders but, respectively, a villa in Bournemouth and a veranda in Samoa, from where RLS wrote to J. M. Barrie:

> It is a singular thing that I should live here in the South Seas under conditions so new and so striking, and yet my imagination so continually inhabits that cold old huddle of grey hills from which we come . . . the sights and thoughts of my youth pursue me; and I see like a vision the youth of my father, and of his father, and the whole stream of lives flowing down there, far in the north, with the sound of laughter and tears . . . And I admire and bow my head before the romance of destiny . . .[79]

The state of exile prompts reflection upon one's identity, codifying a longing expressed by many. Charles Murray's oft-cited, if little-read collection of poems, *Hamewith* (1900) is a classic case in point. The book opens with the epigraph: 'Here on the Rand we freely grant/We're blest wi' sunny weather/ Fae cauld an' snaw we're weel awa/ But man, we miss the heather'. And the poems are replete with wistful couplets:

> There's a wee, wee glen in the Hielan's [sic],
> Where I fain, fain would be;
> There's an auld kirk there on the hillside
> I weary sair to see . . .
> I wander o'er the desert lone,
> There's nae mair hame for me.
>
> I want to wade through bracken in a glen across the sea –
> *I want to see the peat reek rise.*
>
> Hamewith [homeward] – the road that's never dreary,
> Back where his heart is a' the time.[80]

Here is the rallying call to home as shared sentiment, like an after-dinner toast at so many Burns Clubs and Caledonian and St Andrew's Society gatherings throughout the New World. Ironically, of course, these are voices from the same British Empire that so exploited the Highlands as an internal colony. The celebrants' hearts may be in the Highlands, but they often conveniently forget the reasons they left them there. This structure of retrospect, in its collective amnesia as well as its nostalgia, is central to the meaning of Scotland as imagined community.

Likewise with émigré writers: whether in London-based Barrie's cleaving to 'past community as the image of human fulfilment no longer available to the modern world', or Douglas Brown's anti-Kailyard antithesis contrived from Oxford, each 'imagin[es] Scotland as a place exiled to the imagination, incapable of envisaging a future for itself'. Yet, for both there is also a 'double movement of separation and identification'.[81] Grassic Gibbon, writing in Welwyn famously expresses such tormenting liminality in the character of Chris Guthrie, heroine of his trilogy *A Scots Quair* (1946) and herself a metaphor for the nation:

> Two Chrisses there were that fought for her heart and tormented her. You hated the land and the coarse speak of the folk and learning was fine and brave one day, and the next you'd waken up with the peewits crying across the hills, deep and deep, crying in the heart of you and the smell of the earth in your face, almost you'd cried for that, the beauty of it and the sweetness of the Scottish land and skies.[82]

Paradoxically, a full sense of Scottish identity – one that emphasised the coherent peasant and artisan community – could only be maintained where opportunities abroad allowed the aspirant and ascendant to flourish. Had they remained at home the transformation of agrarian society, whether through the drastic clearance, land hunger, and depopulation of the Highlands and Islands or the capitalist reorganisation of farming in the Lowlands, would have put paid to such ambitions. To be sure, it is the social or, at least, human element that is problematic. Where recollection is of the natural, changelessness is what matters. W. H. Murray wrote *Mountaineering in Scotland* (London: Dent, 1947) in the wretched confines of an Italian prison camp during World War II, consoled by the memory of exposure to moor and mountain: 'He knew that these places continued to exist; this is what sustained him'.[83]

But if the Kailyard evidenced a deliberate forgetting, denial or elegy for the pain of internal migration to the cities, emigration, by contrast, produced a new hero: not the peasant determined to stay put and cultivate his parks, nor the lad o' pairts intent on using education or skill as an escape from the peasant community, but the emigrant, able to transport – lock, stock and whisky-barrel – the opportunities of realising the Scots Myth in the New World, New Zealand, Nova Scotia, a phoenix reborn. While in MacDiarmid's vision the margins stand for the centre, here is another displacement, between the material realities of Scottish society and the idealisation of those arrangements from elsewhere. Either way, from the late-nineteenth century and for much of the twentieth, few were sitting at home in urban or suburban Scotland narrating the world about them. The brute material facts of that environment simply 'did not pose a cultural problem that had to be solved in specifically Scottish terms'. So, rather tautologically, intellectuals 'could not deal with modern experience in Scotland because in the relevant sense there *was* no "modern experience": such experience was the product of culture, not its pre-existing social basis'.[84] Instead, so the argument goes, the lacuna was filled by the lumpen popular culture alluded to above.

D. C. THOMSON'S CULTURAL INTIMACY

In this regard, Nairn is particularly scathing about the role of the Scottish-owned and Dundee-based enterprise of D. C. Thomson, publisher of the tabloid *Sunday Post* newspaper.[85] The *Sunday Post* boasts an adult readership of 1,088,000, of whom three-quarters are in Scotland. No less than 64 per cent are aged over 55 (44 per cent over 65) and 72 per cent fall within social class C1, C2 and D (skilled and semi-skilled manual workers) categories.[86] With the tagline 'a thoroughly decent read', the publisher claims that the *Sunday Post* is 'family orientated, with a unique insight into Scottish life',[87] a putative reflection of this being the huge popularity of the children's cartoon strips, 'The Broons' and 'Oor Wullie', which have run as part of the paper's Fun Section since 1936 and are now referred to by academics as 'icons of Scottish culture'.[88] 'The Broons' are redolent of a cultural homology between family and nation and have been variously dubbed 'Scotland's happy family that keeps every family happy' and 'Scotland's First Family'. Inhabiting a tenement flat at 10 Glebe Street,[89] this extended household comprises Granpaw Broon, Maw and Paw, daughters Daphne (large) and Maggie (glamorous), sons Joe (muscular), Hen (gangling), Horace (the boffin), the twins, and the bairn. Their lifestyles and morality are quintessentially respectable working-class (although they own a small cottage in the country, the but 'n' ben, which has presumably passed down through the Broon generations), and their dialect is Dundonian inflected with Glaswegian, as befits 'Auchenshoogle', the fictional town where they reside being an admixture of these two cities. Much of the humour still concerns traditional, and rather antiquated themes involving childhood pranks, the 'generation

Fig. 4.2 The wrong trousers – Paw's in trouble at the brambling.
From *The Broons Annual* 1985.
Image supplied courtesy and © D. C. Thomson & Co. Ltd, Dundee, Scotland.

gap' and the bewilderment of outsiders who get caught up in various plots. Indeed, since the characters and their visual likenesses have barely been updated since the 1930s, remaining constant as life about them changes, it is unsurprising that 'The Broons' have a strong nostalgic appeal amongst

adults, 'characters who remain locked inside the memories of five generations of readers . . . bringing their curious brand or morality to an ever
murkier world'.[90]

More generally, the *Sunday Post* causes intellectuals to cringe because
it presents Scots society and its citizens as *couthy* – genial and folksy,
sometimes to the point of quaintness – conflating thereby a homeliness
of outlook with a parochial narrowness of attitude. Beyond the standard tabloid interest in sport and celebrity, its regular columns include
Francis Gay's highly sentimental, 'heartwarming' stories, medical advice,
consumer problems, and 'Can you do me a favour?' which airs readers'
requests for items such as knitting wool. It also provides a service through
which readers can post messages to trace lost friends and relatives. Yet
while 'The Broons' is certainly the Kailyard portrayal of an idealised
family and community, locked in past time, this does not mean that such
a caricature is left unexamined by its many readers, quite the reverse. For
Herzfeld 'cultural intimacy' entails 'the recognition of those aspects of a
cultural identity that are considered a source of external embarrassment
but that nevertheless provide insiders with their assurance of common
sociality'.[91] Through the exclamations 'Jings!', 'Crivvens!', and 'Help ma
Boab!', sanitised oaths uttered frequently by family members, the image
of 'The Broons' instantly connects readers with a fondly recollected simu-
lacrum of Scotland that is semiotically very much in this zone of humor-
ous but potentially embarrassing familiarity. As time marches on and its
pastness becomes still quainter, Scotland's cartoon family is appreciated
precisely because it has become a parody of itself, hence, for example, the
popularity of Maw Broon's cookbooks.[92]

A comparison of two magazines issuing from the avowedly conservative D. C. Thomson stable reveals how different contents are aimed at
different audiences. *The Scots Magazine* claims 272,000 readers, 53 per
cent of whom live in Scotland. Meanwhile, *The People's Friend* has a total
readership of 554,000. Although only 15 per cent of UK readers live in
Scotland, this figure is disproportionately high relative to background
population size. Each, therefore, has both considerable domestic appeal,
and a broad circulation outside Scotland. Both have long pedigrees, *The
Scots Magazine* being founded in 1739 and *The People's Friend* in 1869.
The publisher's marketing profiles reflect the differing social distributions
('demographics') of the two readerships. Firstly, while *The Scots Magazine*
claims 67 per cent of its sales to be to members of social classes A, B and
C1, *The People's Friend* records 56 per cent in C2, D and in E. Secondly,
although 48 per cent of the *Scots Magazine* audience are aged over 55,
among *People's Friend* readers 79 per cent are over 60. Thirdly, 60 per

Fig. 4.3 *The Scots Magazine* – 'for people who love Scotland'.
Image supplied courtesy and © D. C. Thomson & Co. Ltd, Dundee, Scotland.

cent of *Scots Magazine* readers are male, whereas 88 per cent of *People's Friend* readers are female. *The Scots Magazine* appeals predominantly to a relatively affluent clientele: 'they are generally financially secure, outgoing people with higher than average leisure time and are thus able to enjoy the finer things in life such as travel, dining and gardening'. By contrast, while *The People's Friend* acknowledges that it is 'a publication ideally suited to the female over-50s market', it is basically a 'fiction-based magazine' bought by relatively poor pensioners.[93]

With its logo 'For people who love Scotland' and a front cover that tends to feature a photograph 'of a Scottish scene with a human element in the picture',[94] *The Scots Magazine* places its reader imaginatively within a uniquely Scottish landscape. This distinctive element is played to full effect in the content, which evokes iconic individuals through narratives re-tracing, say, the footsteps of Rob Roy in Balquhidder, or (ironically enough) seeking the spirit of 'MacDiarmid country'.[95] Illustrated itineraries along particular stretches of coast or country, features on indigenous flora and fauna, and spotlights on specific towns, villages, customs, battles and institutions fill every issue, such popular ethnology

Fig. 4.4 *The People's Friend* – couthy stories for older women.
Image supplied courtesy and © D. C. Thomson & Co. Ltd, Dundee, Scotland.

being complemented by reviews and advertisements for books and DVDs about Scotland, especially those with historical, genealogical or 'heritage' themes. Outdoor clothing and holiday accommodation predominate.[96] By contrast, *The People's Friend* is more in line with the stylistic and social tenor of the *Sunday Post*. Its covers are painted in the distinctively romantic, watercolour style of J. Campbell Kerr,[97] depict mainly Scottish landscapes or small-town scenes and carry the tagline 'The famous story magazine' (previously 'The famous story magazine for women'). Romance fiction has always constituted its *raison d'être* – the magazine's early popularity was famously sustained by its serialisation of the stories of Annie S. Swan – although medical advice, recipes 'from Scotland's larder', poetry (accompanied by pastoral scenes), holiday packages and knitting patterns punctuate this theme. Regular features called 'The Farmer and his Wife'('Each column brings a new anecdote from their farm "The Riggin" in Cupar, Scotland') , 'From the Manse Window' and 'Those Were the Days' indicate that the imagined world into which the reader is enjoined to insert herself takes its cue from a morality that is largely rural and situated in the past. Equally, the abundance of advertisements for stair-lifts, supportive underclothing, spectacles and cardigans provides a strong reminder of the present market.[98]

The People's Friend of March 1993 ran a series of articles aiming to get 'Behind the scenes at *Strathblair*', a contemporary television soap opera filmed in Blair Atholl. In reflecting a popular fascination for exploring linkages between period soap operas and real life in their locales, including *Dr Finlay's Casebook* (Callander), *(Take the) High Road* (Luss), and *Monarch of the Glen* (Ardverikie) – all Scottish and rural – these pieces hoped to strike a moral chord with their readership. Consider this extract from an interview with Andrew Keir, an actor who played a leading role in the drama. He comments:

> 'I liked the story of Strathblair immediately: it says something about the disappearing values I admire.'

> So he sees Strathblair as something more than a couthie tale of Perthshire folk? [intones the interviewer]

> 'It is about a fiercely proud and independent people who are intensely human and fall out over petty things, but they would never turn a blind eye to their enemy in need . . . Being your brother's keeper is an age-old tenet . . . You know, this series is being shown in Europe. It might help them to understand our attitudes, our history as a series of small, closely-knit communities.'[99]

This Kailyardist imagery indicates how Anderson's points about the nation also hold for the fictional community. First, like the nation, it is an abstraction created as a result of shared beliefs. Secondly, the fictional community, like the nation, is 'limited' in that it is more or less antagonistic towards those outside the brotherhood: positive images of those within the community logically require negative images of those outside it. Thirdly, like the nation, it is a fellowship of equals. From the vantage point of today's elderly *People's Friend* reader one can see why 'disappearing values' of fierce independence and neighbourly solidarity might appear comforting in a mediated world of muggings, theft, child murder and the 'breakdown of the fabric of society'. Moral panics concern the mores of community and their apparent collapse. *People's Friend* devotees are mostly older working-class women, many living alone. They are more vulnerable than most. Given the urban and suburban milieux in which many must find themselves, the past-situated, fictional rural world lends a comforting vision of an alternative world – indeed, an imagined community – in which justice, safety and caring prevail.[100]

The various D. C. Thomson vehicles occupy different niches, reflecting class-based variations in habitus.[101] However, they share elements of *kitsch* – for instance, all carrying advertisements for tartan teddies – and an interest in dialect. The regular 'Speaking Scots' feature in the *Scots Magazine* examines the etymology of individual words in detail and provides a vernacular dictionary on its web page. This engagement is of a different order to that of the *Sunday Post* which in its use of everyday Scots simply aims to empathise. It is different again from Alexander's Doric, from the Lowland speak, or Lallans, contrived by the Scottish Renaissance poets or, indeed, the phonetic styles of contemporary urban writers such as James Kelman and Irvine Welsh or the poet Tom Leonard. All, however, have the goal of connecting with and replicating the rhythms of everyday Scottishness, of finding a common language of understanding. That some may be, or have been, more effective than others is a moot point however, and those sitting on the high horse of academic vanity do not have the evidence to tell. All one can say with confidence is that D. C. Thomson have a formula and, judging by sales, it works for a great many readers. What they purvey may be so much folksy pabulum, but their popularity cannot be wished away as culturally irrelevant or ushered into place as de-politicised 'sub-nationalism'. To do this is to misunderstand cultural intimacy. The humour of 'The Broons', like many other examples of popular cultural production (as I write, the television comedy series *Still Game* comes to mind) appeals by engendering a degree of homely ridicule, and our laughter here is somewhat more arch than Nairn's argument would suggest.[102]

VISUAL CULTURE AND THE KAILYARD MYTH

Interestingly, while MacDiarmid's peripheral nationalism is fundamentally opposed to the culture of the metropolitan core, Nairn stands accused of adopting 'metropolitan perspectives' in his 'deep aversion to everything native and local'.[103] What they share is a construction of the idea of 'Kailyard as a synonym for myth', in that the word comes 'to signify a particular diagnosis of Scottish culture'; it is a term 'to be used interchangeably with Tartanry to indicate a false historical and cultural consciousness that blighted the nation and impeded meaningful self-definition'. Having created this straw man, both had an ideological foil against which they could assert an authentic alternative. This process inflated the aims and significance of the Kailyard School so that the limited local fantasies and 'country values' of a handful of late-nineteenth century authors were made to stand for a vision of the entire nation.[104] 'Kailyard' has thus transcended its original medium to become the much derided 'hegemonic discourse' of Scottish popular culture.

Those who consider such topics frequently cite Colin McArthur's highly influential *Scotch Reels* (1982) compilation of essays on Scottish film culture.[105] McArthur defines 'Kailyard' films as those 'failing to subvert, or render problematic, existing conceptions about Scotland', and for Nash at least, his subsequent analysis 'strengthened the now almost ubiquitous use of Kailyard in Scottish culture to refer to a fake, regressive, parochial representation of Scotland that was inimical to authentic national expression'.[106] Nash goes on to cite Michael Gardiner's 'excusing' the television series *Hamish Macbeth* because of its 'ironic "postmodern" deployment of "high-tartanry and strategic kitsch"', as though this were an exception.[107] Yet such irony is explicit from the opening pages of *Sunset Song* in 1932 to Bill Forsyth's film *Local Hero* (1983), released half a century later and a year after McArthur's analysis emerged. Intriguingly, when Forsyth was searching for a location at which to shoot his movie, he found himself in a predicament akin to Arthur Freed, the director of *Brigadoon*, the archetypal Hollywood film of a fantasy Highland village, who 'went to Scotland but could find nothing that looked like Scotland'.[108] Forsyth's assistant producer notes: 'We thought we knew Ferness, idyllic, irreplaceable and next to a picture-postcard village, and to our horror, when we started to look for this place on the beach we couldn't find it'.[109] While Freed had visited several sites (Culross, Dunkeld, Comrie, Braemar, Inveraray, and the Brig-o'-Doon of Burns fame), all in vain, Forsyth rendered 'Ferness' from a fabricated amalgam of an east coast fishing village (Pennan) and a west coast bay (Morar). There, of course, the similarity ends, for *Local Hero* presents a heavily parodic take on the vision of Scotland borne by *Brigadoon* and allegedly inspired by 'Kailyard'. As his title implies, the point is that parochial representation, suitably articulated, *is* national expression, even if the local setting required is made elusive by the culturally embedded burden of that representation. There remains, however, a danger in being too clever for the parts of one's audience that might be thought best able to discern this. In 1993, McArthur placed the film within an '"elegiac discourse"', where 'we tend to be written by the dominant Scottish narratives rather than ourselves writing stories about Scotland'.[110] As Bill Forsyth elaborates: 'There was an interesting local reaction to *Local Hero* that I was more or less selling out the screen mythology that Scotland had developed, you know, in terms of Hollywood movies like *Brigadoon*. To my mind, I was subverting as much as I knew about that genre.'[111]

Acknowledging this limitation returns us to the continuing hold of the Kailyard Myth. No-one knew more about audience manipulation than William Robertson Nicoll, whose evangelical objective at the *British Weekly*, and so with his stable of novelists, was 'to unite the disparate nonconformist community [and] to reignite the importance of religion within British national life', hence the appeal to him of Maclaren's 'vision of a universal religious community based on feeling rather than doctrine'.[112] There is a sizeable gulf separating such editorial aims in the late-nineteenth century and the appreciation of popular cultural output in the early twenty-first, and much of the measure of this difference lies in the ironic humour – ranging from the gentle parody of 'The Broons' via the grittier Rab C. Nesbitt to the cynicism of *Trainspotting* and *Taggart* – that attends any reading of much of what now passes as popular cultural output. A cultural ethos remains, while the explicitly religious morality has gone from all but the pages of *The People's Friend*. In search of that ethos, we are not helped by the fact that while critics of the Kailyard Myth have recognised the vibrancy of cultural achievements, particularly of the Victorian period and thus revised their historiography, they still tend to read the Kailyard School itself as a homogeneous movement. Nash shows how the term Kailyard has come to mean such things as 'the "strong comfort factor in recognition" of a "parochial Scottish setting: neutered by diminutives, walled in by teacups" . . . writers are shown to appeal to "the kailyard in the Scottish reader" – to draw from an "emotional parish" . . . and exploit the "kailyard reflex" of reader recognition'.[113] This sense of identification has been exploited most fully in material aimed at the 'women's market', *The People's Friend* being a prime example, and note also the novels of Doris Davidson and, rather less fancifully, Meg Henderson. But the Kailyard = anything about community definition has been used to extend the concept to incorporate writers betraying any devices that embrace locality or group identification – from Neil Munro, A . J. Cronin and Compton Mackenzie to contemporary romantic and not-so-romantic fiction. Indeed, Chris Harvie, pursuing the Nairnite path, has gone so far as to berate Irvine Welsh for 'writing "books for people who don't read books" and thus "exploiting the chemical generation kailyard"'. Nash concludes that 'as a synonym for parochialism, Kailyard thus retains its usefulness'.[114] It does; but this stretches the meaning of 'parochial' somewhat.

INTO THE CITY

The industrial city, which Barrie, Crockett and Maclaren are lambasted for having neglected, has acquired its own 'urban kailyard' myth. The inward-looking world of the Glasgow ghetto suggests its own foreclosure. Yet there is surely something more at stake than parochialism which, although tied to the local, is about modes of identification and belonging.

Because the socialist realism of 'Clydesidism' is 'constructed from "real" images of working-class life', McArthur and Caughie, like Blake before them, contend that it is somehow not mythical, but, of course, by 2010 it most certainly is.[115] In search of sustaining moral fodder, each generation draws on an imaginary idea of society some time in the past to get its bearings about identity. Images of the tenement close in the old industrial city – the hard man, Red Clydeside and the steamie – replace those of kirk and ploughshare, but the nostalgic impetus is substantially the same. The ingredients of remembered urban community are as distinctive and apparently enduring as those of the rural. To a degree, as Chapter 7 will elaborate, visual iconography reflects such stereotyping. The early canvases of Peter Howson, such as *The Heroic Dosser* (1987) and *Game Boys* (1991) with their brutal rendition of working-class masculinity, conjure up images as evocative as Stanley Spencer's wartime *Shipbuilding on the Clyde* (early 1940s) panels of riveters and welders, or the Stakhanovite steel and coal workers of many a Grierson-inspired documentary. Likewise the generations of working-class heroes pictured on the panels of Ken Currie's *Glasgow History Mural* (1987). Popular literature is ripe with gang violence, sectarianism and socialism, from McArthur and Long's *No Mean City* (1935) to television detective series *Taggart* (which reprises their title in the words of its theme song), and the plays of Peter MacDougall and Bill Bryden. In 1965, Edwin Morgan attempted to codify the 'peculiar quality' of Glasgow as 'partly the lingering violent mythology of the slums and the gangs and the sagas of the shipyards, partly what survives in things like the Orange Walk.'[116] However, in the decades since, writers such as Alastair Gray, James Kelman, Janice Galloway, A. L. Kennedy and (for Edinburgh) Irvine Welsh have done much to disturb this urban mythology (and, indeed, Alan Garner does likewise for an urbanised rural Scotland in *Morvern Callar* (1995)).

Cairns Craig claims that: 'Charting the hell of Scotland's industrial squalor has been a fundamental requirement of the modern Scottish novel . . . it is the hell of a world of endless repetition, of endless endurance; the hell of a narrative without end, without purpose. The world of urban Scotland is no longer a stage of history, such as might have been envisaged by the Scottish Enlightenment, which will pass away . . . it is a world where history has ceased to operate.'[117] This is a debatable conceit, since history, or, at least, a vivid recognition of social change pervades much urban narrative. What is more relevant for present purposes is a sense of loss and decline, evident, at least, in some twentieth-century literature about West Central Scotland, that mirrors much of what may be said about its rural counterpart. In an attempt to delineate what has disappeared, William McIlvanney, whose fictional detective Jack Laidlaw steers between older and more modern city cultures, invokes a historicist sense of communal ethics that would not have been entirely strange to Burns or Alexander. In a prefatory essay to a collection of Oscar Marzaroli's photographs of Glasgow between 1956 and 1987, he argues that the city 'has forged much of the essence of modern Scotland'. The experience of 'the brutalising effects of the industrial revolution', together with a pre-existing egalitarianism explains the morality of the street: 'the development of a fierce physical pride, fed partly on circumstances that often left room for little else and partly on the democratic traditions deeply embedded in Scottish life'. In a materially impoverished world where people 'didn't have much more collateral than their sense of themselves . . . [s]tanding up for yourself, sometimes against improbable odds, became a Glasgow convention'. Here are folk 'not averse to taking up arms in causes other than their own if they see what they think is an injustice', where violence is used to defend the neighbourhood and to protect one's own. Like the peasantry before them, they are 'terrible insisters that you don't lose touch for a second with your common humanity, that you don't get above yourself'. Theirs is an attitude evident in the bathos of their patter: 'humane irreverence: more than the big ships, Glasgow's greatest export'. And, most importantly, people take great interest in one another. This is the 'land of the unsolicited confidentiality, country of the unasked for information, city where Greta Garbo wouldn't have been allowed to be alone'; not the metropolis of strangers, of anonymity and civil inattention, but the urban village characterised as 'the city of the stare'.[118]

Or rather, it used to be. In his commentary on the 'apparent decay of honour among hardmen', McIlvanney is scathing about the effects of urban renewal in dispersing this sense of community: 'the post-war annihilation of the tenement in Glasgow wiped out not only buildings but a way of life . . . put together over generations'. Admittedly, much old housing was unfit for human habitation, yet 'what had been fairly coherent communities were either shipped out to housing schemes like penal colonies on the edges of the city or incarcerated in high-rise flats' where the fabric of such coherence – its meeting places, informal institutions, modes of shared survival – was rent apart: no social amenities, heroin freely available in pubs, protection rife, theft endemic, morality gone. With this, McIlvanney sees the withering of 'an old Glasgow art form: the transformation of your circumstances with humour and pride. Never mind the buildings, see the people . . . a skill which has been under increasing pressure over the past 40 years'.[119] Perhaps so, but surely the sardonic wit of, say, Rab C. Nesbitt (unemployed, alcoholic Govan street-philosopher of TV sitcom fame), while acknowledging the supplanting of tenement values by collective 'underclass' pathologies, recognises the folly of both stereotypes in a manner suggestive of precisely such an aptitude.[120]

In his novels, McIlvanney's highly masculine evocation of a lost working-class culture points further to a selectivity of representation, one where 'women's location in the domestic sphere is unproblematic', providing 'a sense of idealised continuity in the face of social transformation'. It follows that 'social realism is thus not what it claims to be. It is dependent on the perpetuation of modernist assumptions about public and private spheres'.[121] In celebrating, amongst other things, 'male family closeness and small-town pride' as well as 'pub culture and loud egalitarianism', his work has been criticised for betraying 'exaggerated respect for physical prowess' but 'an unwillingness to explore ways round the genres of elegiac defeat'.[122] As far back as 1983, Craig suggested that 'the death-throes of industrial West-Central Scotland have become the touchstone of authenticity for our culture . . . That decaying world . . . remakes the emblems of tartanry and kailyard in a new form, for it focuses as the real Scotland an element whose powerless destruction is already inevitable'.[123] So, in the search for a lost Eden in the just-tangible past, continues the infinite regress. The Govan of Rab C. Nesbitt and the Leith of *Trainspotting* (albeit outside the Glasgow radius) are already the stuff of urban legend. Doubtless, our children will eventually long for the fragmented, if demotic malaise of James Kelman's *A Disaffection* (1989), or the displaced, divided selfhood of the protagonist John Thaw in Alastair Gray's *Lanark* (1981), who, in remarking that 'if a city hasn't been used by an artist not even the inhabitants live there imaginatively', opened just such an imaginative dialogue. This indeed is the point of much of this recent material, for the problem with the Glasgow novel is not simply the 'failure to invest the place with aesthetic presence',[124] but also that the essential pastness of its moral message substitutes for an engagement with the ethical ingredients of the here-and-now.

CONCLUSION

Thus is nailed 'Clydesidism', along with its more bucolic cousins. For Craig, it comes as no surprise that 'distrust of the novelistic imagination . . . is the haunting undercurrent of much modern Scottish writing' and that 'a doubtful imagination is the only appropriate medium for a nation founded in the democracy of the commonplace'.[125] Yet if collective representations of intimacy mean that 'cultural idioms become simulacra of social relations' while marginal communities come to 'embody the national quintessence' for the Anglo-American bourgeoisie,[126] tourist trade and, indeed, for some members of the intellectual elite intent either upon appropriating such a vision for the nation or, by contrast, challenging the very basis of such, the perennial embarrassment thus created within popular culture does not merely question the idea of a modern country populated by rationally minded, consensual citizens. It also raises the possibility of what one might call an ironic compromise: people accept fictive constructions of themselves in return for the cultural solace conferred by these fantasies. We know, of course, that 'Drumtochty', 'Auchenshoogle', 'Gushetneuk', 'Ferness' and the rest are mythical, but the communal spirit underpinning these places, however kitsch in its literary manifestation, lends foundation to a self-affirming world view – one that draws on the past to establish the ethics of the present. That is why such allegories persist: myths of community are not just useful in 'branding' Scotland for instrumental purposes; they are also about belonging and self-identity. Against them people test their sense of self, and sometimes they are found badly wanting.

To the extent that myths of community are retailed in our popular media they might nonetheless be regarded as evidence of the 'commodification of longing', a process requiring the application of techniques first elucidated by Walter Scott in the introduction to *Waverley; or 'Tis Sixty Years Since* (1814):

> Too great a temporal distance would give his novel the stamp of the antique, the utterly remote; a modern setting would produce a mere novel of manners. Scott's chosen setting ('sixty years since', forty in George Eliot's case) was not very far removed from current experience, yet distant enough to arouse the reader's nostalgia. If you wrote at this remove, there would be no exotic setting to distract the reader from the internal time of human passion. You could make the past live for the reader: your novel could then effect the integration of the external time of history with the beat of human interiority.[127]

The historical novel was part of a process – 'longing temporalised in the desire for a *particular* past' – that constituted bourgeois nostalgia; a formal appropriation consistent with the preservation of archives, the growth of museums and the development of both history and anthropology as academic disciplines; an attempt to consume the past 'in order to attenuate somewhat its estrangement in the mechanical, segmented present'.[128] After two centuries and several different genres, including the offerings of the popular visual media, this reading of literary production might wear thin. Other contrivances prevail, and Victorian obsessions have long had their day. Meanwhile, an older spiritual susceptibility persists, its influence more benign than Calvinist fear. Herzfeld's concept of cultural intimacy is complemented by what he calls 'structural nostalgia', the means whereby images of lost goodness are developed to resolve tensions between the rhetoric of collective self-presentation and the embarrassment of national self-knowledge. When the present is perceived as flawed, the 'idea of a once-perfect reciprocity' serves to orientate people in understanding the extent and nature of their fall from grace. Notions of moral community become crucial here because 'the virtue that has allegedly decayed always entails some measure of mutuality'.[129] Virtue is perceived through social doing, and in so far as culture is the stories we tell ourselves about ourselves, this is the ethical and genealogical role of the characters populating all our imagined yesterdays.

However, unless one takes for granted the idea of a collective subconscious, a diagnosis such as this asks rather too much of most consumers. Surely most people don't think or feel in such a complex or explicit manner? Sociologists will be familiar with the modernist critique of mass culture, ever since Adorno and Horkheimer's *Dialectic of Enlightenment* (1947), as the imposition of factory produced goods and saleable ideas upon a passive and pacified public. The production of popular culture is driven by quantity rather than quality and false needs are manufactured and reflected in consumption which subjugates the masses to capitalism against their better interests. In gauging the literary response to modernity, and its impact upon cultural awareness, modernism ironically became a crucial means of obfuscation. Because by this logic successful marketing is inimical to the development of good taste and high culture, the Kailyard Myth and its passive consumption rather than active and critical re-negotiation, is given undue prominence in a putative 'eclipse of Scottish culture'.[130] And because anything 'parochial' thereby reflects the false consciousness of low culture, it is anathema to the development of national political consciousness. Certainly this is the message from MacDiarmid, through Nairn to McArthur. Worse still, because of the guile of Nicoll, 'Kailyard' can be seen as a process of domination, 'integrating the masses into a debased form of high culture'. The cultural 'inferiorism' promoted by the D. C. Thomson publications is thus not just about social control by the press; it is also about the generic cultural status – neither 'low' nor 'high' but nationally comprehensive – accorded their output. Yet if this is how 'the Lords of *kitsch* exploit the cultural needs of the masses', these needs remain to be explained.[131] Whether we accept the implication that the subject matter is trivial and 'the masses' don't really think or, by contrast, we regard individuals and groups as having an important function in mediating and adapting cultural products, thus rendering any notion of 'mass' questionable, there are reasons why Scots consume as they do. Feeling comfortable with how the various media mirror their context-bound worldview might well be one of these. Conversely, having a definition of popular culture there to be challenged may be another. Whatever, since myths of community run deep in social memory, the representation of neighbourhood feeling plays a considerable part in evoking the lineages and lineaments of identity. This is the dialectic of the parish paradigm.

NOTES

1. T. Nairn, 'Managed by ghouls' (review of C. Kidd, *Union and Unionisms: Political Thought in Scotland, 1500–2000* (Cambridge: Cambridge University Press, 2008), *London Review of Books*, 30 April 2009, pp. 24–5 (p. 24).

2. R. A. Houston, *Scotland: A Very Short Introduction* (Oxford: Oxford University Press, 2008) takes much store by this view. See also G. Morton, *Unionist-Nationalism: Governing Urban Scotland, 1830–1860* (East Linton: Tuckwell Press, 1999), which highlights the importance of locality in forming identity.

3. G. G. Smith, *Scottish Literature: Character and Influence* (London: Macmillan, 1919), p. 45.

4. C. Craig, *The Modern Scottish Novel: Narrative and the National Imagination* (Edinburgh: Edinburgh University Press, 1999), p. 125.

5. Ibid. pp. 34–5.

6. Ibid. p. 35. See C. Craig, *Intending Scotland: Explorations in Scottish Culture Since the Enlightenment* (Edinburgh: Edinburgh University Press, 2009), which argues for a persistent enlightenment in national culture by reinterpreting the achievements of Frazer, Bell, MacIntosh, Clerk Maxwell and others after 1875 and locating these in a continuing – rather than ruptured – tradition, beginning with the Reid and Hume and going forward into the philosophic and (anti-)psychiatric challenges of Macmurray and Laing respectively.

7. D. McCrone, *Understanding Scotland* (London: Routledge, 1st edn, 1992), p. 90.

8. N. Ascherson, *Stone Voices: The Search for Scotland* (London: Granta Books, 2002), p. 286.

9. Ibid. p. 287.

10. G. E. Davie, *The Democratic Intellect* (Edinburgh: Edinburgh University Press, 1961).

11. F. R. Hart, *The Scottish Novel* (London: John Murray, 1979), p. 401, cited in Craig, *Modern Scottish Novel*, p. 37.

12. Craig, *Modern Scottish Novel*, pp. 200, 211.

13. Craig, *Modern Scottish Novel*, pp. 37, 38.

14. I. Carter, 'The changing image of the Scottish peasantry, 1745–1980', in R. Samuel (ed.), *People's History and Socialist Theory* (London: Routledge, 1981), pp. 9–15 (p. 10).

15. Ibid. p. 11.

16. W. Alexander, 'Aberdeenshire character and characteristics: old and new', *Onward and Upward*, 1 (9), 1891, pp. 218–21 (p. 220).

17. W. Alexander, 'Aberdeenshire character and characteristics: old and new', *Onward and Upward*, 2 (1), 1891, pp. 10–15 (p. 11); *Onward and Upward*, 1 (11), pp. 274–6, (p. 276); *Onward and Upward*, 2 (1), p. 10.

18. See J. P. Collie, 'A Study of the Treatment of the Life of North-east Scotland by Scottish Novelists', unpublished Ph.D. thesis, University of Aberdeen, 1954, p. 21: 'No character pervades the Northeast novel more fully than the land itself', and pp. 46–7: 'The Northeast countryside is at one with the folk who farm it. They cannot successfully stand apart.'

19. Hence the subtitle of I. Carter's book *Farm Life in North-east Scotland: The Poor Man's Country* (Edinburgh: John Donald, 1979).

20. Carter, 'The changing image', p. 10.

21. I. Carter, Introduction to W. Alexander, *Johnny Gibb of Gushetneuk* (Turriff: Heritage Press, 1979), unpaginated, provides a concise summary of the key issues.

22. I. Carter, '"To roose the countra fae the caul' morality o' a deid moderatism": William Alexander and "Johnny Gibb of Gushetneuk"', *Northern Scotland*, II, 1976, pp. 148–62.

23. D. Craig, 'Novels of peasant crisis', *Journal of Peasant Studies*, 1, 1974, pp. 47–68.

24. W. Donaldson, *Popular Literature in Victorian Scotland* (Aberdeen: Aberdeen University Press, 1986) p. 148.

25. Ibid. p. 149.

26. J. Veitch, *George Douglas Brown* (London: Herbert Jenkins, 1952), p. 153; I. Carter, 'Kailyard: the literature of decline in nineteenth century Scotland', *Scottish Journal of Sociology*, 1 (1), pp. 1–13 (p. 3).

27. A. Noble, 'Urbane silence: Scottish writing and the nineteenth century city', in G. Gordon (ed.), *Perspectives on the Scottish City* (Aberdeen: Aberdeen University Press, 1985), pp. 64–90 (pp. 64, 73, 79–80).

28. See A. Blaikie, 'The country and the city: sexuality and social class in Victorian Scotland', in G. Kearns and C. W. J. Withers (eds), *Urbanising Britain: Essays on Class and Community in the Nineteenth Century* (Cambridge: Cambridge University Press, 1991), pp. 80–102, in which I draw my sociological argument from R. Williams, *The Country and the City* (London: Chatto & Windus, 1973).

29. Donaldson, *Popular Literature*, pp. 147–8.

30. G. Blake, *Barrie and the Kailyard School* (London: Arthur Barker, 1951).

31. J. Littlejohn, *Westrigg: The Sociology of a Cheviot Parish* (London; Routledge, 1963).

32. D. Craig, *Scottish Literature and the Scottish People, 1680–1830* (London: Chatto & Windus, 1961, p. 145.

33. Carter, 'Kailyard', p. 8, thus talks of 'Maclaren's place in a different tradition from that elaborated by literary critics: a tradition of writing about the penetration of agrarian capitalism'.

34. Ibid. pp. 8, 9.

35. W. R. Nicoll, *'Ian Maclaren': Life of the Rev. John Watson, DD* (London: Hodder and Stoughton, 1908), pp. 179–80, cited in Donaldson, *Popular Literature*, p. 147.

36. A. Nash, *Kailyard and Scottish Literature* (Amsterdam and New York: Rodopi, 2007), pp. 183, 184. By 1908, 256,000 copies had sold in various UK editions and 484,000 in the US (p. 182).

37. Donaldson, *Popular Literature*, p. 146.

38. Nash, *Kailyard*, p. 185.

39. Ibid. pp. 190–201. Barrie is a different matter and is treated accordingly by Nash (p. 193).

40. Ibid. p. 173.

41. Ibid. pp. 193, 195. He was also adept in the art of multiple reviewing – once infamously debunking Arthur Conan Doyle in six different outlets anonymously – and at logrolling (pp. 191–3).

42. Ibid. pp. 196, 201, 198.

43. J. Veitch, *George Douglas Brown* (London: Herbert Jenkins, 1952), p. 57, quotes the author as claiming: 'No-one pictures the real Scottish village life . . . I will write a novel and tell you all what Scottish village life is like'.

44. Brown comments: 'In every little Scotch community there is a distinct type known as the "bodie." . . . The chief occupation of his idle hours (and his hours are chiefly idle) is the discussion of his neighbour's affairs'. (G. D. Brown, *The House with the Green Shutters* (London: Collins, 1901), p. 39.

45. Carter, 'The changing image', p. 11.

46. Brown, *The House with the Green Shutters*, p. 1.

47. Nash, *Kailyard*, pp. 204, 206.

48. H. MacDiarmid, ed. A. Calder, G. Murray and A. Riach, *The Raucle Tongue: hitherto uncollected prose*, vol. 1 (Manchester: Carcanet, 1996), p. 48, cited in Nash, *Kailyard*, p. 210.

49. N. M. Gunn, ed. A. McCleary, *Landscape and Light: Essays by Neil M. Gunn* (Aberdeen: Aberdeen University Press, 1987), p. 90, cited in Nash, *Kailyard*, p. 215.

50. A. P. Cohen, 'Belonging: the experience of culture', in A. P. Cohen (ed.), *Belonging: Identity and Social Organisation in British Rural Cultures* (Manchester: Manchester University Press, 1982), pp. 1–17 (p. 3). See also F. Barth (ed.) *Ethnic Groups and Boundaries: The Social Organisation of Culture Difference* (Oslo: Universitetsforlaget, 1969).

51. L. Grassic Gibbon and Hugh MacDiarmid, *Scottish Scene; Or, The Intelligent Man's Guide to Albyn* [1934] (Bath: Cedric Chivers, 1974), p. 40, quoted in S. Lyall, *Hugh MacDiarmid's Poetry and Politics of Place: Imagining a Scottish Republic* (Edinburgh: Edinburgh University Press, 2006), p. 116. The following section has benefited greatly from reading Lyall's perceptive thesis.

52. H. Tange, '"Scotland Improper"? How the nationalist landscape failed Grassic Gibbon', in N. McMillan and K. Stirling (eds), *Odd Alliances: Scottish Studies in European Contexts* (Glasgow: Cruithne Press, 1999).

53. Lyall, *Hugh MacDiarmid's Poetry*, p. 4.

54. Ibid. pp. 9, 11, 134.

55. Ibid. p. 78, quoting H. MacDiarmid, *Complete Poems, Vol. II*, eds M. Grieve and W. R. Aitken (Manchester: Carcanet, 1994), 1424.

56. Ibid. p. 43. Lyall renders MacDiarmid a proto- post-colonialist. Against the wasteland of contemporary Scotland, his projected national reinvention emphasises a 'calculatedly rooted . . . geopolitical marginality' (p. 152). Like Yeats, his is a 'poetic project of national reinvention' (p. 134), but in stressing tradition it differs from the attempt to conjure up a new Ireland through post-colonial hybridity, for he stresses tradition.

57. Ibid. p.12. Langholm is a small town very close to the English border; Montrose, a fishing port and market town on the east coast; Whalsay, in Shetland, a windswept island at the extreme northern extremity of the British Isles.

58. Ibid. pp. 18, 17.

59. Ibid. pp. 109, quoting H. MacDiarmid, *Complete Poems, Vol. I*, eds M. Grieve and W. R. Aitken (Manchester: Carcanet, 1993), 144; p. 79, quoting MacDiarmid, *Complete Poems, Vol. II*, 1424.

60. Ibid. pp. 128, 65.

61. C. Craig, *Out of History: Narrative Paradigms in Scottish and English Culture* (Edinburgh: Polygon, 1996), p. 108.

62. Ibid. p. 157. 'Your damned democracy' is a line from H. MacDiarmid, 'The North Face of Liathach', *Complete Poems, Vol. II*, 1055.

63. Ibid. p. 49: 'In his own case erudition originated and was fostered in a close-knit, local environment.'

64. The phrase comes from MacDiarmid's most famous and significant poem 'A Drunk Man Looks at the Thistle' (1926) (H. MacDiarmid, *Complete Poems, Vol. I*, 87).

65. T. Nairn, 'Old nationalism and new nationalism', in G. Brown (ed.), *The Red Paper on Scotland* (Edinburgh: EUSPB, 1975), pp. 22–57 (p. 42) distinguishes between the 'dementia' of MacDiarmid and the lucidity of his alias G. M. Grieve who 'reminds us that it was the situation of the intelligentsia that was hopeless, not that of the country'.

66. Craig, *Out of History*, p. 108.

67. Lyall, *Hugh MacDiarmid's Poetry*, pp. 107–8. 'Although thereby reflection of strategic essentialism, such anteriority has been perceived as both elitist and ethnocentric' (p. 10, citing M. Gardiner, *The Cultural Roots of British Devolution* (Edinburgh: Edinburgh University Press, 2004), p. 29).

68. Ibid. p. 136: 'The Islands of Scotland [H. MacDiarmid, *The Islands of Scotland: Hebrides, Orkneys and Shetland* (London: Batsford, 1939)] can be seen as a nationalist response to *A Journey to the Western Islands of Scotland* (1775), topographically extending yet ideologically troubling the assured Enlightenment metropolitanism of Johnson and Boswell's tour of lonely places incompatible with British civilisation'.

69. Ibid. p. 186, quoting H. MacDiarmid, *Complete Poems, Vol. II*, 788. Lyall recognises 'MacDiarmid's eco-Marxism' (p. 122), particularly evident in 'On a Raised Beach' (1933).

70. Ibid. p. 137, quoting 'Mr C. M. Grieve on Up-Helly-Aa', *Shetland News*, 8 February 1934, p. 4).

71. Ibid. pp. 67, 69, quoting H. MacDiarmid, *Lucky Poet: A Self Study in Literature and Political Ideas*, ed. A. Riach [1943] (Manchester: Carcanet, 1994), 20, 3.

72. Craig, *Modern Scottish Novel*, p. 22.

73. Nairn, 'Old nationalism', p. 22.

74. Ibid. p. 36.

75. Donaldson, *Popular Literature*, p. 149.

76. Nairn, 'Old nationalism', pp. 37, 38 (citing G. Blake, *Barrie and the Kailyard School*, pp. 80–1), 39.

77. Ibid. p. 40.

78. Ibid. p. 38.

79. Dedication to *Catriona* (1893), quoted in D. Daiches, *Robert Louis Stevenson and His World* (London: Thames & Hudson, 1973), p. 11, and cited in Nairn, 'Old nationalism', p. 38.

80. C. Murray, *Hamewith* (London: Constable, 1920), frontis., 'Hame' (pp. 41–2) 'The Alien' (p. 4), 'Hamewith' (p. 1).

81. Craig, *Modern Scottish Novel*, pp. 60–1.

82. L. Grassic Gibbon, *A Scots Quair* (London: Hutchinson, 1946), p. 37. This passage initially appeared in *Sunset Song* (London: Jarrolds, 1932), the first novel in the trilogy.

83. R. Macfarlane, *The Wild Places* (London: Granta Publications, 2007), p. 71.

84. Ibid. pp. 38–9.

85. Nairn was not the first such critic: as he himself acknowledges, in 1951 Blake claimed that the firm 'flourishes largely by the careful cultivation of the Kailyard strain' (Blake, *Barrie and the Kailyard School*, 1951, p. 85). See also M. Lindsay, *By Yon Bonnie Banks: A Gallimaufry* (London: Hutchinson, 1961).

86. www.sundaypost.com. Accessed December 2006. G. Rosie, 'The private life of Lord Snooty', *Sunday Times*, 29 July 1973, cited in Nairn, 'Old nationalism', p. 56, estimated that the paper had million readers overall in 1971. The *Sunday Post* and the *Dundee Courier* (both from the Thomson stable) are the only two newspapers to have been continuously Scottish-owned.

87. http://www.dcthomson.co.uk Accessed June 2009.

88. Nash, *Kailyard*, p. 225. The first 'Broons' annual was published in 1939, with 'Oor Wullie' the following year. They have continued to alternate ever since – save for a brief gap during World War II – with sales regularly placing them in the bestseller lists.

89. The address resonates with ties of community, the glebe being the land adjacent to the kirk and belonging to it.

90. S. McGinty, 'In a land where fun still has a place', *The Herald*, 24 August 1966, pp. 6–7 (p. 6).

91. M. Herzfeld, *Cultural Intimacy: Social Poetics in the Nation-State* (New York and London: Routledge, 1997), p. 3.

92. *Maw Broon's Cookbook* (New Lanark: Waverley Books, 2007), 'a facsimile of Maw Broon's very own cookbook, which we borrowed from the sideboard at No. 10 Glebe Street – first made for her by her mother-in-law when "Maw" married "Paw", and added-to over the years', won a Gourmand Award and was Scotland's Number One bestseller for nine weeks prior to Christmas 2007.

93. http://www.marketing.dcthomson.co.uk/pdf_window.asp?pdf=scots_mag.pdf; http://www.marketing.dcthomson.co.uk/pdf_window.asp?pdf=peoples_friend.pdf. Both accessed June 2009.

94. http://www.scotsmagazine.com/photoguides.asp. Accessed June 2009.

95. Both in *Scots Magazine*, November 2006.

96. Despite this, the ageing character of the target market appears to be acknowledged. For example, the June 2009 issue carries advertisements for reclining chairs and lightweight vacuum cleaners.

97. 'J. Campbell Kerr' is apparently a pseudonym covering a number of artists.

98. Guidance notes for contributing authors characterise typical readers thus: 'They like being entertained – and dislike being depressed. They like realistic material, but not so realistic – with sex, violence, drugs, drink, etc. – that they are frightened or saddened. They still believe in the sanctity of marriage and the importance of the family. Our readers like people – ordinary people, with problems they can sympathise with, and in situations they can relate to. They're optimistic – they like to see something good coming out of a situation, or the redeeming side of a character . . . They're always willing to give a neighbour a helping hand and enjoy being with a group of friends' (http://www.jbwb.co.uk/pfguidelines.htm Accessed June 2009).

99. V. Bissland, 'Behind the scenes at Strathblair, Part Two', *People's Friend*, 13 March 1993, pp. 18–21 (p. 21).

100. See A. Blaikie, 'Imagined landscapes of age and identity', in G. J. Andrews and D. R. Phillips (eds), *Ageing and Place* (London: Routledge), pp. 164–75 (pp. 170–2).

101. A broader analysis might also consider competitors such as *Scotland Magazine*, *Scottish Memories* and *History Scotland*.

102. In the early twentieth century, *Wee Macgreegor*, Para Handy, *Whisky Galore*, and the music hall tradition of Harry Lauder all fell into this category, where 'once again the association with Kailyard turns on the popular appeal and the popular use of humour' (Nash, *Kailyard*, p. 221).

103. D. McCrone, *Understanding Scotland* (London: Routledge, 2nd edn, 2001), p. 141, citing C. Beveridge and R. Turnbull, *The Eclipse of Scottish Culture* (Edinburgh: Polygon, 1989) pp. 61, 58.

104. Nash, *Kailyard*, pp. 234–6, 230–2.

105. C. McArthur, *Scotch Reels: Scotland in Cinema and Television* (London: BFI Publishing, 1982). While D. Petrie, *Screening Scotland* (London: BFI Publishing, 2000) attempts a more positive evaluation of Scotland within a similar frame of reference (see Nash, *Kailyard*, p. 241), in exploring several transnational genres through which Scotland has been imagined in recent years, D. Martin-Jones, *Scotland: Global Cinema* (Edinburgh: Edinburgh University Press, 2009) certainly broadens the scope for cinematic criticism.

106. Nash, *Kailyard*, pp. 239, 241.

107. Ibid. pp. 241–2, citing M. Gardiner, *Modern Scottish Culture* (Edinburgh: Edinburgh University Press, 2005), pp. 179–80.

108. F. Hardy, *Scotland in Film* (Edinburgh: Edinburgh University Press, 1990), p. 1.

109. *Local Hero*, *Movie Connections*, series 2, programme 7, BBC1 Scotland, 18 February 2009.

110. C. McArthur, 'Scottish culture: a reply to David McCrone', *Scottish Affairs*, 4, 1993, pp. 95–106 (p. 102), cited in McCrone, *Understanding Scotland*, 2nd edn, p. 140.

111. *Local Hero*, *Movie Connections*.

112. Nash, *Kailyard*, pp. 175, 192.

113. Ibid. p. 247, citing D. Chapman, 'Designer Kailyard', in D. Gifford and D. Macmillan (eds), *A History of Scottish Women's Writing* (Edinburgh: Edinburgh University Press, 1997), pp. 536–48 (pp. 537, 538, 539, 541).

114. Ibid. p. 248, citing C. Harvie, *Scotland and Nationalism: Scottish Society and Politics, 1710–1994*, 3rd edn, (London: Routledge, 1998), p. 222.

115. McCrone, *Understanding Scotland*, 2nd edn, p. 139; C. McArthur, 'Scotch reels and after', *Cencrastus*, 11, 1983, pp. 2–3; J. Caughie, 'Scottish television: what would it look like?', in McArthur, *Scotch Reels*, pp. 112–22.

116. E. Morgan, 'Signs and wonders', *New Statesman*, 13 August 1965.

117. Craig, *Modern Scottish Novel*, p. 131.

118. W. McIlvanney, 'Where Greta Garbo wouldn't have been alone', in O. Marzaroli and W. McIlvanney, *Shades of Grey: Glasgow, 1956–1987* (Edinburgh: Mainstream/ Glasgow: Third Eye Centre, 1987), pp. 13–36, reprinted in W. McIlvanney, *Surviving the Shipwreck* (Edinburgh: Mainstream, 1991), pp. 163–84 (pp. 165, 167–8, 183–4, 180).

119. Ibid. pp. 169–70.

120. Rab nevertheless remarks that what talent he once had was obliterated by Govanites who, being scared of such a thing, resolved to 'tae batter it tae death wi' empty wine bottles'. Such was the re-channelling of the impulse to violence. See http://en.wikipedia.org/wiki/Rab_C._Nesbitt (Accessed June 2009) for details of this comedy and its characterisation.

121. A. Howson, 'No gods and precious few women: gender and cultural identity in Scotland', *Scottish Affairs*, 2, 1993, pp. 37–49 (p. 43).

122. J. Idle, 'McIlvanney, masculinity and Scottish literature', *Scottish Affairs*, 2, 1993, pp. 50–7 (pp. 50, 57).

123. C. Craig, 'Visitors from the stars: Scottish film culture', *Cencrastus*, 11, 1983, pp. 6–11 (p. 9).

124. Donaldson, *Popular Literature*, p. 149.

125. Craig, *Modern Scottish Novel*, pp. 216, 234.

126. Herzfeld, *Cultural Intimacy*, pp. 6–7.

127. C. Steedman, *Dust* (Manchester: Manchester University Press, 2001), pp. 90–1.

128. D. Lowe, *History of Bourgeois Perception* (Brighton: Harvester, 1982), pp. 40–1, cited in Steedman, *Dust*, p. 91.

129. Herzfeld, *Cultural Intimacy*, pp. 111–12.

130. Beveridge and Turnbull, *The Eclipse*, p. 14.

131. D. MacDonald, 'A theory of mass culture', in B. Rosenberg and D. Manning White (eds), *Mass Culture: The Popular Arts in America* (Glencoe: Free Press, 1957), pp. 59–73 (p. 60).

Chapter 5

Retrieving 'that invisible leeway': landscapes, cultures, belonging

The conventional logic of landscape evaluation is that the Romantic Movement was a conservative response to the onset of modernity, emphasising the need to develop 'culture' as moral salvation against the instability of urbanisation and industrialisation. Its legacy has seen a supposedly preexisting Arcadia touted as 'authentic' for a public that misrecognises fabrication for historical fact. Arguably, alienated from their own acts of creation, cultural producers have reified their own constructions, believing likewise that these reflect a sacred essence of 'natural beauty'. Icons abound. What more can be said about the social construction of the Scottish landscape?

One of the acknowledged paradoxes of modernisation is that the myth of an enduring British countryside emerged precisely at the period of wholesale urban and industrial upheaval. Investigating this myth is compromised by the implication that the tools of its construction and analysis are themselves novel and historically specific in character. For instance, it has been suggested that 'between them the camera and tourism are two of the uniquely modern ways of defining reality'.[1] They are certainly jointly implicated in the emergence of Scottish identity over the past 150 years. Yet, paradoxically again, their relationship to that identity is one that has been troubled by modernity to such a degree that in classifying the country's 'heritage' both have obscured the evidence of the very processes that created it. Consequently, unravelling the texture of landscape imagery requires us to deconstruct not only histories of photography and travel but also how we perceive the relationship between self and national identity.

Highlandism

In April 2006, *The Scotsman* published the results of its 'massive public ballot' in which over 50,000 voters selected their favourite national icon.[2]

The National Trust for Scotland, celebrating its 75th anniversary, partnered the newspaper in this 'Seven Wonders of Scotland' project, where 30 short-listed 'wonders' were championed by famous public figures. With Glencoe polling the fourth highest number of votes, 'natural' landscape featured in fully one-third of the placings and, as indicated in an accompanying essay, the Highlands were heavily over-represented:

> The nation mainly defines itself in terms of its glorious landscape and some iconic physical formations (Forth Bridge and Edinburgh Old and New Towns). The Wonders are also timeless and enduring. Late Victorian Scots would have recognised them all; there is no place for the 20th century in the list. When we define ourselves, we look back for markers of identity [and here the] seductive power of Highlandism on the Scottish imagination . . . shows no sign of waning . . . Apparently for many modern Scots, as for their Victorian ancestors, their hearts are still in the Highlands.

Following a long tradition in cultural historiography, Devine sees in the 'adoption of Highland emblems and associations as the national image for a modernising Scotland' an answer to 'the emotional need to maintain distinctive Scottish identity without compromising the Union'.[3] At a time when most Scots claim to be Scottish before they are British and many disavow Britain altogether, this is not just a consideration of past concerns. Highlandism persists today because it is a reflection of a popular *mentalité* in which Scottishness is imagined not just by seeing landscape in particular established ways but through using it symbolically to connect personal, social and national identities. Like the painters before them early landscape photographers invested their pictures with emotion and spirituality.[4] Yet contrary to the poetic manner in which community is envisaged in popular literature, people are conspicuous by their absence. This lends many images a ghostly quality, for paradoxically yet again, given their utility as a resource for continuity and connection between generations, these portrayals are distinctively landscapes without figures, and, by that fact, exclude the industrial Lowlands. Thus the iconography of Scottish landscape overwhelmingly consists of images of empty places that are distant from where most Scots live. This presents an interesting topophilic puzzle, for while personal connections clearly bind human beings to the physical environment, landscape photographs create the impression that this environment is rarely the immediate, everyday habitat in which people dwell.

In addressing this conundrum, we must first pay heed to the connection between national identities and the cultural frameworks through which these may be imagined. What we understand as 'landscape' is socially constructed, 'its scenery is built up as much from strata of memory as from layers of rock'. Such is 'the annexation of nature by culture'.[5] And, as everywhere, Scottish identity has been premised upon a long history of landscape metaphors. Whereas, in the United States, the wilderness was conceived as 'a democratic terrestrial paradise'[6], or, in England, the village came to signify a vanishing rural world, Scottishness has played heavily on the raw majesty of the Highlands, which contribute in large measure to the 'patriotic topography' of the nation.[7] But it was not always so. In 1730, the Hanoverian officer Edward Burt observed that the hills around Inverness were 'of a dismal gloomy Brown, drawing upon a dirty Purple; and most of all disagreeable when the Heath is in Bloom', yet nowadays, 'trying to see that neutral, unappropriated flower would be like trying to see, say, a swastika as nothing but an abstract design. For us, the moment we set eyes on a heather-covered Highland hillside is . . . the moment when we register the presence of the Highland romance'.[8] During the half-century after the defeat of Jacobitism at Culloden, the Highlands were romanticised to suit the ideological requirements of a Unionist British state. Thus, a region that had been regarded as hostile and alien before 1746 was by the early nineteenth century incorporated and tamed through a semiotics of romantic painting and literature characterised by 'subjugation, survey, and appreciation, very much in that order'.[9] Its landscape, once regarded in a simply utilitarian manner, had been invested with emotive meaning. This sustained cultural resonance, engineered by Scott and Landseer and consolidated by Queen Victoria's eulogisation of Balmoral, was part-and-parcel of an emphatic and well documented alteration in consciousness of the relationship between people and the natural world that has culminated in a potent mythology:

> We know that the Highlands are romantic. Bens and glens, the lone shieling in the misty island, purple heather, kilted clansmen, battles long ago, an ancient and beautiful language, claymores and bagpipes and Bonny Prince Charlie – we know all that, and we also know that it's not real. Not that it's a pure fabrication: on the contrary, all the things on that rough-and-ready list actually exist, or existed. But the romance is not simply the aggregate of the things; it is a message which the things carry.[10]

Significantly, this message is one that has percolated from high to popular culture as it has become geographically hegemonic, such that a once elite visualisation of one part of the country now stands for Scotland *in toto*. If, as Chapter 4 has suggested, nineteenth-century Scottish fiction (or, at least, that consumed by the middle-class cognoscenti) was remarkable in its apparent failure to confront the problems of the industrial city, so a continuing pictorial sensibility – emotions in relation to landscape being categorised as the beautiful, the picturesque or the sublime – rendered the Lowland Scotland inhabited by most of the population at best ambiguous and at worst redundant in the twentieth-century imaginary.[11]

POSTCARDS, PLATES AND TOURIST VENTURES

In the history of photography different genres may be identified and compared on the basis of what pictures themselves include or exclude. Thus a recent survey notes that 'whereas American documentary photographs saturate the photograph with human figures, landscape images empty the land of human presence'.[12] Scottish pictorial traditions reflect this dichotomy, yet this is not simply because photographers have subscribed to global conventions in technique. If the legacy of Hill and Adamson's pioneering experiments of the 1840s was a vision founded on portraiture, the subsequent commercial rivalry between George Washington Wilson & Co. and James Valentine & Sons revolved more around the ready translation of panoramic vistas into prints, cabinet views, albums and lantern slides than any wish to document late-Victorian society. By 1865, George Washington Wilson produced 550,000 prints per annum, with almost two-thirds of the income coming from sales of views.[13] Both firms capitalised upon the rapid development of tourism in Scotland following Thomas Cook's first excursion in 1846 and the expansion of rail travel, and their catalogues provide 'a map and index of popularity of the tourist destinations of Scotland'.[14] The territory expanded as photographers ventured, like the eighteenth-century travellers before them, into remoter parts in search of picturesque scenes, encouraging tourists to follow. In the same way that Boswell and Johnson, Pennant and others marked the bounds of the Scottish grand tour so the photographic tour may be considered as 'a minor cultural form in its own right'.[15] With epic poems like Scott's *The Lady of the Lake* (1810) providing 'not so much a pretext to visit the place (the Trossachs) as a rubric on which to base a pictorial response',[16] the pictures were 'iconic representations of those places most revered in the tourist literature where literary and historical associations reinforced the appeal'.[17]

Photographers' exploits combined expeditionary fervour with delight in the sublime, hence desolation, bleakness and wild grandeur came to be much prized qualities. Meanwhile, since the criteria presumed either timeless rurality or great national monuments, their compass ignored Lowland industrialism. As Durie comments, if these photographs were the only source available for reconstructing nineteenth-century Scotland:

'It would be a land of history, scenery and architecture, with an economy that was largely pastoral and devoted to leisure. There would have been, apparently, almost no heavy industry and the main support of the population other than agriculture would have been fishing and the provision of leisure services'.[18] Exposing social conditions was not on the agenda since slums did not sell, not least because the countryside, and especially the curative influence of clean air, were central to the growing popularity of travel among those who realised the insanitary influences of the urban environment. Those early documentarians who focused on the city scene, like Thomas Annan, had local interests in architecture and latterly portraiture rather than the tourist market.

The demise of Wilson's empire came in 1908 as profits declined with rising competition from cheap postcards and book illustrations made from half-tone prints. Moreover, the rise of artistic modernism after the First World War saw a rapid waning of rural romanticism as 'tourism and fine art ceased to run together'.[19] The following decades saw a democratisation of both experience and image as the aesthetic conventions of landscape art were further transformed via popular magazines and didactic travel guides which 'sought not only to impart information about places and landscapes, but were also keen to say how they should be appreciated'.[20] MacDonald suggests that while early photographic depictions of landscape had followed the picturesque tradition of Sandy and Gilpin in privileging 'picturing' over 'looking', 'representation over observant practice', the guidebook imagery of the Interwar years 'construct[ed] the Highlands as a place for looking', with 'remarks about "skilful gradients" and "strategically-sited lay-byes" [that] were primarily focused on the accelerated focus of the moving landscape'.[21] In 1927 The Scots Magazine, founded in 1739 and the official organ of Scottish Societies around the globe, joined the popular D. C. Thomson group. With a mission 'to present a picture of Scotland as a nation' it was to become the world's best-selling Scottish-interest periodical, its pages including regular illustrated features by renowned landscape photographer Robert Moyes Adam.[22] The following year SMT Magazine began, later to become Scotland's Magazine as an organ of the Scottish Tourist Board.[23] Retrospectively described as 'a wide-ranging and colourful magazine with stories, letters, descriptions of Scottish towns and landscapes; very much the kind of thing one could find in dentists' waiting rooms', it carried 'a strong current of Scottish nationalism'.[24] Significantly, its title, short for Scottish Motor Traction, and publisher, the Scottish Bus Group, reflected the close relationship between changing modes of transport and mass tourism. As Gold and Gold demonstrate, during the Interwar years the motor car increasingly 'gave the middle classes a degree of mobility and control over their travel plans, rather than being confined to accessible channels around rail networks or organised travel parties'.[25] In 1934 the Shell-Mex petrol company began sponsorship of a series of Shell Guides, edited by John Betjeman, although only one Scottish volume was produced before 1939. While a large differentiated market in illustrated tourist literature developed, its mainstay was the discerning, automobile-equipped middle classes.

These developments of the late 1920s and early 1930s coincided with the depths of a global Depression that hit industrial Scotland particularly severely.[26] Yet neither the magazine market nor the more high-minded *Shell Guide to the Western Isles* volume gave any real indication of its impact, while the visual imagery of decayed industrial landscapes was altogether lacking. However, during the early 1930s a distinction arose between the tradition of appreciating Scottishness through landscape and attempts to identify and explain the Scots character. Recognising that Scotland's remoter parts were now within reach of motorists, Batsford's *Face of Britain* series of topographic companions published *The Face of Scotland* in 1933, followed the next year by *The Heart of Scotland*.[27] Their titles presaged an attempt to codify differences between what could be inferred from superficial topography and what might be understood from shrewder cultural investigation. In his foreword to *The Face of Scotland* writer and diplomat John Buchan, no less, provides clarification. Its text, he says, 'is strictly an exposition to accompany some of the finest specimens of the photographic art that I have seen . . . The "Face of Scotland" is not the heart of Scotland, but, if properly discerned it is a clue to it. Much of the idiom of the national history, character and literature can be traced to the landscape'. However, this was a travel book rather than an interpretative essay, the authors acknowledging that it 'attempts to provide a compact outline of Scottish topography . . . chiefly concerned with scenery . . . The inclusion of so many fine photographs largely dispenses with the need for elaborate descriptive writing'. Lavishly illustrated, with some 116 images attributed to 'landscape photographers', the sections were organised regionally with fully half devoted to the Highlands and Islands.[28] Almost a quarter of the photographs used (27) were sourced from the Dundee postcard firms of Valentine's and White's. As Gold and Gold reflect, the pictures 'presented a country of vast open spaces, panoramas of mountain, loch and sky: a depopulated, empty country with scarcely a hint of human intervention'. While this was to some extent a product of contemporary photographic style, displaying 'an aversion to allowing human detail to distract from the serious business of landscape', it was nevertheless remarkable that the cities too 'seem[ed] almost devoid

Fig. 5.1 Motoring through empty Glen Shee in the Grampians –
The Face of Scotland (1933).
© Anova Books Company Limited.

Fig. 5.2 Appreciating Scotland through landscape – *The Face of Scotland* (1933).
© Anova Books Company Limited.

of people'.[29] The 'rhetoric of the open road', a path to discovering this undefiled territory, gave tourists 'the opportunity to go in search of dialogue between the modern world, on the one hand, and the authentic and unchanging traditions of the countryside on the other'.[30]

Ostensibly similar, in that its cover design employed Brian Cook's distinctive pictorial house-style while using some 76 photographic illustrations many of which were rural panoramas, George Blake's, *The Heart of Scotland* set out not to look at scenery but to discover how people lived, thought and felt, to investigate 'a consciousness of Scottishness' in 'what John Buchan excellently calls "the idiom" of the national life'.[31] In a final chapter in the 1951 edition, entitled 'Unconventional Journey', Blake spoke of a proliferation of 'Caledoniana' partly due to 'resurgent nationalism' which had seen a particularly 'dramatic growth' in the years since the 1934 first edition. But he also noted that 'it seems equally true that Mr H. V. Morton's fabulously successful *In Search of Scotland* [1929] – romantic, sentimental, choosey, but immensely competent – set a fashion. The development of hiking and tourism has almost ludicrously stimulated the outflow of topographical exercises. Not a Scottish mountain or glen but has been photographed all ends up. The Leica and the Contax out of industrial Germany raven on the Highland scene'.[32] In literature he detects a division amongst writers about Scotland, who either want romance or realism, such that 'a Scottish norm is most damnably difficult to fix'. Thus he argues that the topographical tourists 'miss much of the quiddity of Scotland' since 'an excessive emphasis on romanticism distorts the picture', but so too – to Blake's mind – does the excessively realist journalism of slums and sectarianism. As he heads east out of Glasgow, the book's final paragraphs present the author's attempt to square the circle, yet the image evoked is certainly not romantic:

> the lorries thunder through mile upon mile of farmland, indeed, but . . . it is obviously related to an urban economy . . . *Dereliction* is the word . . . The stigmata of neglect litter this highway [A80] almost all the way from Glasgow to Stirling . . . let the intelligent traveller consider as he passes through them the nature and provenance of Millerston, Mollinsburn, Cumbernauld and Dennyloanhead. It is impossible to traverse such communities without seeing that something rather horrible once happened to Scotland, something from which it has never recovered.[33]

This is the aftermath of industrialism. It does not present an edifying picture, hence no photographic illustrations. Yet, concludes Blake: 'if Scotland is to be understood rather than merely seen, one may reasonably suggest that its heart is where most of its people live. The scenery will always be there, vestigial and indestructible. It is still a fact that the present state of Dennyloanhead is of much more importance to the living community of Scotland than the bloom of heather, a vegetable of barren places, on Lochnagar.[34] The word suburban does not neatly capture the ambience of such places; they are nonetheless represented as analytically problematic 'edgelands': neither city nor country; thrown up by industry but relevant because they disfigure natural beauty.[35] Davidson has recently argued that: 'One of the starkest differences between Scotland and England is the absence in Scotland of the village in the English sense. In Scotland the break between town and country is absolute. Small settlements are small urban settlements . . . The smallest settlement is a city townscape, on however minute a scale'.[36] Whatever the merits or otherwise of this observation, it suggests that the sociable pastoral upon which much Merrie Englishness is founded may be lacking, leaving thereby no ground for compromise. Instead, Scotland becomes a landscape of singular contrast: sublime, mostly Highland scenery versus contemptible urban sprawl. The reader, meanwhile, may have felt perplexed by the disjunction between Blake's argument and the accompanying illustrations, for realism and romance clearly no longer ran together.

H. V. MORTON'S TWO SCOTLANDS

Relationships between text and image betray to a degree the aims of different publishers. Another trend in popular travel writing at the time was for articles that first appeared in newspapers or weeklies to be compiled into travelogues. H. V. Morton, the prolific and hugely influential travel writer alluded to above, was pivotal here. Following the dramatic success of *In Search of England* (1927), he published *In Search of Scotland* (1929), a book which, like its predecessor, had originated as a series of *Daily Express* essays following his itinerary through the country in his two-seater Bullnose Morris car. It was to become the best-selling of all his works.[37] His English material had clearly been contrived to minimise 'the intrusion into Eden of vulgar modernity', Morton later confessing that he had 'deliberately shirked realities' by making 'wide and inconvenient circles to avoid modern towns and cities'.[38] Meanwhile, regarding Scotland Gold and Gold comment that:

> Morton's tour of enlightenment was no simple exposition of the appeal of the Highlands. As with his writings on Wales and elsewhere, Morton had an interest in industrial landscapes. He approached the shipyards of the Clyde with picturesque sensitivity; workers in the steelworks at Motherwell, in a striking analogy, seem like devils at the mouth of Hell. He admires the spirit of the Glaswegians and the architecture of their central city.[39]

Fig. 5.3 Urban emptiness – H. V. Morton, *In Scotland Again* (1933).
© Methuen Publishing Limited.

This is a sound analysis so far as the book is concerned: Morton does visit Scotland's cities, and a goodly number of towns, and its industries are included as fully as its countryside. But while *In Search of Scotland* contains sixteen photographic illustrations and *In Scotland Again* (London: Methuen, 1933) carries a further fifteen, all but one are scenic views of landscapes or monuments.[40] Aside from a handful of tiny figures on a bridge (Inverness panorama) or loitering in a rather empty square (Dumfries), the crowd witnessing the golf at St Andrews, two old fishermen talking and a solitary close shot of a man feeding tame fish are the only images including any sign of human activity. None at all involve labouring.

In stark contrast, the versions published in the *Daily Herald* are both richly illustrated and somewhat more populated by people at work. Morton had left the staunchly Conservative *Daily Express* in February 1931, joining the Labour and trades-union-orientated *Herald* the next month. This 'signalled no change in his own political outlook' and his collected travel columns 'In Search of Wales' became another Methuen travel volume in 1932 in tried and trusted fashion.[41] Nevertheless, several developments are evident with 'In Scotland Again', a travel column that appeared in 38 instalments, between 29 September and 2 December 1931 – roughly four times a week. The series included 61 photographs taken by Morton's travelling partner James Jarché, a press photographer, who 'in his day, was something of a celebrity'.[42] Jarché had been on the staff of the *Daily Sketch* from 1912 until 1929, but began working for the *Daily Herald* in 1931. Elsewhere I have argued that his pictures complement Morton's rather conservative social analysis of slums and areas of industrial blight.[43] Nevertheless, he had already pioneered new techniques to produce investigative photojournalism in collaboration with Morton, who, despite claiming to be politically non-partisan, produced devastating health and housing statistics and advocated state-directed slum-clearance policies. With their story about Welsh coalminers in 1931 Jarché became the first cameraman to use a flashbulb underground. Meanwhile, his Scottish work that year included a photo-essay on the building of the Queen Mary. Sandwiched between Friday's article 'The watch on the Clyde for work that never comes' (6 November 1931) and Tuesday's 'Heartbreak Close: tenements haunted by life's derelicts' (10 November 1931), the five photographs comprising the spread on 'Building Britain's mammoth liner' (9 November 1931) present awesome images of industry, conveying 'an overwhelming impression of immensity' and contrasting sharply with the social depression so vividly portrayed in the adjacent Glasgow stories.[44]

Yet none of this reportage found its way into the book version, published in 1933. Instead, Morton passes through the city, visiting a bagpipe factory, then quickly traversing 'the miles of ugly streets that lead to Dumbarton' en route between the Isle of Arran and Loch Lomond. He stops briefly to meet a friend in the polished mahogany offices of a shipyard, musing that:

> It impressed me [also] as a fragment of a world that has vanished. Nothing in our world is quite so solid and assured . . . here beside the Clyde, now so tragically silent, this rich, confident room lingers on in a condition of suspended animation . . . I felt that it should be preserved in some museum.

When his friend arrived, Morton 'took him by the arm and led him out into the silent place where the empty slipways go down to the Clyde, in order that the magnificent room might hear nothing of our troubles, and go on dreaming of the old ships and the old times and – the old cheques'.[45]

Taken together the consecutive *Daily Herald* pieces reflect the immediacy of Morton's sojourn, in style and impact very different to the books' sense of thoughts recollected in tranquillity, whereas his diary indicates that *In Scotland Again* was cobbled together from several trips made at different times over a number of years, the construct of the narrator as lone traveller here a literary device rather than the transcript of any actual odyssey.[46] The Morton of the *Daily Express* and Methuen travelogues clearly differs from the Morton and Jarché of the *Daily Herald*. Morton the travel writer evades consideration of Glasgow's economic and social problems. In this version of his itinerary he moves swiftly on to write, as one reviewer put it 'lyrically, picturesquely and freshly of the Romance of Scotland'.[47] In marked contrast, Morton the *Herald* journalist lingers far longer on human activity – particularly employment, unemployment and social hardship. And it is here that Jarché's photographic contribution finds its forte. The newspaper series of 'In Scotland Again' contains no less than 32 images of people doing work – over half of all the photographs used – while others depict unemployed men and their families. Fully ten of the *Daily Herald* articles, including 19 photographs, cover Glasgow, as against a mere four pages (from 407) and no photos in the book version.

As Morton and Jarché proceed up the east coast in their *Daily Herald* guise, aspects of the fishing industry prevail, with descriptions of salmon-netting, fisher lassies, the Peterhead drifters. A major story, taking up four separate articles preceded by a captioned photo-spread, involves them going to sea on a trawler from Aberdeen. Meanwhile, the details of linoleum manufacturing in Kirkcaldy, jam production in Dundee and the women's activities in Perth dye works each command stories, as do the mysteries of jute machines (Dundee again), whisky making and – back over in Glasgow – dredging, India tyres, shipbuilding, steel processing, glass silk, electric cable and chemical dyes. In West Lothian, they find shale oil and coal mining. The ardent activity of contemporary industry conveyed in the majority of the reports contrasts with coverage of those afflicted by its shortcomings. These are twofold, and each is deemed a tragedy: first, there are the unemployed stevedores and cranes of the Clyde in 'River of tragic silence' (5 November 1931); second, the 'fragment[s] of an old Scotland that is rapidly vanishing', like 'the old men and old women who sit baiting the hooks' in 'bits of disappearing Scotland' (Dunbar harbour) and the handloom weavers of Kilbarchan, 'the last vestige . . . all old people . . . they have resisted the modern world' but they will not for much longer. This rhetoric of fading heritage alongside the pain of present-day unemployment is nevertheless consistent with Morton's overall conservatism – little change is for the good, and here are some of its casualties.

Michael Bartholomew suggests that Morton's ability to shift register was helped by a readiness to distinguish himself from the figure of the narrator in his journeys, a point that underscores the artificiality of his 'travel' books.[48] It also explains the sharp differences between his Scottish books and the *Daily Herald* itineraries. *In Search of Scotland* was aimed at the reader looking less for a guidebook than reassurance that a Utopian, cohesive country existed out there somewhere beyond the competing vision of urban-industrial ugliness, to satisfy a yearning for an essence of Scotland which, like England, 'remain[ed] tantalisingly out of reach'.[49] However, this time the search for the nation's soul was not directed to 'a village, deep in the countryside', but to a mythology forged by the trinity of literature, grand historical escapades and notions of race. The narrator is thus 'attracted to landscapes that he encountered first in the pages of Burns or Scott . . . to search out the exact spots at which decisive incidents in Scottish history took place' and to 'interpret the behaviour of the people he encounters . . . by reference to their supposed "Celtic" character'.[50] Places were thus not intrinsically enchanting but made magical by balladry or fanciful prose, often tragic history or social peculiarity.[51] Yet, for all this evocation and imbuing, 'his descriptions of breathtaking landscapes [to] slither together into one composite picture: there is only so much that can be done with mist, loch and heather'.[52]

If the romantic Morton wrote to satisfy a market for the dream that an authentic Scotland unsullied by modern life lay over the horizon, the realist Morton found a very different country. It is a contradiction probably apparent to few in Scotland at the time: one audience consisted of comfortable middle-class motorists; the other working-class newspaper readers. To that extent he might as well have been two different writers, musing, as he did, over two differently constructed realities with associated visual motifs. These mirrored disjunctions in what people saw as much as they reflected their class-based conditions of existence.

EDWIN MUIR'S MORAL INDEX

Scenic views of bens, lochs and glens and grim evocations of depressed industrial landscapes share little; indeed, they signify wholly different aesthetics. Of course, Morton was influenced by the designs of his publishers to produce scenery for the one (Methuen), but social comment for the other (Odhams' *Daily Herald*), and the variations discussed above suggest his pliability, if not a degree of commercial opportunism. Yet through the critique of modernity via the travelogue a meeting ground and symbolic space existed where conservatives like Morton met Socialist writers such as Edwin Muir. The Batsford collections offered 'a remarkably coherent, conservative, backward-looking and nostalgic vision of England [sic]

. . . While Britain faced political uncertainty, strike and depression . . . [they] enacted a powerfully conservative mythology' to build an enduring historical narrative.[53] A similar sense of security underpinned the success of Morton's project, particularly in England where the mythical pre-industrial village atmosphere provided psychological anchorage for those whose lives had been ruptured by the horrors of the Great War.[54] Both saw people alienated from their homes and lives in urban industrial society. However, unlike Morton, who arrogates no specific blame for perceived social decay, Muir, a key figure in the Scottish cultural renaissance during the 1930s, lays responsibility *à la* Marx squarely at the door of capitalism. For him, while it would be an act of madness to discard industrialism for an ideal of simple agricultural harmony, nevertheless only a socialist pro-gramme could rid Scotland of the worst ravages of its capitalist version.

As a social investigation into the condition of the Scottish people, Muir's *Scottish Journey* (London: Heinemann and Gollancz, 1935) – pub-lished as a companion to Priestley's *English Journey* (1934) – is a work whose landscapes are pictured entirely through word-imagery.[55] These nevertheless present striking visualisations that are highly polarised, the Dantésque vision of industrial purgatory being pitched against a prelapsarian rural idyll. He opens with an observation:

> The first thought of writing this book came to me two years ago after I had driven through the mining district of Lanarkshire. The journey took me through Hamilton, Airdrie and Motherwell. It was a warm, overcast summer day; groups of idle, sullen-looking young men stood at the street corners; smaller groups were wandering among the blue-black ranges of pit-dumps which in that region are the substitute for nature; the houses looked empty and unemployed like their tenants; and the road along which the car stumbled was pitted and rent, as if it had recently been under shell-fire. Everything had the look of a Sunday which had lasted for many years, during which the bells had forgotten to ring – a disused, slovenly, everlasting Sunday.[56]

Here, in these 'grotesque industrial towns . . . the heart of Scotland':

> iron-coloured brooks sluggishly oozed, and [where] stringy gutta-percha bushes rose from sward that looked as if it had been dishonoured by some recondite infamy . . . defaced and suffering patches of country . . . as if in this region nature no longer breathed . . . The forlorn villages looked like dismembered parts of towns brutally hacked off . . . The towns themselves, on the other hand, were like villages on a nightmare scale, which after endless building had never managed to produce what looked like a street, and had no centre of any kind . . . merely a great number of houses jumbled together in a wilderness of grime, coal-dust and brick, under a blackish-grey synthetic sky . . . bloated and scabbed villages . . . these black slag peaks and valleys make up a toy landscape

... dwarf-like and sinister, suggesting an immeasurably shrivelled and debased second-childhood ... This scene really seemed to be more like an allegorical landscape with abstract figures than a real landscape with human beings. The abstruse ugliness of this black iron and coal region is such a true reflection of the actual processes which have gone on in it during the last hundred years that the landscape has acquired a real formal and symbolical significance which one cannot find in the slatternly chaos of Glasgow.[57]

For Muir, the visual impression of a place was directly symbolic of the effects of industrialisation upon it. Thus he laments the 'untidy, draggled appearance of most small Scottish towns' and the 'decay of the villages of Scotland ... insensibly and silently dying'.[58] However, this perception is limited to those places where industry has ruptured social continuity, for in the industrial Border towns – Hawick, Kelso, Galashiels and Selkirk – he finds 'a curiously wakeful and vivid air', explained by the imputation that they 'have kept their old traditions more or less intact': 'the weaving of tweeds and other woollen cloths, which, being essentially local and distinctive, [have] survived the intensifying onset of Industrialism that has eaten into the core of other communities'. Here, he claims, 'history goes back without a break', the Reformation 'was never so complete as in the rest of the Lowlands, for the genius of the Border people was already too completely formed to be fundamentally altered, its 'most essential expression' being found in the ballads, which unlike the oeuvre of the Protestant Robert Burns represented 'an unchanging pattern of the Scottish spirit'. In the Borders, 'one can feel the presence of history, in the landscape and in the faces and manners of the people. Over the rest of Scotland one has to dig for history beneath a layer of debris left by the Reformation and the Industrial Revolution'.[59] Muir does not venture to the Northeast, although there is a passing reference to 'towns like Montrose and Kirriemuir [where] there is none of this vigorous public life, and no common object'. Instead, the 'spectre of Industrialism' provides a recurrent theme, personified in the vivid evocation of small-town life as that of a decadent and aged crone: 'most of the ... towns I have seen in Scotland are contentedly or morosely lethargic, sunk in a fatalistic dullness broken only by scandal-mongering and such alarums as drinking produces; a dead silence punctuated by malicious whispers and hiccups ... private lives ... forced indeed to become fantastically private beneath a reciprocal and insatiable scrutiny'.[60] Muir acknowledges that he borrowed this evocation of suffocating and constricted parochial gossip from George Douglas Brown's singular classic of counter-Kailyard, *The House with the Green Shutters* (1901). And the Kailyard School is itself regarded as a by-product of economic change, for it was, he argues, 'the increasing bestiality of industrial Scotland that turned the countryside of fiction into a *Schlaraffenland* [fool's paradise], and made Scottish literature for a time mainly a literature written by sentimental ministers'. The industrial system was 'so sordid and disfiguring' that people sought escape in a fictional structure of retrospect that deliberately evaded the hard facts of Scottish town life: 'The flight to the Kailyard was a flight to Scotland's past, to a country which existed before Industrialism'.[61]

So much for the towns and villages. Having asserted that all Scotland's cities are 'monuments of Scotland's industrial past, historical landmarks in a country which is fast becoming lost to history', Muir devotes his first chapter to Edinburgh's 'excessive stiffness combined with excessive conviviality' a reflection of the contrast between 'its legendary past and its tawdry present'.[62] While the capital of Scotland is portrayed as the capital of anachronism, Glasgow symbolises the most brutal effects of urban industrialisation. In his long disquisition on the city (a third of the book is about Glasgow) fear and contamination blend in equal measure: 'I have passed through most of the slums of Glasgow, but I have never done so unless when forced by necessity, and I have never attempted to investigate them, and would not do so at any price . . . There can be hardly any decent Glaswegian but has seen some sight in passing through the slums which he afterward wanted to erase from his memory'. While Muir is at pains to indicate that until such recollections are confronted the health of society will continue to suffer, in the meantime, 'the whole soil for miles around is polluted . . . a debased landscape in which every growing thing seem[s] to be poisoned and stunted'. Environmental decay is mirrored in social degeneracy as Muir, like many of his contemporaries, slides into a categorisation of urban types. Not only does he observe 'stunted naked boys' playing in the filth, but 'a [sadder] distinguishing characteristic of the Glasgow man (and it cuts across all classes) is the mark that has been visibly impressed upon him by Industrialism, in the lineaments of his face and the shape and stature of his body'.[63]

The topography of *Scottish Journey* is schematic rather than representative, covering only the Borders and parts of the Southwest, Edinburgh, Glasgow, and the Highlands. Comparisons between these regions – with added allusion to his homeland – suffices to make Muir's political point. The Highlands provide stock enchantment, but only in their wildest state where they possess 'a thing which is common no doubt to all wild and solitary scenery: that is, the added value which every natural object acquires from one's consciousness that it has not been touched by the human will'. Here people 'had a different look on their faces . . . were a different race'; 'the scent of birch . . . [was] different from ordinary air, something along with which one inhaled the fine essence of the free things growing round about'. In those zones tamed by agriculture, however, Muir finds the farm labourer's status 'too like slavery to be agreeable', while 'many of the children look half-starved'.[64] Meanwhile, his native Orkney is cast as 'a country community where it was a tradition among the small farmers to help one another when help was needed'. He writes that 'if, in my description of the rural community of the Orkneys . . . the colours will be pleasing, that is partly because they are actually so, but mainly because I wish to deepen the darkness of my picture of industrial Glasgow by contrasting it with a normal traditional mode of existence'.[65]

This dichotomous picture was to a degree a rationalisation of bitter personal experience. In 1901, when Muir was 14, his father had lost his farm in Orkney and the family had moved to Glasgow. Within a year his parents and two of his brothers had died. As Richman notes, 'the change forever marked Muir', for suddenly he saw 'slum dwellers on whose faces was etched what [he] described as "depraved and shameful knowledge"'.[66] It was a traumatic encounter with the 'fallen' world after Edenic Orkney:

> Orkney was still more or less untouched by the industrial revolution. The undesecrated landscape set the stage for an idyllic childhood . . . Orkney natives were ignorant of modernity and its discontents. They did not 'know what competition was . . . they helped one another with their work . . . following the old usage; they had a culture made up of legend, folk-song' . . . There was also a rude economic self-sufficiency.[67]

Muir recalled being 'absorbed in my own dissociation' and writing poems with titles like 'The Lost Land' that turned to the past for solace. He subsequently underwent Jungian analysis, coming to see his own life as the unfolding of an archetypal fable, the 'ancestral pattern' whereby 'the life of every man is an endlessly repeated performance of the life of man'.[68] In *The Estate of Poetry* (1962) he elaborates: 'Hugo von Hofmannsthal once said that true imagination is always conservative. By this he may have meant that it keeps intact the bond which unites us with the past of mankind . . . [or] it sees the life of everyone as the endless repetition of a single pattern . . . We become human by repetition'.[69] From this perspective, he explains his concern for continuity and horror at its rupture as an existential dilemma:

> I was born before the Industrial Revolution, and am now about two hundred years old. But I have skipped a hundred and fifty of them. I was really born in 1737, and till I was fourteen no time-accidents happened to me. Then in 1751 I set out from Orkney for Glasgow. When I arrived I found that it was not 1751, but 1901, and that a hundred and fifty years had been burned up in my two day's

journey. But I myself was still in 1751, and remained there for a long time. All my life since I have been trying to overhaul that invisible leeway.[70]

While a life of constant travel did indeed reflect Muir's abiding sense of displacement, his recognition of a personal need for connectedness between past and present relates to a more general and profound aspect of the contemporary human condition. To quote Christopher Lasch, the past is a 'psychological treasury' from which we have become separated via modernity.[71] The claim, following Freud, is that in order to maintain a symbolic sense of identity, continuity and ancestral allegiance, we deny that separation has occurred by imagining ourselves either to be in a state of complete self-sufficiency or by regressing into an ecstatic and painless reunion with our mythical roots. Or, at least, people attempt to explain the severance, the better to devise repair strategies. Edwin Muir's wish to do this is exceptionally well articulated through the projection of his personal discontents onto the national scale. Arguably, however, he expressed a common desire for continuity and order in an age where the life course of the average Scot saw considerable biographical disruption, marked either through their own geographic migration and social mobility, or in the effects of economic and social change upon their home environment.[72]

DOCUMENTARY DIVERSIONS

Given the significance of place in grounding the sense of self, it may thus appear surprising that landscape photography has sought either to deny the dialogue between people and setting or to lament its attenuation. Victorian and Edwardian topographical scenes rarely included people. If the emptiness of many Highland views reflects 'the duplicity of landscape'[73], 'wilderness' disguising clearance, immiseration and eviction of humans to make way for sheep and deer forest, then the photographs of Wilson and others must be judged in the main by what they fail to show. Where people do appear, they are generally in self-conscious poses, 'studied figures at toil in a landscape of privation'.[74] Meanwhile, photographers were 'struck by the almost barbarous character of the domestic architecture, and made special arrangements to seek out and photograph the most dilapidated example'.[75] The material and cultural dominance of the British metropolitan centre over the 'Celtic fringe' persisted in the ideological opposition forged between the 'improved' and 'civilised' core and an 'uncultivated' and 'primitive' periphery. On one level, there were 'the "empty" landscapes of the colonial imagination'.[76] But also, as Chapter 6 argues, these assumed distinctions did much to create stereotypes of rural recalcitrance, not least through an anthropological 'othering'. Here lies a further historiographic twist, for among Hill and Adamson's most pioneering works were their 130 photographs on 'The Fishermen and Women of the Firth of Forth', a conscious attempt 'to depict the complete life of a community' whose only precedent lay in anthropological drawings brought back from the colonies. The object was to show in the religious, working and family life of the Newhaven fisherfolk a moral contrast to the destitution and squalor of the Old Town of Edinburgh, to demonstrate 'not just that it was an admirable society, but how and why'. It was, as Stevenson remarks, 'a most interesting expression of nationalism'.[77]

This documentary and evaluative strain in the genealogy of photography was later reiterated in deliberate attempts to record the lives of communities threatened by the advances of modernity. During the twentieth century, photographers who pictured people rather than landscapes were largely moved by ethnological concerns, resulting again in a somewhat selective inventory. Thus the six main photographic collections in the National Museums' Scottish Life Archive indicate distinct skewness towards fishing and crofting, focusing respectively on Fife fishing villages, Foula (Shetland), the Uists, Coll, Ardnamurchan, Morar and Arisaig, St Kilda and Lewis.[78] Meanwhile very few images of heavy industry exist, perhaps because the technology was inadequate when it came to photographing people in dark places like mines. Fisherfolk, crofting and island life have not been regarded as central to mainstream economic history, but they have been culturally important as emblems of difference, hence their appeal to preservationists, albeit that the photographers, far from being driven by an impulse for social realism, were romantically motivated. Alistair Alpin MacGregor's picturesque images of the Western Isles even provoked The Lewis Association into publishing a critique of his over-sentimental visions of Gaeldom.[79]

In the mid-twentieth century, the influence of Robert Flaherty's film-making affected visual attempts to convey realist scenes of life and labour, the photographs of Werner Kissling, M. E. M. Donaldson and Margaret Fay Shaw representing folkloric attempts to create a material and cultural record of the disappearing crofting community.[80] These have been important in highlighting an imagery of remote and final outposts of a traditional way of life in the throes of irreversible change. The stance was partly ideological, Shaw's husband John Lorne Campbell standing for 'a school of thought, born out of Catholic conservative reactionism, which railed against the threat of modernism'.[81] By contrast, again, the

Fig. 5.4 Two women walking near a blackhouse, 1936. One of hundreds of photographs taken by Werner Kissling that complement his film, *Eriskay – A Poem of Remote Lives* (1935).
© University of Edinburgh – Dept of Celtic and Scottish Studies.
Licensor wwwscran.ac.uk

critique of modernity offered by Paul Strand – the only photographer of major international repute to have worked in the Hebrides – applies considerable intellectual sophistication in making images, requiring an equal refinement in their interpretation. There is always a human presence, thus his landscapes may appear empty, but there is a sense in which they are 'only extensions of people who happen to be invisible'.[82] As a deliberate aesthetic effect this is not something broadly evident in Scottish landscape imagery. And unlike landscapes, whose vantage point implies the position of privileged outsider (either as onlooker or as honoured 'guest'), the figures who stare at us from Strand's images question the observer's assumptions about crofters as romanticised subjects. From his Marxist viewpoint, so far as social and visual perspectives coalesce, the tenacity of Hebrideans against an extreme environment finds expression in the motif of portraits of islanders besides the evidence of their work upon the land, the artefacts, buildings, and farming tools. His aim is very different from that of the Victorian pictorialist carefully siting crofts in the foreground as evidence of civilisation amid the fastness. In his major work *Tir A' Mhurain* (1962), a book of photographs, the juxtaposition of faces with

Fig. 5.5 Paul Strand: *Mr and Mrs Angus MacLean*, South Uist, Hebrides, 1954.
Copyright © Aperture Foundation, Inc., Paul Strand Archive.

natural objects and features is designed to display an ecological symbiosis.[83] There is a homology between society and the surrounding habitat, but rather than being that of an uncouth people in a wild landscape it is one of harmonious consubstantiation. Meanwhile, evidence of constant adaptation belies the myth of unwordliness conveyed by more sentimental imagery and literature. In his efforts 'to render history visible', to make 'plainness' itself exotic, to provide a sense of deliberately arrested time, Strand's formalism renders him very much a modernist photographer, yet his celebration of native virtue set against the oncoming rupture of the nuclear missile range planned for the Uists is fundamentally opposed to modernity, or at least its capitalist version.[84] As Chiarenza indicates, 'there is never any evidence of the materialism of modern society in his photographs'.[85] Instead, his attempt to 'excavate the meaning of the past from the appearance of the present', signals motives similar to the ethnologists or oral historians.[86]

By geographical definition, the Outer Hebrides signify remoteness. In allying this spatial aspect to one of temporal backwardness, most photographers have contributed to the manufacture of an ongoing cultural fabrication of 'the Celtic periphery'. Thus, twenty years after Strand's sojourn, and very much in his shadow, if influenced more by the documentary realism of Walker Evans, Gus Wylie aimed to capture 'the last region of Britain to be black and white':[87]

> His pictures, particularly his intimate interior shots, are of a very specific time in the islands – the dawn of the Formica age when the huge Welsh dressers and the tongue-and-groove wall panelling were being thrown out to make way for the essentials of modernity: chipboard, plasterboard, televisions.[88]

In more recent, if partly retrospective work he uses colour, presumably to indicate a more contemporary flavour.[89] Nevertheless, the more general point is that whether the photographs are taken in the 1930s, 1950s, 1970s or later, each time the theme is one of islands on the threshold of modernity, as though in citing traces of the past in the present the photographers have salvaged something of a unique and ongoing tradition. Their accompanying images of bleak, starkly illuminated landscapes suggest the beauty of harsh, windswept places against which people struggle to maintain a living.

If Strand's 1954 work in the Uists represents 'a significant stage in the construction of Scotland as a Modernist subject', its impact has nevertheless been far greater outside Scotland than within, his Hebridean masterpiece being 'marginal to the dominant visual content of Scotland as a sign' and thus having done little to alter the 'dominant canon of the picturesque'.[90] Clarke comments that: 'Much of the strength of a great deal of post-war British landscape photography lies precisely in the way it seeks a path between the two poles of its traditional reference: a settled English lowland and its Highland alternative, the traditional difference between the Burkean sublime and the beautiful.'[91] Neither Strand nor Wylie can be – or would have wished to be – construed as contributors to this dialogue, although in highlighting the distinctiveness of their chosen region they do reinforce a discourse of romantic exoticism. More generally, while it is argued that several British photographers have deconstructed cultural myths of landscape by reducing the countryside to a pastiche of popular signs as the natural has all but disappeared, others such as Fay Godwin, with her formal and purist images of Sutherland, or Raymond Moore, whose portfolio ranges from the 'Taoist vision of unity' of *Benbecula* at evening to the misty *Dumfriesshire*, where 'natural images are as much hemmed in by manufactured signs as the land is controlled by human activity', indicate that it would be foolish to apply a singularly realist reading.[92] Furthermore, such intellectualisation does not reflect everyday perception and, although it is important to compare the counter-narratives underwriting the work, it does not carry the same demotic – or, indeed, semiotic – freight as the populist imagery circulating in leisure magazines or tourist guides.

Belonging: An Emotional Geography

Evidence of the relationship between socially constructed ideas of landscape, national and personal identity may certainly be found in the commonsensical reflections of coffee-table literature. A Sense of Belonging to Scotland (2002) and A Sense of Belonging to Scotland: Further Journeys (2005) are the fruits of a project in which Andy Hall approached 105 famous Scots and offered to photograph their favourite places.[93] He then asked each to describe what made their choice special. The result is mostly a celebration of a scenic sense of locality that appears to revel in a twenty-first-century sublime. The contributors vary in age from their early thirties to late eighties, while three-quarters (seventy-seven) are male. As celebrities, none are presently working class, with nine bearing titles such as 'Lord', 'Sir' or 'Dame'. The majority now live, or spend much of their time outwith Scotland. Such geographical absence resonates with emotional attachment: 'It was clear that for people who could not be at home at this dawn of the new century, there was a strong sense of longing for and belonging to [Scotland]', hence 'the beautiful melancholia experienced by Scots away from home'.[94] Equally, near-ubiquitous allusion to youth, childhood and family memories – discussed directly by no less than sixty-three contributors, and indirectly by many others – vividly accentuates the temporal aspect of longing. Without suffering for the cause with quite the same vehemence as Muir, most people make a village out of their childhood. Here indeed is evidence of Peter Berger's 'homeless mind', of isolated, migratory moderns seeking meaning in the return to roots or hearing 'the Siren call of this wild land'.[95] The places envisioned are catalysts for connection and continuity with a deep-seated sense of self and family, and, in many cases, form the milieu in which a consciousness of appropriate ethics is grounded, be it one that 'evokes the moral compass that guided my grandfather' or one that 'taught him the value of friendship and humour'.[96]

The locations indicate a strongly outdoor rural bias, with only fifteen urban scenes. Just one image – Charles Rennie Mackintosh's House for an Art Lover, chosen by Carol Smillie, presenter of a popular television programme on redecorating family houses – portrays an interior. Aside from the occasional miniscule figure in the background or a few grazing sheep, only one picture – of yachtsman Chay Blyth on a horse – includes persons or animals. This absence is the more striking when one considers that normally heavily populated locations such as Ibrox football stadium are included.[97] Aside from half-a-dozen castles, few individual buildings appear. Eight sportsmen selected golf courses. For the rest, water seems especially significant, with no less than seventy-eight including lochs, rivers and the sea (thirty-one seascapes and bays; eight harbours and coastal villages). The dichotomous manner (rural/urban, then/now, leisure/work) in which a great many rural scenes reminiscent of growing up or childhood holidays (all sixty-three of them) are set against the individual's current situation reflects elements prevalent in Urry's 'tourist gaze', whereby holiday destinations are premised upon the appeal of their difference from daily life.[98] Focus is directed to features which are out-of-the-ordinary but which also convey recognisable signs of socially constructed beauty, leading to a series of popular icons – the Forth Rail Bridge, Glencoe, Gleneagles, the Trossachs and *Rob Roy*, Culzean Castle, Arthur's Seat, the Wallace Monument, the filmic backdrop to the *Monarch of the Glen* television drama. As with tourism and heritage, novelty is also evident in the effort to illuminate new objects for our gaze – the counter-sublime industrial fantasy suggested by Grangemouth oil refinery, 'the finest display of fairy lights in the land' – but this is a singular exception.[99]

In so far as the composition of each photograph reflects 'a much greater sensitivity to visual elements . . . than is normally found in everyday life', Hall's images are conventionally touristic. Urry notes that: 'people linger over such a gaze which is then visually objectified or captured through photographs, postcards, films, models and so on. These enable the gaze to be endlessly reproduced and recaptured'.[100] By publishing his images, many of which are taken from hillsides or hilltops, from the standpoint of surveillance, Hall has contributed to the ongoing presentation of Scottishness through landscape already advanced in the popular books of Colin Prior, Colin Baxter and Craig McMaster.[101] Together they constitute an exercise that has effectively institutionalised how we look at Scotland as scenic vistas, hence the apparent paradox of highly personal reflections being represented through a collectively acknowledged frame of reference. If Hall's subjects are individualised travellers rather than mass tourists, the ambience they speak of is nevertheless one that is commonly understood: 'the 'lonely grandeur' of Dollar Glen, 'sheer desolation' of the Summer Isles, 'places of sanctuary and contemplation . . . where the physical and spiritual landscapes unite'.[102]

To be sure, in most instances this speaks of Urry's 'romantic gaze', stressing 'solitude, privacy and a personal, semi-spiritual relationship with the object of the gaze . . . "the romantic notion that the self is found not in society but in solitudinous contemplation of nature"', in what we like to call 'undisturbed natural beauty' – empty beaches, Highland glens, the play of light and land.[103] Yet these pictures are more than aggregations of stereotypical signs denoting rural romance. Because a personal inter-pretation appears on the page opposite each, we are enjoined to share an otherwise private experience. There is thus a direct dialogue, the autobio-graphical words in the text lending each image a necessary authenticity. However, the contributors are not tourists, but exiles (either physically or in the mind). Their journeys into belonging are not temporary visits from which they will return home, for 'home' lies in the very places pho-tographed. A journalist talks of his 'spiritual home of Buchan, where I still come from time to time in search of peace and harmony', another of a place 'that I return to in my mind when I am in far-flung places'.[104] For a Skye musician, 'to return to that space where you feel utterly connected' is to stop time still and 'for a moment, to make sense of all things'.[105] 'Peace', 'harmony', 'tranquillity', and 'serenity' are sentiments mentioned in fully twenty-one narratives, different senses of time, including stillness and timelessness, in another ten. The steadfast, pastoral imagery of places frozen in time and space by implication contrasts with the uncertain sense of movement and migration characteristic of contemporary urban life, hence 'the security of the surrounding hills' and 'the sense of being cosseted by the land', an 'antidote to [the] turmoil and change' where it is 'easy to forget the hustle, bustle and stress'.[106]

The sites photographed are thus more than just the locales for remem-bered experience. In their spiritual clarity, visually associated with quality of light in several commentaries, such places provide a strongly therapeutic function which, since it is difficult to rationalise, is often simply referred to as 'beauty', 'a beauty that is timeless' or essential.[107] But, *pace* romanticism, this is not simply a matter of forsaking society for nature. Remarks such as 'home is where the heart is . . . I have been to many beautiful places around the world, but none please me more than this' are redolent of an atavistic impulse, suggesting ancestral ties, while several see continuity in bringing their children to places they themselves loved when young: 'I will return to it time and time again, now with my children, and, who knows, maybe they will return one day with theirs!'[108] Anecdotes about connections to parents abound – 'As I walk in Dunkeld to this day, my father is by my side'; 'Whenever I look over the rocks, I can see my mother as a little girl playing'; 'a symbol that bore a direct connection to your father and grandfather before you and probably to your son and grandson'; 'I always feel that [my father's] spirit

Fig. 5.6 'Shipyard cranes, Govan.'
By Andy Hall from A *Sense of Belonging to Scotland* (2002), reproduced by kind
permission of Polygon, an imprint of Birlinn Ltd, www.birlinn.co.uk

is there watching, waiting for me to come home' – each testifying to the
transcendent importance of generational ties through place.[109] For some,
the blood connection is associated less with family than nationhood, the
beauty of the landscape evoking pride in being Scottish, rootedness in
the country and connection with 'the essence of Scotland'.[110] For most,
the links are emotive, 'part of the furniture of my spirit'; for others, more
corporeal: 'These hills are as familiar to me as my knees', 'part of my DNA
and I cannot do without it'.[111] There is much reflection, the panoramic
image 'almost like looking in [on oneself] from the outside'. As Alan
Sharp avers, meaning is attached to 'origins, or shaping source' and 'the
imprinting remains as much metaphor as memory'. In this 'primeval . . .
allegorical description of the human spirit', all see a landscape then seek
to place themselves within it.[112]

This is the generality, yet there are also sights that puncture the sooth-
ing vision, such as the disturbing image presented by the dockscape of
urban Govan: 'Look how serene the picture is, and then think back and
you realise that the very heartbeat of the Clyde is missing – the ships . . .
the ghost of the Clyde . . . I can't help but feel the sadness'.[113] Loss vividly
complements longing from the outset, the first writer in the selection
'hunting for the township where my people came from' and discovering

'one of those sad and empty places you find all over Mull, relics of a lost community', yet also a place that feels 'rather touchingly domestic . . . overwhelmingly homely'.[114] The picture is of evening sunlight cast against ruined crofts. In itself, this suggests desolation, and it is the commentator, not the photographer, who populates the scene. Similarly, when contemporary towns and villages are pictured, their significance lies not in anything that might be read off from the image – for none at all show people – but in the accompanying explanation. The photograph of the ornamental arch framing the village of Edzell is simply pretty. Its enchantment and import are only conveyed by the accompanying text: 'Scottish villages as a rule tend to be workmanlike rather than beautiful, but now and again one comes along which manages to combine both qualities'.[115] Vistas of Langholm, Lossiemouth, Greenock and Ullapool, nestling in the middle distance, do not in themselves indicate the welcome and warmth of their people alluded to in the surrounding commentary. The fishing boats of Eyemouth suggest work, but will only echo 'an enormous sense of the continuum of life' after one has read John Bellany's remarks. Likewise with the close-up of a bar sign that connotes for Ian Rankin 'a tradition of friendship and storytelling'. This everyday humanity stands in stark contrast to the awe inspired by the age and permanence of features like the Callanish Stones, where confronted with human remnants 5,000 years old and 'standing [there] on the geology of twenty million years, one is forcibly faced again with one's own insignificance'.[116] Nevertheless, whatever the focus, the common element lies in the way in which the written word supplies an explanation for what are otherwise scenes devoid of active human presence.

Strikingly, although Hall's pictures convey the chosen scenes of over a hundred individuals, they are easily located within a recognisable pictorial tradition:

> The American can still, at least, contemplate a wilderness condition. In the British tradition the photographer is pushed to the margins of the landscape, using such habitats to recover a sense of isolation. The photographs make available icons of an alternative existence: primary spots of release and contemplation as if they, literally, stand in for a landscape that we rarely see but need to know. . . . areas which bring to us evidence of another land and another time. To read them from our predominantly urban perspectives is to return to a strange, almost forgotten, Britain.[117]

Yet it is not a return so much as perpetuation: the reproduction of iconic images in personal remembrance, and, in turn, their retailing in popular literature, creates a hermeneutic circle of representation.[118] Because we

Fig. 5.7 'Callanish Stones, Isle of Lewis.'
By Andy Hall from *A Sense of Belonging to Scotland: Further Journeys* (2005),
reproduced by kind permission of Polygon, an imprint of Birlinn Ltd,
www.birlinn.co.uk

tend to reify 'the land' as primordial space, we become time travellers in search of the past in the borders and interstices of the present. However, the constant repetition of landscape imagery merely creates a heritage that is taken for granted.[119] We envision places that are at once both precious and clichéd. It is only in the rare physical encounter with foreboding empty space that we sense the limit and contradiction of our aesthetic, as the charm of 'wilderness' gives way suddenly to the fearsome face of awe. Here is H. V. Morton in an uncharacteristic moment of panic, motoring late in the day around the very perimeter of Sutherland:

> As it grew dark, and the long northern twilight fell over Loch Eriboll, all sense of adventure deserted me. I wanted to hear someone speak. I wanted to see a fire. I wanted to get away from the threat of the hills and their implication that I, and all men, were intruders on the surface of the earth.[120]

CONCLUSION

Edwin Muir despaired of the deviation in Scottish social life from that of his remembered origins, so much so that he placed his childhood figuratively in the mid-eighteenth century. Had he examined 'that invisible leeway' between 1751 and 1901 – the real conceit lay in suggesting he could not see it – he may have discerned not just the hidden hand of capitalism, but also the workings of a set of cultural processes conspiring to create the imagined idyll to which he alluded. In 1935 he concluded his journey by noting: 'I did not find anything which I could call Scotland; anything, that is to say, beyond the vague and wandering image already impressed upon me by memory: the net result of my having been brought up in it, and of living in it until I was nearly thirty, and lastly of belonging to it. . . My deepest impression . . . was one of emptiness, and that applied even more to the towns than to the country-side'.[121] Those few contemporaries, like Blake, who urged readers to look at the unpleasant reality of industrialism seem a long way adrift of the effete anachronism of Scott's 'Crags, knolls, and mounds, confusedly hurled,/ The fragments of an earlier world'.[122] Indeed, in a largely post-industrial environment the sense of loss implied in Muir's statement has turned to a recognition of the precious uniqueness of places that connote a deep sense of belonging. For many these places are past-related and idealised, with social scientists and historians contending that, rather than confront the pressing problems of the moment, people tend to seek refuge in their history: 'Scotland has problems of housing, unemployment and religious bitterness which make it a society torn by class and racial tensions. Scots often prefer not to discuss these, and when they think of Scotland they conjure up a picture of the past'.[123] If in large measure this has been a pre-modern hinterland, latter-day reminiscences of the urban/industrial Scotland of yesteryear are equally nostalgic, and for similar reasons, as Chapter 7 indicates. Longing and belonging are undergirded by the deep emotional appeal of particular places, not necessarily rural ones. However, what the discussion has aimed to point out is that the imaginaries from which we draw when explaining such appeal to ourselves and to others are limited by codes and conventions that owe much to the history of image-making.

Clarke avers:

> Perhaps even more than the portrait, landscape photography remains encoded within the language of academic painting and the traditions of landscape art . . . viewed through a highly developed and popular picturesque aesthetic . . . As a cultural index, the picturesque [thus] sought visual confirmation of a timeless Arcadia; a unified image of social life.[124]

This is the Eden myth, that somehow 'natural' landscapes beget 'right' ways to be. Yet the rhetorical force of Scottish landscape imagery has lain less in forging a distinction between the Highland sublime and the English pastoral than as a critique of the damage wrought by two centuries of industrialism – an indictment that effectively erased the places where most Scots live from the aesthetic map. It was not just that Scottish Lowland landscapes did not fit or were constrained by conventional distinctions, or simply that they came to represent the despoilation of the land in the now futile service of industry (for just as devastatingly the Highlands had been emptied by 'Improvement'); rather, that in alienating people from their natural domain, disrupting its ecology, economic change was seen to have perverted the psycho-social order of things. For Morton and Muir, the decaying towns of the Central Belt were no longer communities providing the basis for an ethic of living, transmittable through generations.[125] By extension, some sixty or seventy years on, many appear to acknowledge that to reconnect with that ethic we must by-pass the urbanisation of our own times to find comfort in scarce fragments of a more innocent rural landscape, albeit one that is an artefact of our aesthetic invention. Equally, those whose forebears were displaced by emigration or migration to the cities may justifiably hanker for the hills of home. It is because we are deracinated, late-modern beings that we strive so, as though in eliding the 'leeway' of a difficult and tainted recent past we might capture traces of a deeper truth. Modernisation begets anti-modernism. The visualisation of this historical escape attempt is evident in landscape photographs, which, in their appeal to the highly personal spirit, are paradoxically devoid of humans themselves. This Scottish imaginary is thus not that of the imagined community – a collectivity nonetheless found in popular fiction, as we have seen – or one involving the physical engagement and placing of self within a specific everyday environment. It is instead one of 'unspoilt' nature. Nevertheless, it does partake of an impulse to trace the lineaments of a common identity.

For the Irish revivalists Yeats and Synge the reason for celebrating the pre-modern west of Ireland was 'not the existence of an undefiled state of nature, but the possibility of renewing a sense of community'.[126] In Scotland that sense is often sought in and through the landscape itself. That this should be so is testimony to the peculiarities of a nation wishing not so much to evade its recent past as to invoke physical terrain as a geologically abiding template for its identity. Other nationalisms, Scots among them, rely upon other ideas and other foundations yet the conviction, even the empty realisation, that, in the final instance, 'nothing endures but the land' remains a bedrock of belief.[127] The myth of the Highlands and, by extension of Scottish landscape more generally, is one of nature 'as left behind, as lost wholeness'.[128] It is a land of lost content in both senses of the word. The sublime irony is that in 'look[ing] upon a land denuded of cultural reference'[129] we are doing something that is, of course, supremely cultural.

NOTES

1. D. Horn, *The Great Museum: The Re-presentation of History* (London: Pluto Press, 1984), p. 12, cited in R. McKenzie, 'The "photographic tour" in nineteenth-century Scotland', *Landscape Research*, 17 (1), 19, 1992, pp. 20–7 (p. 26).

2. *Seven Wonders of Scotland* supplement, *The Scotsman*, 8 April 2006.

3. T. Devine, 'Our hearts are in the Highlands', in *Seven Wonders*, pp. 4–5. C. Withers, 'Picturing Highland landscapes: George Washington Wilson and the photography of the Scottish Highlands', *Landscape Research*, 19, 2, 1994, pp. 68–79 (p. 74) refers to 'that enduring resonance between wilderness, the Highlands, historical event and poetic tradition'.

4. S. Stevenson, 'The Scottishness of Scottish photography: discoveries and exploration', in S. Stevenson et al., *Revisions – Zeitgenösischte Fotografie aus Schottland* (Munich: Nazraeli Press, 1994), pp. 82–9 (p. 83).

5. S. Schama, *Landscape and Memory* (London: Harper Perennial, 2004), pp. 7, 12; see also p. 15n: 'National identity . . . would lose much of its ferocious enchantment without the mystique of a particular landscape tradition: its topography mapped, elaborated, and enriched as a homeland.'

6. Ibid. p. 7.

7. Cf. S. Daniels, *Fields of Vision: Landscape Imagery and National Identity in England and the United States* (Princeton: Princeton University Press, 1993), p. 5.

8. P. Womack, *Improvement and Romance: Constructing the Myth of the Highlands* (London: Macmillan, 1989), p.1.

9. Schama, *Landscape and Memory*, p. 466, who notes a 'peculiar alliance between drawing and subjugation'. For example, given the period, Paul Sandby's pen drawing 'View in Strathtay' (1747) 'necessarily reflects the obedient topography of pacification . . . delicate and unfearsome', looking, 'so very *English*'. Sandby worked for the Ordnance Office, surveying the conquered Highlands. However, by 1780, with the sense of Jacobite threat gone and the Scottish elite co-opted into 'a reminted Hanoverian union', Sandby responded to the 'market for more picturesque depictions' by 'drastically altering his drawings for the engraver. The identical view of Strathtay which had looked so innocuous in 1747 was made more dramatic, with loftier peaks and crags; the upland meadows replaced by the suggestion of gorse and heather'. Tellingly, the foregound now included a kilted Highlander, unthinkable thirty years before when wearing the tartan had been a criminal offence (pp. 466–7. Both images are reproduced on p. 468). See also G. Clarke, *The Photograph* (Oxford: Oxford University Press, 1997), p. 55: 'The photograph allowed land to be controlled, visually at least – to be scaled and ordered, in the way that white colonial settlement attempted politically.'

10. Womack, *Improvement and Romance*, p. 1.

11. The introduction of a picturesque aesthetic, embracing the sublime and involving travel in the conscious pursuit of scenes as objects for observation and appropriate emotional response is generally accredited to William Gilpin. On the application of his techniques to photography in Scotland see R. Taylor, *George Washington Wilson: Artist and Photographer, 1823–93* (Edinburgh: Mercat Press, 1982), pp. 51–2.

12. Clarke, *The Photograph*, p. 64.
13. A. Durie, 'Tourism and commercial photography in Victorian Scotland: the rise and fall of G. W. Wilson & Co., 1852–1908', *Northern Scotland*, 12, 1992, pp. 89–104 (p. 93); Taylor, *George Washington Wilson*, p. 112.
14. R. Smart, '"Famous throughout the world": Valentine & Sons Ltd., Dundee', *Review of Scottish Culture*, 4, 1988, pp. 75–87 (p. 86).
15. McKenzie, 'The "photographic tour"', p. 20.
16. Ibid. p. 22.
17. Taylor, *George Washington Wilson*, p. 50.
18. Durie, 'Tourism and commercial photography', p. 100.
19. J. R. Gold and M. M. Gold, *Imagining Scotland: Tradition, Representation and Promotion in Scottish Tourism since 1750* (Aldershot: Scolar Press, 1995), p. 119.
20. Ibid. p. 130.
21. F. MacDonald, 'Geographies of Vision and Modernity: Things Seen in the Scottish Highlands', unpublished D.Phil. thesis, University of Oxford, 2003, pp. 46, 50, 49; C. R. Steve, 'Smoothing the tourist's way', *Scottish Field*, April 1962, pp. 54–7. MacDonald cites *inter alia*: W. A. Poucher, *Scotland through the Lens: Loch Tulla to Lochaber* (London: Chapman & Hall, 1943), J. Baikie, *Things Seen in the Scottish Highlands* (London: Seeley Service & Company, 1932), and A. Alpin MacGregor, *Behold the Hebrides! Or Wayfaring in the Western Isles* (London: W. & R. Chambers, 1925).
22. A collection of 14,495 negatives of Adam prints is housed in the Library Photographic Archive, University of St Andrews.
23. *Scotland's Magazine* ceased publication in 1975. The SMT collection, which includes many photographs by David Innes, is part of the Scottish Life Archive, National Museum of Scotland. See also *Scottish Field*, aimed at the higher social circles.
24. National Library of Scotland Rare Books – Important Acquistions Notes (Accessed June 2009 at: http://www.nls.uk/collections/rarebooks/acquisitions/index.cfm).
25. Gold and Gold, *Imagining Scotland*, p. 122.
26. At the height of the depression in 1933, 30 per cent of Glaswegians were unemployed. H. V. Morton's *In Search of Scotland* (London: Methuen, 1929) was published in August 1929, three months before the Wall Street Crash. The National Trust for Scotland for Places of Historic Interest or Natural Beauty was founded in 1931.
27. H. Batsford and C. Fry, *The Face of Scotland* (London: Batsford, 1933); G. Blake, *The Heart of Scotland* (London: Batsford, 1934).
28. Batsford and Fry, *Face of Scotland*, pp. v, vii–viii, ix.
29. Gold and Gold, *Imagining Scotland*, p. 133.
30. Ibid. p. 138. As Gruffudd points out, this literature created a ruralist discourse 'stressing the integrity of rural life and landscapes'. It was, nevertheless, a one-sided process, the road itself irreversibly drawing once-hermetic or remote parishes into the modernising frame of the broader national culture (P. Gruffudd, 'Selling the countryside: representations of rural Britain', in J. R. Gold and S. V. Ward (eds), *Place Promotion: The Use of Publicity and Public Relations to Sell Towns and Regions* (Chichester: Wiley, 1994), pp. 247–63 (p. 247), cited in C. Brace, 'Publishing and Publishers: Towards an Historical Geography of Countryside Writing, c. 1930–1950', *Area*, 33 (3),1991, pp. 287–96 (p. 292).
31. References here are to G. Blake, *The Heart of Scotland* (London: Batsford, Third Edition, 1951), pp. viii, 1. Interestingly, John Grierson made films entitled *The Face of Scotland* (1938) and *The Heart of Scotland* (1961).

32. Ibid. pp. 100, vii.
33. Ibid. pp. 101, 111–12.
34. Ibid. p. 112. Lochnagar is a mountain on the Balmoral Estate.
35. Cf. F. Rapport, P. Wainwright and G. Elwyn, '"Of the Edgelands": broadening the scope of qualitative methodology', *Journal of Medical Ethics; Medical Humanities*, 2005, 31, pp. 37–42, which includes reference to techniques of photo-elicitation in the imagination and interpretation of 'the area between urban and rural landscapes' (p. 37).
36. P. Davidson, *The Idea of North* (London: Reaktion Books, 2005), p. 237. Intriguingly, one historian repeats Blake's observation some sixty years later: 'A combination of policies to attract work to areas of unemployment and to disperse the congested population of the Glasgow conurbation has created a new Scotland, neither urban nor rural, which straggles westwards from the fringes of the Firth of Forth to the lower Clyde. It is this unknown Scotland, not in the guidebooks, away from the motorway, seen fleetingly from the express, that holds the key to the modern politics of the country' (C. Harvie, *Scotland and Nationalism: Scottish Society and Politics, 1707–1994* (London: Routledge, 1994), p. 116, cited in C. Craig, *The Modern Scottish Novel: Narrative and the National Imagination* (Edinburgh: Edinburgh University Press, 1999), p. 21).
37. Morton wrote some 50 books and pamphlets. *In Search Scotland* (London: Methuen, 1929) sold 30,000 copies in its first five months of publication. While *In Search of England* (London: Methuen, 1927) was already in its 29th edition by 1943 and had sold a third of a million copies by 1969, the Methuen Archive indicates that with sales of 333,900 by 1964 – as against 330,850 – *In Search of Scotland* was still more successful (M. Bartholomew, *In Search of H. V. Morton* (London: Methuen, 2004), pp. 133, 109; C. R. Perry, 'In Search of H. V. Morton: travel writing and cultural values in the first age of British democracy', *Twentieth Century British History*, 10 (4), 1999, pp. 431–56 (p. 434n).
38. Bartholomew, *In Search*, pp. 33, 32.
39. Gold and Gold, *Imagining Scotland*, p. 131.
40. The exception – two fishermen engaged in conversation – is the only image supplied by Jarché.
41. Bartholomew, *In Search of*, p. 141; H. V. Morton, *In Search of Wales* (London: Methuen, 1932). Bartholomew, *In Search of* (p. 173) notes that Morton's politics were built around a series of 'powerful prejudices' rather than any coherent creed. He 'championed the cause of slum-dwellers and had praised Labour councils' slum clearance programmes, but in his diaries he regularly expressed hatred of democracy, affection for monarchism and resentment of having to pay taxes to support those he saw as the idle and feckless', while he privately supported the general principles of the British Union of Fascists.
42. C. Jacobson, 'The importance of being there', *Independent*, 14 November 1999.
43. See pp. 331–3. In 1933, the Labour Party published *What I Saw in the Slums*, a pamphlet containing several of Morton and Jarché's *Herald* articles about six English cities. Bartholomew (*In Search of*, pp. 146–7) remarks that unlike George Orwell, who stayed among his subjects in squalid lodgings while researching *The Road to Wigan Pier* some four years later, Morton had only the vantage point of the visiting outsider. Meanwhile, Jacobson contends that Jarché's images – even those designed to evoke social concern – rarely departed from the posed arrangements of most press

photography of the time, and it was not until he joined *Weekly Illustrated*, founded in 1934 as Britain's first popular illustrated paper, that he came under the influence of the refugees Lorant, Hutton and Man from whose techniques the documentary humanism of *Picture Post* was born. Jarché was not recruited by that illustrious magazine, a fact that Jacobson regards as indicative of his being 'at ease with the world': he failed to challenge the status quo, and was 'not really a storyteller, but a one-picture man' (Jacobson, 'The importance').

44. All articles cited appeared in the *Daily Herald*. Microfilm copies of the newspaper, together with daybooks and negative index to Jarché's photographs are housed at the National Museum for Photography, Film and Television, Bradford, UK as part of the *Daily Herald* photographic archive.

45. Morton, *In Scotland Again* (London: Methuen, 1933), pp. 142, 144, 143.

46. Bartholomew, *In Search of*, p. 131.

47. A *Sunday Times* writer quoted on the dust-jacket of *In Search of Scotland* (London: Methuen, 1929).

48. M. Bartholomew, 'H. V. Morton's English Utopia', in C. Lawrence and A. K. Mayer (eds), *Regenerating England* (Amsterdam: Rodopi, 2000), pp. 25–44 (p. 35).

49. Ibid. p.25.

50. Bartholomew, *In Search of*, pp. 122, 123.

51. In describing his 'map of romance', Morton alludes to such things possessing: 'an arresting importance, almost as if some part of their passion had soaked itself into the grass and into the hard surface of the rocks' so rendering them emotively meaningful (*In Search of Scotland*, p. 6).

52. Bartholomew, *In Search of*, p. 131.

53. Brace, 'Publishing and publishers', p. 293.

54. Bartholomew, *In Search of*, pp. 25–6.

55. Brace explicitly compares Victor Gollancz's anti-totalitarian and leftist publishing aims with Batsford's conservatism (Brace, 'Publishing and publishers', p. 293).

56. E. Muir, *Scottish Journey* (London: Heinemann and Gollancz, 1935), p.1.

57. Ibid. pp. 2, 167–70.

58. Ibid. pp. 80, 87.

59. Ibid. pp. 45, 44, 45, 46, 45.

60. Ibid. pp. 43, 103, 43. The crone is a trope used in similar acerbic vain by his contemporary Lewis Grassic Gibbon, who talks of Edinburgh as 'a disappointed spinster with a hare-lip and inhibitions', Dundee as 'a frowsy fisher-wife addicted to gin and infanticide' and Aberdeen as 'a thin-lipped peasant-woman who has borne eleven and buried nine' (L. Grassic Gibbon, 'Glasgow', in L. Grassic Gibbon, *A Scots Hairst*, ed. I. S. Munro (London: Hutchinson, 1967), pp. 82–94 (p. 82). Like Grassic Gibbon, Muir was at a loss to personify the manifold horrors of the nation's largest city, Glasgow, although the ways in which they characterise the relationship between urban and human degeneracy in the city share many similarities – see p. 221n.

61. Muir, *Scottish Journey*, pp. 68, 67–8.

62. Ibid. pp. 4, 34, 38.

63. Ibid. pp. 115–16, 122, 123, 124, 124, 156. Muir cites Blake on 'the Glasgow man' (p.158).

64. Ibid. pp. 187, 188, 184.

65. Ibid. pp. 111, 105.

66. R. Richman, 'Edwin Muir's journey', *The New Criterion*, 15 (8), 1997, pp. 26–33 (p. 27).

67. Ibid. p. 26, quoting E. Muir, *An Autobiography* [1954] (Edinburgh: Canongate, 1993), p. 54. Muir is regarded as the mentor to the novelist George Mackay Brown, whose own biography reflects a life and art haunted by 'the childhood Eden of Orkney' and who 'wrote extraordinary columns for the *Orkney Herald* – full of bitterness and bile at modernity'. However, Mackay Brown's 'pronounced agoraphobia' – he rarely left Stromness – contrasts markedly with Muir's unsettled wandering around Europe (A. Greig, Review of M. Fergusson, *George Mackay Brown: The Life* (London: John Murray, 2006), *The Scotsman*, 15 April 2006).

68. Muir, *An Autobiography*, p. 39.

69. E. Muir, *The Estate of Poetry* (London: Hogarth Press, 1962), p. 86.

70. Muir, *An Autobiography*, p. 289 (Appendix II: 'Extracts from a diary 1937–9').

71. See C. Lasch, *The Culture of Narcissism: American Life in An Age of Diminishing Expectations* (London and New York: Norton, 1991), p. xviii.

72. This desire is frequently referred to as the wish for ontological security. Prominent among the sociologists of late modernity, Anthony Giddens (*Modernity and Self-Identity* (Cambridge: Polity, 1991), p. 243) borrows the term from the Scots anti-psychiatrist R. D. Laing who refers to the existential need in everyone for 'a centrally firm sense of his own and other people's reality and identity' (R. D. Laing and A. Esterson, *Sanity, Madness and the Family, Vol. 1: Families of Schizophrenics* (London: Tavistock, 1964), p. 39. Such self-concern is itself a consequence of (late-) modern life where the struggle to maintain a personally secure reality requires a workable world-view.

73. Withers, 'Picturing Highland landscapes', p. 74, citing S. Daniels, 'Marxism, culture and the duplicity of landscape', in R. Peet and N. Thrift (eds), *New Models in Geography, Vol. 2* (London: Unwin Hyman, 1989), pp. 196–220.

74. Ibid. p. 75. See T. Pringle, 'The privation of history: Landseer, Victoria and the Highland myth', in D. Cosgrove and S. Daniels (eds), *The Iconography of Landscape* (Cambridge: Cambridge University Press, 1989), pp. 142–61.

75. McKenzie, 'The "photographic tour"', p. 24.

76. T. Cusack, 'A "countryside bright with cosy homesteads": Irish nationalism and the cottage landscape', *National Identities*, 3 (3), 2001, pp. 221–38 (p. 238).

77. Stevenson, 'The Scottishness of Scottish photography', p. 88.

78. The collections are: William Easton Collection, H. B. Curwen Collection, Cathcart Collection, Robert Sturgeon Collection, Mary Ethel Muir Donaldson and Alasdair Alpin MacGregor Collection. See D. I. Kidd, *To See Oursels: Rural Scotland in Old Photographs* (Glasgow: HarperCollins, 1992), pp. 10–13 provides outline details.

79. Kidd, *To See Oursels*, p. 11.

80. M. Russell, *A Different Country: The Photographs of Werner Kissling* (Edinburgh: Birlinn, 2003); J. T. Dunbar, *Herself: the Life and Photographs of M. E. M. Donaldson* (Edinburgh: William Blackwood, 1979); M. F. Shaw, *Folksongs and Folk-lore of South Uist* (London: Routledge, 1955). In 1935, Kissling made *Eriskay – A Poem of Remote Lives*, the first moving picture to use spoken Gaelic. He later took hundreds of photographs on Eriskay and South Uist, many of which portrayed people involved in traditional crafts. As Chapter 3 indicates, Flaherty's *Man of Aran* (1934) was also a seminal influence upon John Grierson.

81. J. Burnett, '"Into the whirling vortex of modernity": cultural developments in the Scottish Gaidhealtachd, 1935–1965', in R. J. Morris and L. Kennedy (eds), *Ireland*

and Scotland: Order and Disorder, 1600–2000 (Edinburgh: John Donald, 2005), pp. 175–88 (p. 281 [sic] n82). Burnett also cites G. Scott-Moncrieff, The Scottish Islands (London: Batsford, 1952) as 'a classic example of presenting the "rural" as a bulwark against socialism, urbanisation and industrialism' (ibid. p. 282).

82. J. Berger, About Looking (London: Writers & Readers, 1980), p. 46.
83. P. Strand and B. Davidson, Tir A' Mhurain/Outer Hebrides (London: MacGibbon & Kee, 1962).
84. F. MacDonald, 'Geographies of Vision', p. 283.
85. C. Chiarenza, 'Review: Tir A' Mhurain /Outer Hebrides', Contemporary Photographer, 4, 1963, pp. 63–5 (p. 65), cited in MacDonald, 'Geographies of Vision', p. 350.
86. MacDonald, 'Geographies of Vision', p. 361.
87. R. Hutchinson, 'Striking Images of the Islands of 30 Years Ago', West Highland Free Press, 22 August 2003. Wylie has copied Strand's technique of pairing images of individuals and nature: the viewer is invited to compare, for example, the colour and texture of lichen with a crofter weaving Harris tweed. See G. Wylie, Hebridean Light (Edinburgh: Birlinn, 2003).
88. T. Crichton, 'Last Glimpse of a Disappearing World', Sunday Herald, 11 December 2005.
89. Wylie, Hebridean Light; G. Wylie, The Hebrideans (Edinburgh: Birlinn, 2005).
90. MacDonald, 'Geographies of Vision', pp. 287, 286, 359.
91. Clarke, The Photograph, p. 68.
92. Ibid. pp. 70–1; R. D. McClelland, 'The light and the vision: the work of Raymond Moore', British Journal of Photography, 29 August 1969; Clarke, The Photograph, p. 71.
93. A. Hall, A Sense of Belonging to Scotland (Edinburgh: Mercat Press, 2002) [hereafter Hall (1)]; A. Hall, A Sense of Belonging to Scotland: Further Journeys (Edinburgh: Mercat Press, 2005) [hereafter Hall (2)].
94. Hall (1), pp. vi, 54.
95. P. Berger, B. Berger and H. Kellner, The Homeless Mind: Modernization and Consciousness (London: Pelican, 1974); Hall (2), p. 28.
96. Hall (2), p. 86; Hall (1), p. 62.
97. Hall (1), p. 42; Hall (2), pp. 104, 52.
98. J. Urry, The Tourist Gaze: Leisure and Travel in Contemporary Societies (2nd edn, London: Sage, 2002).
99. Hall (1), p. 38.
100. Urry, The Tourist Gaze, p. 3.
101. C. Prior, Highland Wilderness (London: Constable & Robinson, 1993); C. Prior, Scotland: The Wild Places (London: Constable & Robinson, 2001); C. Baxter, Scotland (Grantown-on-Spey: Colin Baxter Photography Ltd, 1999); C. McMaster, Elements: The Landscape of Scotland (Edinburgh: Mercat Press, 2004). Baxter is the best known and most prolific, his catalogue extending to regional guides, postcards, calendars, mousemats and keyrings. See also Craig Aitchison's Land and Light panoramas (http://www.landandlight.co.uk/calendar.html Accessed June 2009).
102. Hall (1), pp. 14, 92; Hall (2) p. 46.
103. Urry, The Tourist Gaze, p. 43; C. Crawshaw and J. Urry, 'Tourism and the photographic eye', in C. Rojek, Touring Cultures (London: Sage, 1997), pp. 176–95 (pp. 176–7) note that 'different gazes are '"authorized" by different discourses' and 'imply different socialities'. In the 'romantic' gaze, 'the presence of other people detracts

from the quality of the experience', but 'the "collective" gaze by contrast involves conviviality. Other people are necessary to give atmosphere to the experience of place, which then becomes a shared process of visual consumption'.

104. Hall (1), p. 28; Hall (2), p. 92.
105. Hall (1), p. 6.
106. Hall (2), pp. 24, 64, 92, 102.
107. Hall (1), pp. 16, 58.
108. Hall (1), p. 76, and see p. 32; Hall (2), pp. 94, and see Hall (1) pp. 12, 14, Hall (2) pp. 12, 18.
109. Hall (1), pp. 16, 100; Hall (2) p. 52; Hall (1) p. 52.
110. Hall (1), pp. 40, 86, 58.
111. Hall (2), pp. 38, 28, 10.
112. Ibid. pp. 22, 70, 60.
113. Hall (1), p. 36.
114. Ibid. p. 2.
115. Ibid. p. 20.
116. Hall (2), p. 108; Hall (1) p. 74; Hall (2), p. 82.
117. Clarke, *The Photograph*, pp. 67–8.
118. O. Jenkins, 'Photography and travel brochures: the circle of representation', *Tourism Geographies*, 5 (3), 2003, pp. 305–28.
119. Cf. M. Billig, *Banal Nationalism* (London: Sage, 1995).
120. Morton, *In Scotland Again*, p. 290.
121. Muir, *Scottish Journey*, p. 243.
122. W. Scott, *The Lady of the Lake* (Edinburgh: J. Ballantyne, 1810), Canto I. XIV.
123. J. G. Kellas, *Modern Scotland: The Nation since 1870* (London: Pall Mall Press, 1968), p. 17, cited in A. A. MacLaren (ed.), *Social Class in Scotland: Past and Present* (Edinburgh: John Donald, 1976), p.1.
124. Clarke, *The Photograph*, p. 55.
125. To a degree their views were echoed in the arguments of ethical socialist sociologists during the 1990s in the moral panics surrounding the apparent rise of a British 'underclass'. See for instance N. Dennis and G. Erdos, *Families Without Fatherhood* (London: IEA Health and Welfare Unit, 1993).
126. Cusack, 'A "countryside bright"', p. 227, citing L. Gibbons, 'Romanticism in Ruins: Developments in Recent Irish Cinema', *The Irish Review*, 2, 1987, p. 60.
127. See L. Grassic Gibbon, *Sunset Song* [1932] (Edinburgh: Canongate, 1988), p. 119: 'And then a queer thought came to her in the drookèd fields, that nothing endured at all, nothing but the land she passed across, tossed and turned and perpetually changed below the hands of the crofter folk since the oldest of them had set the Standing Stones by the loch of Blawearie'.
128. Womack, *Improvement and Romance*, p. 174.
129. Clarke, *The Photograph*, p. 58.

Section III

Local Visions

CHAPTER 6

A pattern of islands: photographs in the cultural account

INTRODUCTION

Torgovnick's literary analysis of primitivism in Freud, Malinowski and Mead suggests that the impulse to record 'other' cultures represents a means of 'handling, through displacement, the series of dislocations that we call modernity and postmodernity'.[1] While archivists have collected and classified, the better to re-present the past for contemporary consumption, the socio-historical critique of heritage and 'museumry' has properly castigated selective and ethnocentric interpretation.[2] Cultural studies includes among its nostrums the need to 'honour the plurality of perspectives'[3] in a world where 'above all, and directly contrary to the form in which they are constantly invoked, identities are constructed through, not outside, difference'.[4] And an emergent visual anthropology has been deployed to lend graphic evidence, the gaze behind the fading photographs of distant islanders being exposed as that of Western imperialism.[5] The assertion of 'otherness' is seen to have driven an ideological wedge between 'modern' civilisation and its 'traditional' absence.

It seems that, in the very creation of display, indigenous readings have been elided. The ensuing discussion elaborates some of the ways in which this process has occurred. However, a second thread in the analysis examines how photographs have also been drawn upon to affirm local worldviews that may offer competing historical accounts. Given that during the course of the last century or so photography has become a fundamentally democratic medium, it is possible to contend that images might consist of resources for identity formation and maintenance as much as sources of subjectification.

'Otherness': The Gaze from Without

The primary sources referred to in this chapter are housed in the archive collections of local museums, chiefly those of the Northern Isles of Orkney and Shetland.[6] In the old Shetland Museum, as I crossed the threshold between the display area and the backstage archives,[7] I was struck by the sight of two sets of partly-catalogued objects: one was a set of filing cabinets and boxes housing collections of the works of local photographers plus a selection of recently donated family albums; the other was a group of ancient human bones with name-tags attached, lying on open shelves.[8] The scene implied that in so far as it is the curator's role to present the life of the islands to its people as well as tell a story about Shetland to all comers, pictures and bones are handy vehicles: both are witness to genealogical roots, one in archaeology, the other a kind of pictorial ethnology. Indeed, if we follow Bourdieu, then photographs, like standing stones, are themselves 'part of the solemnisation and celebration of collective life', and should be examined as such.[9] But museums, as Victorian edifices designed to house exhibits brought home from the dark recesses of Empire, also share similarities with zoos. The prevailing evolutionary paradigm was much influenced by the claim advanced by E. B. Tylor that existing 'primitive' societies held vestigial cultural survivals from earlier stages of human social development.[10] It was thus urgent that disappearing peoples be recorded before it was too late.[11] In that photographs of distant peoples were thought to capture vanishing traces of ancestral custom, they had perhaps more in common with taxidermy. Indeed, a Foucauldian reading regards both as 'realist practice[s] of domination', stuffing animals as a visual technology being the precursor to collecting images of 'the natives'.[12]

In winter 1982 journalist Ian Jack wryly concluded a visit to the Western Isles of Scotland by asserting that, 'the Hebrides, in fact, have not become what some of the rest of us may have wanted. They have not become a human game reserve'.[13] Notwithstanding the modern reality he observed, his allusion pointed to the continuing tendency to imagine the societies of the Scottish islands as an antique curiosity held in aspic from former times. As Chapter 5 has suggested, some photographs have had a significant role in purveying such a misplaced perception. By contrast, the visual record has also contributed much as a valid historical source for ethnological understanding, providing details of dress, custom, craft skills, building styles and other aspects of material culture.[14] The potential danger facing historical interpretation lies in a failure to appreciate how the mythical aspects of the medium are implicated in its utility as a treasury of illustrative evidence. In highlighting this collusion, the researcher must engage in a cultural analysis both of the communities at issue and of those who have pictured them.

The very act of taking a photograph transforms its subject into an object. Moreover, Barthes has argued that whether we categorise a set of photographs empirically, rhetorically or aesthetically, 'the distributions we impose upon it are . . . external to the object'.[15] The apparently raw 'reality' of island culture has already been appropriated and ordered. These layers of objectification and classification render the roles of both photographer and curator inherently problematic since the idiosyncrasies of each affect who or what is identified – and how – thus limiting the character and extent of the preserved record.[16] The museum, as a repository for the collections of various photographers, cannot naively be regarded as an agent enabling mediation between insiders and outsiders.

Conventional histories of the Scottish islands rely heavily on a traditional versus modern polarisation in which visual images are employed to demonstrate a critical severance between past and present. Early photographs, like bones or standing stones, inhabit the romantic reliquary of a dead society. They are thus used to represent the simple Arcadian life of the Noble Savage. Whilst Victorian investigators built on this imperialist interpretation, the fisherfolk, crofters and peasants were portrayed with a homely social realism characteristic of European art, in which the 'salt of the earth', or of the sea (the classic image of an aged seafarer being George Washington Wilson's 'An Old Salt') were considered closer to nature, thus less sophisticated than their urban counterparts.[17] Subsequently, other media such as film emphasised this distance between image and audience, spatially, temporally and culturally.[18]

Over the past century, social scientists have done much to emphasise – indeed reify – this dichotomy.[19] Community studies have taken their cue from Tönnies's distinction between traditional *gemeinschaft*, translated as 'community' and referring to pre-industrial, small scale societies in which people were bound in harmony by extended kin relationships and a shared culture, and *gesellschaft* ('association'), seen as characterising modern relationships that are individualistic, impersonal, competitive and calculative.[20] The Chicago School, notably Robert Redfield, codified the distinction by applying the ideal-typical concept of folk society to denote small, isolated groups, in which kinship predominates and culture is transmitted orally, while Durkheimians later refined the notion of the rural-urban continuum by demonstrating roles to be less clearly differentiated, but networks denser towards the rural end of the spectrum.[21] It is unsurprising, therefore, that until the wave of 'white anthropology' swept over them in the late1970s, coincident with the impact of the oil industry in Northern Scotland, Scotland's outer isles were conventionally perceived as socially marginal and culturally backward.[22]

The archetype is St Kilda, Britain's remotest island, some 90 kilometres west of the Outer Hebrides and just 5 kilometres long. The last thirty-six inhabitants were evacuated, at their own request, in 1930. Although interest in their unique way of life has grown particularly since then, outsiders have long chronicled the traditions of St Kilda. In the late seventeenth century Martin Martin wrote of 'People in the Golden Age . . . in Innocency and Simplicity, Purity, mutual Love and cordial Friendship', an evocation further developed in Victorian travel writing which stressed continually the Utopian ideal, with the representation of life as both primitive and democratic enhanced considerably through the photographic postcards mailed by early tourists from the island's tiny post office.[23] Then, as now, George Washington Wilson's images of the 'St Kilda Parliament' – the daily meeting of the menfolk – and of fowling – men scrambling over precipitous cliffs to take the seabirds that supplied their food, bedding, lamp oil and much else – contributed the basic iconography. In line with the imperialist image, Spring refers to a later film voiceover in which the St Kildans are spoken of as being like 'animals in a zoo' by camera-toting tourists.[24] As he observes, maintaining such a fiction perhaps served the islanders well by ensuring a gullible, but lucrative audience. He continues, however: 'Of the various photographs that constitute an ethnographic reading of the St Kildan way of life, several characteristics . . . stand out – notably a concentration on the "otherness" of their way of life with its emphasis on work rather than leisure activities . . . the self-conscious employment of direct address, and the clear association of the inhabitants of the island with the landscape they inhabit or the natural things they harvest', a juxtaposition also marked in early documentary films where 'the weatherbeaten faces of those portrayed are often cut into scenes of rocks or storm-ridden seas'.[25]

The images of American photographer Paul Strand, who visited the Uists in 1954 (see Chapter 5), were accompanied by text from African anthropologist Basil Davidson, who remarked: 'with the rain and wind and rock and shallow soil of their land they have woven a strong individuality, a strong determination to resist and to survive'.[26] Of the rural communities he had studied elsewhere in the 1940s Strand himself noted that 'nature and architecture had come to reflect the personality of the people'; hence close-up images of people juxtaposed with pictures showing wave-sculpted (or eroded) rocks.[27] Similarly, in a retrospective publication of a native Lewisman's photographs, the editor notes how 'the fertile machair soil of Ness, at the extreme north-westerly tip of the Outer Hebrides, has sustained a strong Viking-derived community for over a thousand years'.[28]

This symbiosis between people and place as represented in visually distinctive physiognomic and other traits has been a central theme in the construction of the putative character of picturesque 'types' throughout the British Isles.[29] The eugenicist overtones evident in the inclusion of photos of 'pure highlanders' amongst the British Association's 'Racial Committee' Albums of the 1870s gives way to a more sentimental imagery.[30] Finlay, for example, portrays 'Scottish types', including the 'Highland crofter', 'Lowland miner', 'Hebridean woman' and 'East Coast fisherman',[31] whilst railway advertising posters of the 1930s depicted a series of 'East Coast Types'. At the same time the *Illustrated London News* referred to a tableau of St Kilda images as 'island types'.[32] The distinctiveness of each is also intended to signal a folkloric distance from the urban or suburban mainstream of 'modern' everyday life.

Yet there are also indications of a collapsing idyll (and it is telling that photography gained ascendancy in the nineteenth century just as urbanisation reached its zenith), as closeness to nature lapses into social regression. Like the sketches from Van Gogh's Nuenen period, in which peasants sometimes resemble apes, so the Aran Islanders pictured by Frank Stephens off the West Coast of Ireland during the 1930s seem stolid and uncomprehending.[33] Meanwhile, elderly eccentrics, with bizarre nicknames (such as the midget 'Coconut Tam' from Edinburgh's Old Town) and afflicted by odd facial features, outsize feet (like Tain's town crier 'Rory Toe'), imbecility and other abnormalities, abound among museum and postcard archives: here lie legendary 'characters', such as Willie Laughton alias 'Skatehorn', who trolled about Orkney in his bowler hat and on a penny farthing bicycle, or Annie Harper, the bearded fortune-teller whose 'clothing defied description', carrying her dogs, named after the minister's wife and a notorious local laird.[34]

As localism disintegrates with migration, transport advances and the rise of broadcast and visual media, the uniqueness of island cultures becomes both a rare commodity and an untenable reality. Nostalgia kicks in. The sagacious 'man who told the stories',[35] once vital as the vehicle for passing on the wisdom of the community, like the aged oddballs who defined its boundaries, has his likeness captured on camera. As Benjamin says, 'only in extinction is the collector comprehended'. And the two archaic figures, past masters of the art of storytelling, the peasant and the seaman – the one earthbound, rooted in local ways and traditions, the other who has

Fig. 6.1 Willie Laughton alias 'Skatehorn'.
Photographer Tom Kent.
Reproduced by kind permission of Orkney Library & Archive.

travelled and brought back his store of parables – are nowhere better represented, indeed massively over-represented, than in the photographic record.[36] As experience became devalued, so its protagonists – be they craftspeople, wise men or simply witnesses to events long past – became quaint curiosities from another world, ultimately anachronisms. The image simply confirms their redundancy; they no longer possess anything to pass on but their memory. Since knowledge is now separated from its source, knowledge itself and the receiver of knowledge, the wisdom of elders has been supplanted by their 'ascribed worthlessness'.[37] Yet in a discourse where older people symbolise the last of the old order, photographs become precious as final traces of the existence of bearers of vanishing skills (like sound recordings of people speaking a disappearing language). Here questions of staged authenticity arise over the proliferation of images of old women carrying peats and knitting at the same time; in Orkney 'traditional' straw-backed chair makers abound (although straw-making had long been a domestic craft, straw plaiting only became a cottage industry following its introduction by a London company in the early 1800s)[38]; matriarchs with spinning wheels are ubiquitous. The image of an old woman carrying a creel seems so definitively associated with the past that 'if ever she put it down the world would go out like a light'.[39] The older the photograph, the more precious the image.

Coull, discussing Shetland, provides typical textual backdrop:

> The nineteenth century was still the time of big families, and population continued to increase until 1861 ... Subsequently numbers fell with accelerated emigration, which was linked in part to clearances of crofters by appropriation of their scattald [hill] grazings; and with the trend toward smaller families from the end of last century, the population continued to fall for a full century to 1961 ... While numbers of small islands have become deserted ... none have actually been abandoned in the last 50 years, although the population in some is now around one-tenth of their nineteenth century peak. The survival of the communities in the remaining small islands is now delicately poised.[40]

Stalwart survivors thus act as commentary on the state of the community, the perilous predicament of islands on the verge of irreversible transformation. In the *Third Statistical Account of Scotland* (1985), for example, the longevity of the people of Unst is remarked upon, over 40 islanders (from a mean population of around 2,000) having attained 95 years in the period since 1851.[41] Meanwhile, at Westray in the Orkneys, Scotland's longest married couple celebrated their 75th anniversary in 1998: they had lived on the same 19-acre croft since 1923.[42] Nonetheless, Westray's 'fast becoming an island of old people' is attributed in part to 'a strong tendency for young people to move out of the island in search of work'.[43] This compositional shift is also detected in Walls parish (Shetland), where the number of households containing children in 1983 was just sixty-six, against 162 with no children; over half of all households comprised one or two people only, most of whom were elderly.[44] While Westray is particularly well served by proud photographs of its ancients – 'Willie o' the blacksmith's' featuring among these – the age-selectiveness of emigration has elsewhere contributed to a vision of crumbling elders who appear as relics of dysfunctional communities. This alternative view (see, for instance, the Skye crofters depicted on one of the 'Nostalgic Images' postcards, or photographs of couples entitled 'The Last of the Cottars') pictures elders beside their decrepit crofts and black houses, part of the landscape of decay.[45] Such metaphorical association is reinforced by the fact that many images are themselves blurred or the negatives damaged by mildew, so that faces appear to be fading into oblivion. More deliberately, the technique of tinting originally monochrome images

Fig. 6.2 Fading into oblivion – the image as vanishing trace.
Photograph by John Irvine. Reproduced by kind permission of
Shetland Museum & Archives.

so that they appear in sepia is a commonly practised means of evoking
antiquity.

A more upbeat version of remembrance becomes evident in the 1970s
and 1980s. While photographers like Tom Kidd aimed to illustrate that
'underneath the veneer of oil-age sophistication, there is abundant evidence of the old Shetland', culture clash remained heavily implicated:
'Inevitably the photographs highlight the difference between the old and
the new, contrasting the ugly steel structure of the oilmen with the simple
basic tools of the crofter as he wields his scythe or tar brush.' His narrative
foretells demise while the spirit of the people endures in the expressions
of his subjects: 'the strength and determination of the fisherman, the
humour that shines in the eyes of an old lady as she introduces her pet
lamb, the quiet commonsense that shows so clearly in the faces of the
crofters and the resignation shown by the very old whose only concern
is that someone else should keep them warm, clean and well fed'.[46]
Tellingly, however, these last are in nursing homes, not in the bosom of
their loved ones.

REFLECTIONS FROM WITHIN: CONTINUITIES IN THE CULTURAL ACCOUNT

Such is the reading from without. However, in direct contrast to the apparent hegemony of what has been termed the 'Grand Dichotomy by which peripheral cultures are both romanticised and marginalised',[47] it is possible to claim an indigenous appreciation of the role of imagery that emphasises continuity over change, adaptation rather than schism, generational solidarity against attenuation. Cohen argues that in Shetland routinised crises – clearances, emigration and oil – have had the effect of promoting and strengthening a collective self-identity.[48] This proposition may be extended to other Scottish islands, notably the Hebrides, while food shortages and famine may be added to the catalogue of woes threatening, and often succeeding in devastating communities. Although remoteness might have bred a certain confident distinctiveness, contact with and intrusion by outside forces has produced an enhanced awareness of the need to retain and assert that distinctiveness. It is this consciousness of difference that prompts cultural accounting: 'Once one has become conscious of culture, it must be perceived and handled in a different way than previously. Hence the recounting of what life was previously like must always be, to some extent, a *reconstruction* rather than a mere recall . . . The past, in cultural accounting, becomes a powerful guide to the interpretation of the present'.[49] In evoking continuity it becomes a critical resource.

On the island of Whalsay, kinship was the sheet anchor of symbolic survival:

> Even relatives at a further remove were classified genealogically. The detail was bewildering and awesome . . . it suggested to me, first, the importance of genealogy to Whalsay people as a means of mapping their social knowledge; and, second . . . the remarkable intensity of kinship on the island . . . Three-quarters of the population could be related to each other through their grandparents' generation. This is explained by two factors: the historical preponderance of local endogamy; and the much lower rate of out-migration from Whalsay than occurred in other areas of Shetland. This, in turn, has produced a powerful sense of historical continuity in which the present and the past are curiously merged. The past is ever present, in yarns about characters of old, in the minutiae of place names . . .
>
> Conversation thus spans and concertinas the centuries. In this and in the extensive knowledge of genealogy and kinship history there is a pervasive sense of rootedness, of belonging, as if people were as immovably and inherently part of the island as the very features of its landscape.[50]

Anthropologists have noted this phenomenon elsewhere; Hugh Brody's analysis of the Tory islanders referring to 'the reckoning of kin' and naming of family boats,[51] and arguably, Sontag's claim that photographs allow people to take possession of the places in which they are insecure imputes a similar psycho-social requirement.[52] Eccentrics clearly supply fodder for humour which binds people in a specifically local way, especially when kinship becomes an ever more fragile source of cultural affirmation. As Malinowski asserts, 'the last stronghold of [national] peculiarity can be found in its traditional diversions, and without diversion and amusement a culture and a race cannot survive'.[53] Thus Up Helly Aa persists as an annual Viking Festival in Lerwick and the New Year 'Ba" game takes place every New Year in Kirkwall.

Particular characteristics are attributed to people from particular families or places, be these facial or bodily features or local practices. The islanders of Sanday were made fun of throughout Orkney because they used cow-dung for fuel, while the people of Fair Isle have fared rather more famously with their sweaters.[54] Likewise, more generic commentary on the 'Character of the People' is found in the *Statistical Account*. For example, it was noted in 1845 that 'the people [of Shetland] are not remarkable for size or muscular strength, but chiefly for hardihood and endurance of fatigue'.[55]

Despite this, Cohen contends that since accounting is largely a mental construct it is difficult for the anthropologist to document: consciousness inheres in the thoughts behind the image, rather than in the image itself. However, the ways in which photographs have entered the vernacular are themselves remarkable. Folk histories derive from a collective vocabulary incorporating 'personalities' (often aged), nicknames, events, customs, skills and local humour. Several local photographers appear to have amassed images of 'personalities', hence the sub-categories 'Kay personalities', 'personalities – Rattar', 'Stout personalities', 'personalities – Peterson', 'Manson – personalities' and 'personalities – smaller collections' in the catalogue files of the Shetland Museum. A discourse may be formed using such pictures as catalysts, prompts that trigger collective remembrance. As we have seen, an outsider may of course construct a similar inventory, but it would be devised and interpreted in quite different ways. The indigenous articulation is one in which the past initially appears to be contrasted with the present, but where continuity is delivered 'as a kind of *coup de grace*'.[56] The dialectic between then and now is held by threads of kinship and association. Thus, when Cohen gathered with some islanders to look at 'Henry's collection of photographs of some old Whalsaymen', taken before 1900:

not everyone present was able to identify the people in the photographs, though the names were known, as, in varying degrees and with differing emphases, were possibly apocryphal stories associated with them. That much was common currency. But behind this common property were the unique connections each person present traced to the historical characters, through their own genealogies, their associations with parents or grandparents, stories about them peculiar to their childhood households, and so on.[57]

In contrast to the wistful world we have lost depicted from the outside, this is a tangible world gained through kinship – a 'carrier concept' through which the world is made meaningful. The stereotypical qualities of kin become 'a treasury of public knowledge . . . like compass bearings . . . means of social orientation', indicators of 'the authenticity of the community . . . [T]hey relate its present generations to their lineal predecessors'.[58]

Photographs thus remind friends and relatives how far they have changed, but also how much remains familiar. The 'Birthday Greetings' section of the *Shetland Times*, in common with many local newspapers in Britain and North America, prints a weekly gallery of snapshots of today's forty-year-olds as children, or youngsters from 50 years ago beneath headings such as '8/11/95. Happy 70th Birthday Shu's [she's] worn weel!' They may look different, yet here too is confirmation that they are the same people. Such accounting is of a different domain to a request from outside appearing in the same paper entitled 'Hunt for ancestors' and reading: 'A woman from England is researching her husband's family tree and has discovered she has ancestors from Shetland . . . She is having difficulty tracing this line and would like to hear from anyone with any information'.[59]

To regard images simply as memory triggers is to neglect their wider role as a medium through which communities express their past identities. Like Bourdieu, Kopytoff makes the Durkheimian observation that 'cultural systems of classification reflect the structure and cultural resources of the societies in question'.[60] This is not to say, however, that only one system of classification exists locally, or that communal identifications necessarily coincide with the 'symbolic inventory of society' held in the museum.[61] In so far as photographs have social biographies these may be fragmented at different career stages as the physical evidence passes from photographers, to families, to curators and back again. Given the subject matter and, in some instances the provenance (family albums) of such material, we might expect a degree of negotiation and renegotiation of meaning between curator and community.[62]

An aspect of the collaboration between museums, or local history societies, and indigenous knowledge is the publication of photographs in local newspapers requesting further information. These appeals are often followed up by articles packed with anecdotal detail. Evidence of this reflexive relationship may be found in the Shetland Museum. Peter Halcrow was born in Shetland in 1865, but in his early twenties left for Edinburgh where he was a grocer until his death in 1955. On a visit home at some time before 1914 he photographed his elderly mother. He also supplied a Victorian portrait which the curator had captioned 'Robert and Laurina Smith, Aith'. Subsequently, however, a line was drawn through this text and the scribbled lines 'Peter says no!! Possibly one of his brothers' added below. Years later, in common with many photographs in the Museum's keeping, several pictures from Halcrow's family collection formed part of a local community exhibition in Cunningsburgh, his birthplace. Locals who viewed these images did two significant things: firstly, they helped to name the places where the pictures had been taken and the individuals and their family relationships; secondly, where captions already existed, they queried the details, frequently amending or supplementing them. For example, a group pose of the Smiths of Sabre and Aith has been dated; the individual who was once labelled John is now thought more likely to be Peter, 'Brother to William, the smallest, broadest and perhaps strongest, 5' 11'", while the figure thought to be Robert is in fact Arthur (home on leave). Someone has added 'There were 8 Smith Brothers [only three appear in this shot] and all looked very similar, very tall and well built. William in the photo could step a sixen mast hisel'. Tellingly, nevertheless, the card mounts on which such valuable information has been amassed have now been separated from the photographs which, in the process of digitalisation, stand to lose a degree of local and genealogical meaning: the catalogue entry reads simply 'Unknown elderly couple'.

Photographs may be a primary data source, but their messages depend upon context.[63] Having no innate narrative, they require language to fill the gaps in understanding. As Kracauer remarks of one picture: 'were it not for the oral tradition, the image alone would not have sufficed to reconstruct the grandmother . . . it's any young girl in 1864 . . . This mannequin does not belong to our time; it could be standing with others of its kind in the museum, in a glass labeled "Traditional Costumes, 1864" . . . an archaeological mannequin which serves to illustrate the costumes of the period'.[64] Likewise with the debate over captioning: not only is the process of interpretation controlled by the interaction of image and text,[65] but it also reflects a series of iterative interventions as the community adjusts the museum's assignment. While the Shetland Museum has

Fig. 6.3 Robert Smith or his brother? Negotiating identity.
Photograph by Peter Halcrow. Reproduced by kind permission of
Shetland Museum & Archives.

welcomed such information, contestation and corroboration, the people's
eagerness to ensure a correct record represents a strong sense of ownership
and attachment to their ancestors. Talk of tribespeople who shy away
from the camera for fear it will steal their souls has become clichéd. But
here we have an instance of people retrospectively asserting the claims
of local knowledge in order to reclaim traces of their history. Such investigation of the tensions between photography, identity, resistance and
consensus finds cross-cultural resonance in explorations of 'Indianness' by
Native American artists and writers.[66]

   In the indigenous worldview, cultural distinctiveness is illustrated by
expressions of idiomatic behaviour.[67] 'Personalities' are less likely to be
isolated eccentrics establishing the boundaries of normality than individuals whose conduct or bearing typifies specific places or small islands.
Interestingly, however, the provenance of images drawn upon appears
to be rather less relevant than what they have come to signify. Thus,
although the database for picture research will mostly consist of collections of thousands of images by single photographers, and the investigator

will accordingly subject each practitioner to biographical scrutiny and seek evidence of bias, the connection between producer and consumer will often be tenuous, even immaterial. A locally produced study of *Orkney's Pictorial Heritage* remarks that the work of locally born photographer Tom Kent comprises 'by far the most important contribution to our photographic archive'.[68] He it was who saved the aforementioned 'Skatehorn' and Annie Harper for posterity, and his Birsay lobster fisherman adorns not just the cover of this book, but – in sepia reproductions – several hotel bars, shops and even a set of coasters available on the Orkney Mainland. Such portraits are highly iconographic and spoken of with pride. Yet Kent is remembered with some ambivalence. Despite his achievements as a professional, chronicling Orkney life and landscape for thirty-eight years, he had learned his trade working in a Chicago drugstore as a young man, setting up shop in Kirkwall after his return aged thirty-four.[69] His work gained him national fame as a contributor to *Country Life*. Nevertheless, his death at age seventy-three 'passed almost unnoticed'.[70] As Tinch comments: 'Success did not treat him kindly, [however], and at the time of his death in 1936, he appears to have been largely shunned by the society that he so faithfully and brilliantly recorded'.[71] Rumour tells he had a drink problem. Unlike, say George Washington Wilson or James Valentine, both of whom operated companies that generated vast numbers of images for the burgeoning tourist market,[72] or those thousands of anonymous individuals who contributed to private family albums, Kent cannot be easily accommodated by either outside or indigenous renditions. Nevertheless, the fact is that over time his images have been claimed by both points to the manner in which photographs can readily take on fresh meanings independent of, or uncoupled from their immediate source. When this occurs, images become ripe for fabrication.

AMBIGUITIES OF THE IMAGE

In a compilation of Scottish women in photographs, historian Leah Leneman captioned a picture of an old woman knitting with the following text: 'Mrs Gillies, one of the last St Kildans, seated in front of her house. This photograph was taken the day before St Kilda was evacuated, in August 1930. She calmly continued to knit, using wool plucked from the local Soay sheep and spun at home. Most of her own clothes would have been dyed and woven or knitted on the island'.[73] Naïvely interpreted, the image suggests a degree of staging in order to blend old age and a dying local craft, the portrayal being lent added poignancy by its timing: this is a classic memento of the end of a marginal way of life. However, a more

Fig. 6.4 The last of the St Kildans. Mrs Gillies knitting: natural pose or staged portrait?
Photograph from Alasdair Alpin MacGregor collection.
© National Museums Scotland. www.scran.ac.uk

precise understanding of the context in which the photograph was taken
tells a rather different story. Spring's analysis of films made about St Kilda
reveals 'the camera-shy "natives" of 1923 onwards hiding their faces from
the inquisitive gaze of the tourists', an aversion symptomatic of a community in decline, 'a symbol of their unhappiness that their once happy way
of life was finally and irrevocably at an end'.[74] But by 1930, shyness had
shifted to an altogether more confrontational stance, the shot list for John
Ritchie's (suppressed) documentary film *Evacuation of St Kilda* reading:

> Old woman knitting socks outside her cottage. Photographer paid her £2.00 for
> the privilege of taking this shot . . . Another woman knitting outside her house
> takes fright at the camera and three times runs away to escape into the house
> . . . One woman hides her face. Woman's back to camera . . . Old man smoking
> pipe outside his house. Younger man picks up stone to throw at the camera . . .
> Group of people outside house. Woman sitting disconsolate.[75]

Thus, the superficially composed Mrs Gillies disguises a scene of sharp
social tension. It is far easier to romanticise – and simplify by aesthetic

— 189 —

distancing – such moments than to articulate their complexity. Like earlier images of destitution, clearances and emigration they have lent themselves to a nostalgic interpretation that renders the subjects passive victims.

Barthes contends that photographs are inherently elegiac since by definition they are snapshots in time.[76] Equally, however, the image 'preserves a fragment of the past that is transported in apparent entirety into the present'.[77] The effect is often a synchronic functionalism that denies the passage of time by presenting the historically exotic as the 'ethnographic present'. Frequently photographs inhibit rather than aid the process of historical recovery. There is also the intention of the photographer to consider. Certainly, photographic artists have been at pains to reflect how contemporary life (including family relationships) is fragmented and dispersed, yet despite an awareness of such fracturing, means of documenting the past which account for dispersion had seldom been articulated until relatively recently.[78] This presents particular difficulties for the Scottish islands, where for generations depopulation has combined with seasonal and return migration to produce decidedly well travelled families. Since photographs are by definition snapshots, they – like the census – can produce fallacious impressions of family and social composition. One of Dan Morrison's 1950s images from Ness in Lewis provides a good example:

> Such communities are highly mobile and far-reaching. The men in the bothan [drinking den] ([Fig.] No. 25) would have sailed the seven seas, in peace and war. Every week, money earned on the Clyde or on the prairies boosted the local economy. Every family had its graduate and every township its welcoming caucus in the cities of the Empire . . . At one level, the photo of the bothan bespeaks community. The men clubbed together to buy liquor and distributed it according to clearly understood rules. But at another level it bespeaks segregation. Only half the menfolk of the village are here. The other half are probably in the Prayer Meeting.[79]

Without this accompanying textual insight, which ruptures the fallacy of traditional, place-bound cohesion, we would simply see a group of men who happen to be together in an act of celebration. Of itself, the image provides no clues to the complex patterns of kin mobility, interdependence and social cleavage both within and beyond the locality. The same applies to images of women on the island, many of whom 'had long years of experience as domestic servants in Glasgow, Toronto or Boston'.[80]

A second, more general sense in which photography misleads is due to the nature of the medium itself. Photography allows an image to be endlessly reproduced and distributed so that almost immediately from the moment of its being taken a picture can be separated from its origin and reproduced in any number of contexts.[81] The very condition of modernity means that whereas in the traditional setting, time and space 'are connected through the reliable boundedness of place, [and] an affiliation of place with kinship relations', now social relations have become 'disembedded' from their context through transportable visual media.[82] In turn, these elements may be recombined in reworked versions of history. Computer touch screens in heritage centres allow consumers to negotiate the past, albeit from a limited range of source materials, while, of course, a huge amount of archive-based visual material is accessible on the internet. The very ambiguity and malleability of photographs, their resistance to definitive explanations, allows us to devise alternative narratives. Photographic recording involves the storage of phenomena that may have been overlooked when an image was taken only to assume relevance for future viewers. Against such creative manipulation, the researcher must resolve the 'hermeneutic entanglement of observer and observed'.[83]

CONCLUSION

The need for images to be, as it were, re-immersed in the developing fluid from which they first formed is a crucial one. Contextualisation needs to be applied as a corrective, for until that ethnographic aim is realised, the researcher's role, at best, involves adjudicating between competing, and as we have seen, somewhat flawed accounts. A sense of place needs a sense of narrative, and the ways in which families and communities are summoned into being, both from the inside and from without, are linked in important ways to how societies remember. Mary Douglas argues that 'public memory is the storage system for the social order'.[84] Like parish registers, a collection of photographs consists of a set of discrete memorials, yet the pursuit of a documentary impulse to record collective life is just one of several routes by which reality may be interpreted. Images of crofters standing by their homes might suggest respectability (upright, sprucely-dressed families in well-tended gardens) or poverty (arthritic peasants beside crumbling walls). Such association could imply social comment (documentary), or testimony to a declining way of life (romanticism), or simply be interpreted as realist depiction.[85] Rather than looking *into* culture and *at* photographs, Edwards suggests that by rendering images problematic researchers may 'look *into* photographs and through them into culture'.[86]

Berger has argued that before the invention of photography, memory served a similar role, in that, like the camera, it 'preserve[d] an event from being covered and therefore hidden by events that [came] after it'.[87] Pictures can perform 'an important mnemonic function amidst the cultural dislocations of [modernity]'.[88] While the simultaneous emergence of 'documentary' photography and the Victorian transition to 'modernity' witnessed a paradoxical focus on unchanging and exotic social representations linked to a certain romantic melancholy,[89] the advent of popular photography in the 1920s coincided with transformations in agriculture and the fisheries that were to impact upon family life in the Scottish islands. In considering archives rather than the images themselves, we must ask further questions concerning the intersection of vision and power, not least the extent to which museums underwrote (and perhaps sometimes still underwrite) the imperialist view from without.[90] Much of the authenticity of a museum inheres in the auratic flavour of its artefacts: objects acquire a patina of pastness that lends them legitimacy, regardless of their actual provenance.[91] In this sense the bones in the Shetland Museum differ from the photographs, since the latter, by their very reproducibility, lack a place-bound uniqueness. They may be corrupted by being positioned out of context: they can become commodities, so acquiring exchange value divorced from their initial utility. Nevertheless, as the example of the re-captioning of the Halcrow prints illustrates, images are capable of being locally re-appropriated by their subjects (or their ancestors, neighbours and relatives).

Sociologists have often used photographs rather uncritically to illustrate their arguments. Arguably, this has had the effect of sustaining a textual critique of modernity whilst the veracity of accompanying pictures remains unchallenged. The recent upsurge of visual sociology and anthropology, together with an (auto-) ethnographic problematisation of memory, has surely argued for an 'historically grounded sociology of the image'.[92] At the same time, all histories – scholarly, popular or mythical – are themselves cultural artefacts, imbued with 'imagination'.[93] Thus, as Macdonald's research on the Gaelic renaissance in Skye reveals, in its 'quest for order' modernity differentiates between traditional and modern, authentic and inauthentic cultures, and the researcher's role must be to unravel this developing fiction.[94] The task is one of constructing an appropriately intertextual reading, a very different exercise from classifying data in the museum manner where the form of visual knowledge constructed 'gives the illusion that crucial features can be abstracted and recorded, [t]hat identity can be catalogued through defining traces'.[95] Rather, in respecting the non-linear laws of memory, 'a radial system has to be constructed around [each] photograph so that it may be seen in terms which

are simultaneously personal, economic, dramatic, everyday and historic'
via the 'documentation of places and objects which surround and construct the "life" of the subject'.[96] The discourse surrounding the images
is multi-vocal rather than simply third-person.[97] Thus, far from reflecting the panoptic gaze of the perspective from without, but also lacking
the empathy of participant observation, such a methodology is designed
to yield a series of refracted insights that, taken together, endorse the
tensions framing each image. Instead of polarising categories of observation, description and ideology, this entails an openly reflexive position,
beginning with the acknowledgement that both history and photography
are perspectivist in character, thus inherently provisional and negoti-
able.[98] It means allowing for the deconstruction of invented tradition and
the recognition of staged authenticity, but perhaps more importantly,
since history is not the historian's prerogative, the acknowledgement of
co-existing indigenous readings.[99]

NOTES

1. M. Torgovnick, *Gone Primitive: Savage Intellects, Modern Lives* (Chicago: University
   of Chicago Press, 1990).
2. G. Rosie, 'Museumry and the heritage industry', in I. Donnachie and C. Whatley
   (eds), *The Manufacture of Scottish History* (Edinburgh: Polygon, 1992), pp. 157–70;
   S. Macdonald and G. Fyfe (eds), *Theorizing Museums: Representing Identity and
   Diversity in a Changing World* (Oxford: Blackwell, 1996).
3. F. Inglis, *Cultural Studies* (Oxford: Basil Blackwell, 1993), p. 227.
4. S. Hall, 'Introduction: who needs "identity"?', in S. Hall and P. du Gay (eds),
   Questions of Cultural Identity (London: Sage), pp. 1–17 (pp. 4–5).
5. J. R. Ryan, *Picturing Empire: Photography and the Visualization of the British Empire*
   (London: Reaktion Books, 1997).
6. Archives consulted include: Orkney Library, Kirkwall (Horne, Hourston, Kent,
   Robertson and Wood Collections); Noel Hill Collection, Kirkwall; Shetland
   Museum, Lerwick (Halcrow prints); George Washington Wilson Archive, Aberdeen
   University; the Scottish Ethnological Archive, Edinburgh.
7. It is coincidental, but apt, that Erving Goffman began the fieldwork that was to
   provide empirical material for *The Presentation of Self in Everyday Life* (New York:
   Anchor Books, 1959) on the Shetland isle of Unst. See E. Goffman, 'Communication
   Conduct in an Island Community', unpublished PhD thesis, Department of Sociology,
   University of Chicago, 1953. Some twenty years later, via the notion of 'staged
   authenticity', MacCannell adapted Goffman's concepts of 'front' and 'backstage'
   regions to explain the carefully managed contrivance of tourist and 'heritage' experiences (D. MacCannell, 'Staged authenticity: on arrangements of social space in
   tourist settings', *American Journal of Sociology*, 79, 1973, pp. 589–603).
8. A major new Shetland Museum with a different configuration of space and arrangement of acquisitions opened in May 2007.

9. G. Hamilton, 'The snapper as nerd' (review of P. Bourdieu, *Photography: A Middle-Brow Art* (Cambridge: Polity, 1996)), *Times Higher Education Supplement*, 15 November 1996, p. 29.

10. E. B. Tylor, *Primitive Culture: Researches into the Development of Mythology, Philosophy, Religion, Art and Custom*, (2 vols, London: Murray, 1871).

11. R. Poignant, 'Surveying the field: the making of the RAI photographic collection', in E. Edwards (ed.), *Anthropology and Photography, 1860–1920* (Newhaven and London: Yale University Press), pp. 42–73 (p. 42).

12. G. Born, 'Public museums, museum photography, and the limits of reflexivity', *Journal of Material Culture*, 3, 1998, pp. 223–54 (p. 252).

13. I. Jack, *Before the Oil Ran Out: Britain 1977–87* (London: Fontana, 1987), p. 180.

14. Cf. D. Kidd, *To See Oorsels: Rural Scotland in Old Photographs* (Glasgow: Harper Collins, 1992); A. Fenton, *The Northern Isles: Orkney and Shetland* [1978] (East Linton: Tuckwell Press, 1997).

15. R. Barthes, *Camera Lucida* (London: Vintage, 1993), p. 4.

16. J. C. Scherer, 'The photographic document: photographs as primary data in anthropological enquiry', in Edwards (ed.), *Anthropology and Photography*, pp. 32–41.

17. A. Blaikie, 'Photographic memory, ageing and the life course', *Ageing and Society*, 14, 1994, pp. 479–97.

18. I. Christie, 'Introduction: returning to the edge of the world', in M. Powell, *Edge of the World: The Making of a Film* (London and Boston: Faber & Faber), pp. vii–ix.

19. S. Macdonald, *Reimagining Culture: Histories, Identities and the Gaelic Renaissance* (Oxford: Berg, 1997), p. 8.

20. F. Tönnies, *Community and Association* [1887], ed. C. Loomis (New York: Harper, 1957).

21. R. Redfield, 'The folk society', *American Journal of Sociology*, 52, 1947, pp. 293–308; R. Frankenberg, *Communities in Britain* (Harmondsworth: Penguin, 1966).

22. M. Chapman, *The Gaelic Vision in Scottish Culture* (London: Croom Helm, 1978); A. P. Cohen, 'Oil and the cultural account: reflections on a Shetland community', *Scottish Journal of Sociology*, 3, 1978, pp. 129–41; J. Ennew, *The Western Isles Today* (Cambridge: Cambridge University Press, 1980); D. Forsythe, *Urban-Rural Migration, Change and Conflict in an Orkney Island Community* (London: Social Science Research Council, 1982); A. P. Cohen (ed.), *Belonging: Identity and Social Organisation in British Rural Cultures* (Manchester: Manchester University Press, 1982); R. Byron, 'Oil and changing concepts of community in Burra Isle, Shetland', *International Journal of Sociology and Social Policy*, 3, 1983, pp. 47–54. P. G. Mewett, 'Peripheral waywardness in the development of Scottish ethnographic studies', *International Journal of Sociology and Social Policy*, 3, 1983, pp. 74–81; J. Wills, *A Place in the Sun: Shetland and Oil – Myths and Realities* (Edinburgh: Mainstream, 1991).

23. M. Martin, *A Late Voyage to St Kilda, the Remotest of all the Hebrides* (London: D. Brown and T. Goodwin, 1698); I. Spring, 'Lost land of dreams: representing St Kilda', *Cultural Studies*, 4, 1990, pp. 156–75 (p. 157).

24. Spring, 'Lost land', p. 171.

25. Ibid. pp. 157, 161, 163.

26. P. Strand and B. Davidson, *Tir A' Mhurain: The Outer Hebrides of Scotland* [1962] (New York: Aperture, 2002, with preface by C. Duncan), p. 17.

27. M. F. Shaw, *Paul Strand: The Hebridean Photographs* (Edinburgh: Scottish Photography Group, 1978), unpaginated.

28. D. Macleod, *Nis Aosmhor: The Photographs of Dan Morrison* (Stornoway: Acair, 1997), p. 5.

29. Cf. D. Poole, *Vision, Race and Modernity: A Visual Economy of the Andean Image World* (Princeton: Princeton University Press, 1997), p. 103.

30. Poignant, 'Surveying the field', pp. 55–9. The Royal Anthropological Institute [RAI] Photographic Collection contains photographs of native 'types', e.g.: '"Murdoch McRae, a pure highlander living at Fort Augustus; native of Kintail . . . never had trousers on but once" – Carte-de-visite, photographed by MacFarlane, c. 1878. Type "B", vol. 2, no. 24. Selected by Dr Beddoe, BAAS "Racial Committee" Albums (RAI 2987)' (Poignant, 1992, p. 59).

31. I. Finlay, *Scotland* (Oxford: Oxford University Press, 1945), p. 9.

32. Spring, 'Lost land', p. 166.

33. F. Orton and G. Pollock, *Vincent Van Gogh: Artist of his Time* (Oxford: Phaidon, 1978). Stephens' Irish photographs are housed in Trinity College Dublin (MS 10842).

34. F. Thompson, *Victorian and Edwardian Highlands from Old Photographs* (Edinburgh: Tantallon, 1989), unpaginated; D. M. N. Tinch, *Shoal and Sheaf: Orkney's Pictorial Heritage* (Belfast: Blackstaff Press, 1988), p. 299.

35. J. M. Synge, *The Aran Islands* (Dublin: Maunsel, 1907), pp. 180–6.

36. W. Benjamin, *Illuminations*, ed. H. Arendt, (London: Fontana, 1992), p. 68; R. Samuel, *Theatres of Memory, Vol. 1: Past and Present in Contemporary Culture* (London: Verso, 1994), p. 323.

37. H. Hazan, *From First Principles: An Experiment in Ageing* (Westport, CT: Bergin and Garvey, 1996), pp. 8–9.

38. Fenton, *The Northern Isles*, pp. 270–2.

39. K. Jamie, 'The Creel', in *Waterlight: Selected Poems* (Saint Paul, MN: Graywolf Press, 2007), p. 31.

40. J. R. Coull, 'Introduction', in J. R. Coull, (ed.), *Third Statistical Account of Scotland: The County of Shetland* (Edinburgh: Scottish Academic Press, 1985), pp. xix–xx.

41. A. T. Cluness, (revised by A. J. Irvine and J. Renwick, 'The island and parish of Unst', in Coull (ed.), *Third Statistical Account*, pp. 176–90 (p. 180).

42. 'Islands Pair Hit 75th Year Together', *Teletext*, 15 February 1998.

43. H. R. M. Fraser, 'The parish of Westray', in R. Miller, (ed.), *Third Statistical Account of Scotland: The County of Orkney* (Edinburgh: Scottish Academic Press, 1985), pp. 231–52 (p. 240).

44. A. Pearson, 'The parish of Walls and Sandness', in Coull (ed.), *Third Statistical Account*, pp. 191–217 (p. 199).

45. See for example B. Charnley, B. and R. Miket, *Skye: A Postcard Tour* (Waternish: MacLean Press, 1992).

46. J. R. Nicolson, 'Introduction', in *Life in Shetland: Photographs by Tom Kidd* (Edinburgh: Paul Harris, 1980), unpaginated.

47. Spring, 'Lost land', p. 168.

48. Cohen, 'Oil and the cultural account', p. 131.

49. Ibid. p. 137.

50. A. P. Cohen, *Whalsay: Symbol, Segment and Boundary in a Shetland Island Community* (Manchester: Manchester University Press, 1987), pp. 8–9.

51. H. Brody, *Inishkillane: Change and Decline in the West of Ireland* (London: Allen Lane, 1973), pp. 132–3.

52. S. Sontag, *On Photography* (Harmondsworth: Penguin, 1979).

53. B. Malinowski, *Argonauts of the Western Pacific* (London: Routledge, 1922), cited in Brody, *Inishkillane*, p. 142.

54. Fenton, *The Northern Isles*, p. 208.

55. L. Edmonston, 'General observations on the County of Shetland', in *New Statistical Account of Scotland, xv: Sutherland, Caithness, Orkney and Shetland* (Edinburgh: Blackwood, 1845), pp. 145–74 (p. 156).

56. Cohen, *Whalsay*, p. 133.

57. Ibid. p. 134.

58. Ibid. pp. 58–60.

59. *Shetland Times*, 10 November 1995, pp. 15, 6.

60. I. Kopytoff, 'The cultural biography of things: commoditization as a process', in A. Appadurai (ed.), *The Social Life of Things: Commodities in Cultural Perspective* (Cambridge: Cambridge University Press), pp. 64–91 (p. 70).

61. Ibid. p. 73.

62. Family albums present major methodological difficulties. Several investigators (e.g. G. Kirkup, 'The family album: past, present and absent', in M. Drake and R. Finnegan (eds), *Sources and Methods for Family and Community Historians: A Handbook* (Cambridge: Cambridge University Press, 1994, pp. 149–54) have noted that they reveal an *ideology* of continuity through images of happy occasions that disguises such important aspects as death, divorce, estranged relatives or partners, poverty or untidy domestic interiors. In this domain, photography – like memory – is highly selective, and it behoves the researcher to seek out absences.

63. Scherer, 'The photographic document', p. 33.

64. S. Kracauer, *The Mass Ornament: Weimar Essays* (Cambridge, MA: Harvard University Press, 1995), p. 48.

65. E. Edwards, 'Introduction', in E. Edwards (ed.), *Anthropology and Photography, 1860–1920* (Newhaven and London: Yale University Press, 1992), pp. 3–17 (p. 11).

66. L. R. Lippard, *Partial Recall: With Essays on Photographs of Native North Americans* (New York: The New Press, 1992).

67. Cohen, 'Oil and the cultural account', p. 135.

68. Tinch, *Shoal and Sheaf*, p. 182.

69. Ibid. p. 182.

70. G. Wright, *Orkney from Old Photographs* (Edinburgh: Gordon Wright, 1981), unpaginated.

71. Tinch, *Shoal and Sheaf*, p. 182.

72. A. Durie, 'Tourism and commercial photography in Victorian Scotland: the rise and fall of G. W. Wilson & Co., 1852–1908', *Northern Scotland*, 12, 1992, pp. 89–104; R. Smart, '"Famous throughout the world": Valentine & Sons Ltd., Dundee', *Review of Scottish Culture*, 4, 1988, pp. 75–87.

73. L. Leneman, *Into the Foreground: A Century of Scottish Women in Photographs* (Stroud: National Museums of Scotland/Alan Sutton Publishing, 1993), p. 72.

74. Spring, 'Lost land', p. 164. Predominant among the 'realist' films about the struggle to survive on small islands made in the 1930s are Robert Flaherty's *Man of Aran* (1934), and Michael Powell's *The End of the World* (1936). Powell intended to film on St Kilda, but the owner's refusal forced him to substitute the Shetland isle of Foula.

75. Ibid. p. 164.

76. Barthes, *Camera Lucida*, p. 96.

77. Edwards, 'Introduction', p. 7.

78. M. Hirsch, *Family Frames: Photography, Narrative and Postmemory* (Cambridge, MA: Harvard University Press, 1997) began a trend towards increasing recognition of such fractured narratives.

79. Macleod, *Nis Aosmhor*, p. 6.

80. Ibid. p. 7.

81. Benjamin, *Illuminations*, pp. 211–44 ('The work of art in an age of mechanical reproduction'). Such recodability has to be set against the scarcity value of many images. For instance, television reports of flooding sometimes present individuals who are distraught since precious family photos have been irreparably damaged; only one image exists, and the negative has long since been lost or discarded. Indeed, the perishability and uniqueness of many old photographs is one reason why private collections are held in trust by museums. The ur-image is frequently the only image.

82. J. Evans, 'John Berger, "Ways of remembering"', in J. Evans, (ed.), *The Camerawork Essays: Context and Meaning in Photography* (London and New York: Rivers Oram, 1997), pp. 39–41 (p. 39).

83. D. Barnouw, *Critical Realism: History, Photography, and the Work of Siegfried Kracauer* (Baltimore: The Johns Hopkins University Press, 1994), pp. 202, 217.

84. M. Douglas, *How Institutions Think* (London: Routledge, 1987), p. 70, quoted in D. Chaney, *Fictions of Collective Life: Public Drama in Late Modern Culture* (London: Routledge, 1993), p. 88.

85. R. Kolodny, 'Towards an anthropology of photography: frameworks for analysis', unpublished MA thesis, Department of Anthropology, McGill University, 1978, cited in Edwards, 'Introduction', pp. 8–10.

86. Edwards, 'Introduction', p. 14.

87. J. Berger, 'Ways of remembering', in Evans (ed.), *The Camerawork Essays*, pp. 42–51 (p. 42).

88. C. Waters, 'Landscapes of memory: art and everyday life in Postwar Britain', *Ideas from the National Humanities Center*, 5, 1997, pp. 5–19 (p. 15).

89. I. Mydin, 'Historical images – changing audiences', in Edwards (ed.), *Anthropology and Photography*, pp. 249–52.

90. Poole, *Vision, Race and Modernity*, p. 12.

91. S. Macdonald, 'A People's Story: heritage, identity and authenticity', in C. Rojek and J. Urry (eds), *Touring Cultures: Transformations of Travel and Theory* (London: Routledge), pp. 155–75 (pp. 169–70).

92. G. Fyfe and J. Law (eds), *Picturing Power: Visual Depiction and Social Relations* (London: Routledge, 1988); E. Chaplin, *Sociology and Visual Representation* (London: Routledge, 1988); A. Sekula, 'On the invention of photographic meaning', in V. Burgin (ed.), *Thinking Photography* (Basingstoke: Macmillan, 1988), pp. 84–109 (p. 87).

93. G. Dening, *Performances* (Chicago: University of Chicago Press, 1996).

94. Macdonald, *Reimagining Culture*, p. 4.

95. Chaney, *Fictions of Collective Life*, p. 99.

96. Berger, 'Ways of remembering', p. 47; H. C. Chapman, *Memory in Perspective: Women Photographers' Encounters with History* (London: Scarlet Press, 1997), p. 34.

97. C. Geertz, *Available Light: Anthropological Reflections on Philosophical Topics* (Princeton: Princeton University Press, 2000).

98. Kracauer, *The Mass Ornament*, p. 62; Barnouw, *Critical Realism*, pp. 12–14; J. Tagg, *The Burden of Representation: Essays on Photographies and Histories* (Basingstoke: Macmillan, 1988).
99. T. O. Ranger and E. J. Hobsbawm (eds), *The Invention of Tradition* (Cambridge: Cambridge University Press, 1992); MacCannell, 'Staged authenticity'; Samuel, *Theatres of Memory*.

CHAPTER 7

Remembering 'The Forgotten Gorbals'

INTRODUCTION

Bert Hardy's 'Gorbals Boys' is an iconic image.[1] It depicts two lads aged about ten, strolling arm-in-arm and glancing pertly at the camera. From their clothing and hairstyles, the rain-washed pavement and tall buildings framing them, the casual spectator would conclude that they are working-class, the period is sometime between 1930 and 1950 and the setting is an industrial city with a cool climate. Rendered 'sepia', the picture adorns the cover of the first volume of an autobiography by Ralph Glasser, as it does the front of a monograph about Hardy, and it is also available from numerous outlets as a wall poster.[2] It has even been mimicked by professional photographers chronicling contemporary village life in Africa.[3] While such broad quotation reflects its popularity, understanding the underlying reasons involves a complex interrogation. This begins with the distant circumstances in which the shot was taken and concludes with considerations of the role of photographic representation in contemporary social remembrance.

Hardy travelled to Glasgow on New Year's Day 1948 with the reporter A. L. Lloyd for the weekly news magazine *Picture Post*. As he later wrote, 'our story was to be the Gorbals, Britain's most notorious slum', and the article was published on 31 January under the banner 'The Forgotten Gorbals'.[4] However, the photograph in question, despite being 'one of the best known and admired documentary photographs of the era', was not included. 'It was the best picture', recorded his widow, herself a researcher for *Picture Post*, 'but it just didn't fit the layout'; rather, the image later became famous 'because Bert was always being asked to write for photo magazines and he always sent the picture as an illustration. It went on the cover of books everywhere. It reminded him of his own boyhood in

— 199 —

Fig. 7.1 Bert Hardy, 'Gorbals Boys', 1948.
Copyright Hulton Archive, Getty Images.

the slums of London. He always kept close to his roots'.[5] Indeed, Hardy himself later reflected that 'this is by far my favourite photo'.[6] Unlike many of his striking pictures, this one did not involve a conscious pose; nor was it a second attempt.[7] Here there was no negotiation, spoken or otherwise, between the cameraman and his subjects. The *Times* photography reviewer writes:

> Compositionally, Hardy was a genius. For this shot he came around the corner, spotted the boys, raised the camera and got it all: the cheeky faces, the tiny sliver of space between the elbow and the lamppost, the long, grey vista of the street behind. Of all the images in the roll, this is the most unimpeachably frank, intensely emotional and at the same time fragmentary, *reproducing the texture and flavour of the moment without explaining its meaning* [my italics]. They didn't exchange a word. Hardy just took the picture and walked on. He knew he'd got it because he didn't take another.[8]

Photographer and critics concur over its impact. Yet the reality it purports to convey travels without baggage: the picture side-steps its own context. What is it telling us historically or sociologically? By its very spontaneity the shot defies ready classification. But it emphatically does not evade interpretation. On the contrary, the Gorbals boys invite the viewer to speculate, to infer, to construct stories 'which trace a past and future for [the] image'.[9] Such placement is not simply chronological for

we will inevitably situate the scene according to pre-conceived categories of understanding, the more so since the picture is removed from any
reference or captioning. Saturated with pastness, 'work such as Hardy's
may function on a collective level as snapshots do in personal life: as a
touchstone for memory, an external witness to the value of experience,
recollection and belief'.[10] Yet although his documentary style aimed to
reveal and castigate poverty, it is broadly acknowledged that latter-day
consumers affect voyeuristic or romantic responses to such images.[11]
Reflecting how times, people and places have changed, these provide an
index of altered perceptions.

In studying urban communities, still photographs have been accessed
as much as illustrative sources of 'authenticity' as they have been deconstructed as quite the reverse.[12] Though commonly regarded as central to
remembered experience the streets and the tenements pictured represent
contested epistemological space, different 'ways of telling about society'.[13]
The ensuing analysis is thus neither an eclectic overview of images of
childhood poverty in one city, nor an evaluation of a single discourse and
its reception, but a demonstration of how meanings have been inscribed
into the fragmentary moment when Hardy's camera caught the Gorbals
Boys, of how the image acquired its significance.

The Moment of Photojournalism

In both technical and sociological senses, the picture sits squarely within
a straightforward historical narrative. The inclusion of photographs in
newspapers had begun with the *Daily Mirror* in 1904, but until the 1930s
taking pictures depended on heavy, single-shot machines that precluded
spontaneity while severely restraining dexterity. The small 35mm Leica A
allowed cameramen 'to insinuate themselves into situations from which
in the past they had been excluded'.[14] This access to candid, covert and
informal imagery was exploited by picture magazines, whose brief but
influential heyday in Britain extended from the late-1930s to the mid–
1950s, when they were eclipsed by television[15]. The photo-essay was the
medium of *Picture Post*, a popular weekly that epitomised the era. It was
part of a developing public rhetoric, inspired by social ameliorism and
sharing its cultural politics with the ethnography of Mass Observation,
Grierson's film-making, and Orwell's attempts to describe a reality
unamenable to conventional prose. Neither sociology nor literature,
documentary humanism forged an emergent structure of feeling that by
juxtaposing analysis and image 'opened up the difficult space between the
"free movement" of art and the social engagement of *rapportage*'.[16]

Between 1947 and 1950 Hardy worked with reporter Bert Lloyd on many *Picture Post* assignments. Both came from very poor families and aspired to be the self-conscious voice of ordinary people, shocking readers by revealing the intimate worlds of society's most humble. If their empathy and insight lent a strong sense of authenticity, the evidence of otherness in places unknown to the wider British public was deliberately disconcerting. Lloyd's prose lends a strong interpretative steer to Hardy's pictures, although its socialism was necessarily tempered. He was a card-carrying Communist, and in the worsening Cold War climate of the late forties, the editor, under pressure to sack him from Hulton, the magazine's Conservative owner, ensured that stories 'were strictly "human interest" in focus and showed no ideological leanings towards the left', thus defining exploitation as 'problems' but offering no structural analysis.[17] Within this tricky remit, Hardy's stylistic aim was to freeze the moment, to capture the activity and quality of everyday life. The immediacy of the street was the grail of his profession, testimony to an uncanny ability to see into experience from outside as though from within.[18] His narrative realism was one of striking verisimilitude, yet because of the framework in which he operated we would be mistaken to see in his prints an unmediated black-and-white reality.

Hardy was not the first documentary photographer to cover Glasgow's social conditions in *Picture Post*, for nine years previously Humphrey Spender's photo-essay 'Glasgow' (*Picture Post*, 1 April 1939) had already included children in street scenes. 'Gorbals Boys' cannot be understood in isolation from this historical context. Moreover, it was never intended as a standalone image anyway, being just one of over fifty prints shot during the 'Forgotten Gorbals' assignment (see *Appendix*). The subsequent article forms part of a collection of classic Lloyd/Hardy pieces about urban deprivation and human resilience, including 'Life at the Elephant' (London 1949) and 'Down the Bay' (Cardiff 1950). Its six pages comprise approximately 3,000 words and thirteen photographs. The title itself berates 'the nation' for overlooking 'an area that provides a very special version of the slum problem', yet paradoxically the article affords several clues to the anatomy of social remembrance.[19] Its gist is that with mass immigration of unskilled Irish labourers in the nineteenth century speculators built shoddy tenements that had become the present squalid and overcrowded ghetto. All here lived in abject poverty, yet associated problems such as violent crime and illegitimacy were not especially great despite gambling and drinking offering obvious escapes. Gorbals was an 'evil quarter . . . not because of the people in it. But because of the way they must live'.[20] Theirs was a critical exposé of the Postwar affluence thesis, similar in approach to much later monographs like Coates and Silburn's *Poverty: The Forgotten Englishmen* (1970).[21] It was, however, the narrative form that was most vivid. Here was the dread, poetic illumination of documentary humanism:

> At midnight, if you stand on any of the four bridges that run across the Clyde into the Gorbals, you see the windows still lit; for when the gas goes down, the rats come out in strength. So the lights burn dimly all night, and they shine on the huddled sleepers, on the delicate faces of the girls, and on the ravaged faces of the women who were once girls, and on the men's faces that look like the broken slabs of every commandment in the decalogue.[22]

The main themes are articulated in the captions beneath each picture. There is overcrowding, with attendant poor hygiene and claustrophobia: 'In a thousand rooms, no bigger than this, some Gorbals folk sleep four to a bed'; 'Mrs Greenan has borne 13 children, lost 7 from pneumonia'; 'No room to sit around at home. No place to sit around in the yard'. Pleasures, like escapes, are few but precious, wholly justifiable: 'Crowded homes. Crowded streets. Nowhere to go'; 'One of the few places . . . is Diamond's Dancing Academy'. Or there are pubs: 'There are 174 of them . . . But the idea that the Gorbals is peopled by roughnecked boozers is erroneous. The area is remarkable for kind, friendly folk, with a strong feeling for social justice', and 'though the district is rough, it is not remarkable for serious crime'. Children inhabit strange juxtapositions of poverty and play, hence a caption reading 'the back-courts of the Gorbals. Broken concrete, flooded pools, heaps of ill-smelling rubbish. And rat-runs that often straggle halfway up the street' beneath the profile of a girl bouncing her ball against the wall – 'a scene that is repeated a thousand times' we are told. And the boys? 'Some see them as hooligans and vandals. Some see them as ordinary children, hungry for a decent place to play . . . the cemetery is the only bit of green', so they leap-frog over the gravestones. The sense of people trapped by their circumstances is suffocating: 'scores of faces at open windows'. The largest, most emphatic image is of a sixteen-year-old girl sitting at a cluttered kitchen table in the most cramped of rooms. The caption title reads: 'In a Gorbals front room, a girl finds her dreams are slipping out of her grasp'. If it is a 'front room' it is also the kitchen, while less than two feet behind her a small child lies on a bed let into the wall. Tiredly propping her face up with her wrist, the girl's expression is reminiscent of Dorothea Lange's 'Migrant mother', although more deeply resigned than careworn: 'Already futility and frustration stretch ahead'.[23]

All this paints a dismal portrait, albeit entirely consistent with its

Fig. 7.2 Bert Hardy, 'Scottish Slum', *Picture Post*, 31 January 1948.
Copyright Hulton Archive, Getty Images.

humanist message. Yet the images at the head of the article present 'Surrealist vistas of de Chiricoian streets and silhouetted statuesque police-men . . . that had to be given monumental connotations', hence a caption 'The Classical Landscape of the Gorbals' beneath a picture of looming tenements receding to vanishing point. This is because these photographs were taken not by Hardy, but by Bill Brandt. Brandt had originally been commissioned to take the photographs for the story. However, on seeing the contacts the editor (Tom Hopkinson) immediately sent Hardy to replace him.[24] The policemen were captioned 'The Sight Sensationalists Expect to See' while the text 'the air of calm that covers a multitude of horrors' was added to the 'Classical Landscape' image, the steer being that readers would find another story as they turned the page, this grand but superficial outdoor scene masking the domestic interiors and 'real life' revealed in the ensuing shots. Brandt had produced many startling images for the magazine, but significantly this assignment signalled the end of his photojournalism, a mutual break in that Hopkinson wanted 'documen-tary' not 'artistic' copy: 'The distance and strangeness of Brandt's Gorbals pictures were utterly different from Hardy's humanitarian populism with

The Classical Landscape of the Gorbals
The air of calm that covers a multitude of horrors. Nearly 40,000 people live in Gorbals. They live four, six, eight to a room, often thirty to a lavatory, forty to a tap. They live in Britain's most abandoned slum.

Fig. 7.3 Bill Brandt, 'The Classical Landscape of the Gorbals', *Picture Post*,
31 January 1948.
Copyright Bill Brandt © Bill Brandt Archive Ltd.

its point-of-view close to the scene, discovering picturesque families, communities, and pub life'.[25]

HEARTBREAK CLOSE: MIDNIGHT'S CHILDREN

But for an editorial decision, therefore, Glasgow's slums might have looked rather different to *Picture Post's* readers in 1948. As it was, Hardy's images realised many traits common to Glasgow's association with children, slums and street photography, a lineage initiated by Thomas Annan 80 years earlier and stretching forward to Oscar Marzaroli and Joseph McKenzie in the 1960s and after.[26] Phases in the photographic account parallel successive waves of demolition and rebuilding, a palimpsest backdrop to the successive generations populating the tenement scene, its ubiquitous 'urchins'. Commissioned by Glasgow City Improvements Trust, Annan took several photographs of east-end closes between 1868 and 1871. The aim was to record a built landscape shortly to be razed.[27] Limited camera technology meant all pictures were taken outdoors and during daylight, without access to the internal world so critical to Hardy's success. Yet people abound in most images, children fidgeting in the foreground: 'Unwilling or unable to pose for the lengthy exposure time required, they appear as blurred ghosts, in varying degrees of detail. Phantom inhabitants of the dingy underworld . . . confined and defined by the very crumbling sandstone walls that surround them'.[28] In 1924, illustrating his argument by means of several photographs attributed to James McKissack, William Bolitho sought to explain how the roots of the 'menace of Red Glasgow' lay not so much with political mobilisation by the astute skilled artisan, as in the desperation of an underclass condemned to life in overcrowded 'backlands' and farmed-out houses, characterised by an 'undending dark gloom' that rendered the Glasgow slum 'the *nearest* suburb to hell'.[29] This enclosed environment fixes the frame around Glasgow's children, as the new tenements of the late-Victorian period become in their turn the slums of the mid-twentieth century. In composition, lighting and subject-matter there are many thematic continuities and, indeed, visual similarities between the images of earlier and later photographers of the Scottish city. Significantly, however, their motives varied: although each presented images of ragged children in faintly-lit closes, the nostalgic pictorialism underlying, for example, the earlier twentieth-century photographs by Coburn in Edinburgh was wholly at odds with the documentary critique of Hardy's Postwar Glasgow.[30] The former was a picturesque retreat from modernity; the latter exposed a lack of social progress and the need for change.

Stylistically, 'The Forgotten Gorbals' is more immediately prefigured by the Glasgow pieces in a series of travel articles in the *Daily Herald* written in 1931 by H. V. Morton with photographs by James Jarché.[31] As with his enormously popular English equivalents, Morton's Scottish writings sought Utopia in a rural myth while bewailing urban degeneration (see Chapter 5). Like Lloyd, he interleaves statistics of overcrowding – and, in 1931, unemployment – with investigative anecdotes culled from discussions with the residents. 'Heartbreak Close' tells of 'tenements haunted by life's derelicts'.[32] There are two photographs: one of a Clydeside street and houses receding to the horizon on which a shipyard crane stands idle; the other, a mother holding her baby and talking to an older woman, presumably her mother. Taken alone, these anodyne illustrations in no sense hint at the message in the text, at once an indictment of public health failings and a description of urban primitives. Cheek-by-jowl among 'the bent forms of women nursing children' live 'a half-starved girl with . . . the appearance of having shrunk' who will soon 'contribute another child to the hundreds who crawl and play about the dark tenement stairs', and an unemployed stoker, his wife and child living in one room: 'She has had five children, four of whom are dead. "What did they die of?" "This house," she says, looking round the room. "The doctor blamed the house."' Meanwhile:

> The boys play noisy and warlike games; the girls spread sacking on filthy stone stairs and put bits of rag to sleep. This is a pitiful instinct, because the less said, thought or done about maternity in Heartbreak Close the better. There ought to be a notice to unborn children written across it: 'Don't be born here, it's too dangerous.' But the fact remains that children swarm in Heartbreak Close. It seems from the way they infest road, alleyways and stairs that the inhabitants have done nothing for ten years but increase and multiply.[33]

This evocation of sub-cultural poverty reflects Morton and Jarché's patrician relationship with the people they encountered. Their frame of reference is conservatively romantic. They 'present the slums as a particularly grim legacy of the aberrant industrial revolution that has blighted an essentially green and pleasant land'.[34] By contrast, Lloyd and Hardy, being originally of the slums, are empathetic, their frame contrastingly progressive. Their accounts have a personal resonance, as with the Cardiff images of 1950: 'Generations of residents and former residents . . . have felt deeply aggrieved about the ways in which "Outsiders" have represented them. With one exception: they like the photographs of them done by Bert Hardy'.[35] Significantly, this insider quality renders Hardy immune from the 'otherness' evident in Morton's loaded language, and, indeed, most ethnographic writing about slums. Yet he does not evade its imagery. As Spring clarifies, historically 'the Glasgow of representation' was Manichean, the 'social photographs' of 'Shadow's' pamphlet *Midnight Scenes and Social Photographs* (1858) being, like Mayhew's London vignettes, written snapshots designed as realist description of the depraved east end.[36] Here was a naïve sociology of the 'dark side' in dire need of moral redemption – by day, Brandt's 'air of calm', or the busy street life; by night, the huddled horrors, lit only to deter the rodents. Here too, Engels' 'race apart', a vision that fundamentally affected the way slum children were perceived and presented.

This dualist symbolism informed philanthropic organisations concerned to 'save' children – morally and physically – from such evils. The NSPCC and Dr Barnardo's Homes later photographed ragged children ('street arabs') before and after 'rescue' and relocation to children's homes, starkly contrasting clothing, posture and facial expression suggesting the transformation from 'savage' to 'civilised'. The historiography of childhood is one dense with diagnostic archetypes and attendant discourses, vulnerability being the common criterion. From 1800 to 2000, Hendrick considers a chronology of classifications: from the romantic, through evangelical, factory, delinquent, schooled, psycho-medical, welfare, psychological, family to the public child.[37] Similarly, in her survey of children from Scotland's broken homes, Abrams discusses the homeless child, boarded-out child, orphanage child, emigrant child, problem child, and the child in danger. Images may be found typifying each, hence, for instance, 'problem children' in a clinic, pictured wearing goggles to receive sun-lamp treatment for rickets – a common disease in Glasgow due to lack of sunlight – or 'orphanage children' working in the laundry of a children's home.[38] These categories reflected a growing objectification that used images of the body to discriminate between 'deprived' and 'delicate' types, size, thinness, dirt, spots and nits becoming motifs of disorder and outsiderhood. Perceptions of 'normality', developed from the identification of specific diseases located in the body, 'extended to the social space surrounding the child', pathologising those who lived outside 'the limits set for "childhood"'.[39]

Slum children were by definition problematic, encoded visually by an obvious raggedness of dress, particularly footwear (or lack thereof), and evidently poor physical health, but there were also more sinister eugenic suggestions. If Annan's view is inadvertent, 'the top lighting giving them Neanderthal brows and lost chins', it nevertheless contributed to a pervasive myth of urban degeneracy.[40] This is well illustrated in the paintings of Joan Eardley, whose portraits of 'street urchins in a ramshackle environment' are deceptively realistic.[41] Eardley spent years in her Townhead studio 'so near the slum parts of the town that I draw', painting mostly the eight children of the Samson family, her favourite willing models. While sentimental reviewers lauded her ability 'to depict these waifs with their knobbly knees emerging stalk-like from flower-pot wellington boots', their 'tousled hair' and 'truculent round-faced' gawps, there was a fine line between artistic integrity and an unwittingly patronising quest for the grotesque, witnessed in her reaction to the news that Pat Samson had had her 'violent squint' straightened: '"Oh hell!" said Joan. "She won't be much use to me now"'.[42] Whatever the intention, her art struck an uneasy chord. In 'Brother and Sister' (1955) a very small girl clings to the hand of her protective older brother, who clutches a milk-bottle, in front of a wall of peeling paintwork and graffiti. This Samson family portrait was considered for purchase by Glasgow's municipal collection, 'but rejected because one councillor . . . complained that the children looked unhealthy and that that would reflect badly on Glasgow'.[43]

Fig. 7.4 Joan Eardley, 'Brother and Sister', 1955.
Aberdeen Art Gallery & Museums Collections.

Nevertheless, 'Brother and Sister' challenges 'Gorbals boys' as the single most iconic image of tenement poverty, not least because its aesthetic is ramified in Edwin Morgan's poem 'To Joan Eardley', in which he wanders through the rubble and graffiti, 'a blur of children at their games', while on his wall he sees details in her painting 'that fix what the pick and bulldozer have crumbled to a dingier dust'.[44] In the following decade, Oscar Marzaroli was the city's most prolific photo-documentarist. He deliberately sought children as subjects to stress the vibrancy of collective life in otherwise derelict environments, a point not lost on later commentators: 'the children are everywhere . . . in ill-fitting shoes, gazing out of windows, watching the demolition of their houses'.[45] Those houses, making way for tower blocks, were the very tenements that had framed the characteristic images of the 1940s and 50s. If the Samson children had been immortalised in Eardley's canvases, Marzaroli's homage, by way of a 1962 photograph of them in a likeness that bears uncanny resemblance to their painted form, surely confirms a legend of the old Gorbals at the very moment of their dissolution.[46]

RECOGNITION, LOSS AND REMEMBERED COMMUNITY

Glasgow's urban imaginary centres on the tenement and its aftermath in ways that stretch far beyond aesthetics.[47] As Spring has it: 'There is a potent narrative that informs all Glaswegians of their collective tenement experience. It is that tenement life was the essence of the collective community'.[48] This way of being, implying the importation of rural parish values to the city, finds sociological form in the 'urban village', a place where neighbourly ideals of integrity and social cohesion, close kin ties and face-to-face relationships prevailed, where despite the violence and poverty there was guaranteed human warmth among 'kind people who batter unkindness'.[49] Whatever the reality, in literature the tenement provided 'the *mise-en-scène* of urban life', as it did for autobiographical recall, the two intertwining to produce a vivid stereotype.[50] Thus, while 'Gorbals Boys' illustrates the front of Glasser's *Growing up in the Gorbals* (1986), the back-cover blurb reads: 'All the "No Mean City" ingredients – the filth and the squalor, the gang fights, the religious bigotry, the violence of the "tallymen", the mating rites of the midden, the pleasure of the "steamie" [public wash-house] – are present'.[51]

While this mythology carries an undue hegemonic force, many autobiographies of the post-war period have centred on the authors' memories of childhood rather than the early years as simply the first episode in narratives focused on adult life. One effect has been to give a sense of entire lost ways of life, rather than just glimpses of individual experience.[52] This genre reflects the fragmentation caused by social and geographical mobility, writers having distanced themselves from their class and locality by their success. Glasser, for instance, was born in poverty in Glasgow in 1920, the child of Jewish immigrants, who left school at fourteen but, following years of night study, won a scholarship to Oxford to become a psychologist and economist of international repute. The second effect is of discontinuity, rendering roots wholly 'other': for Glasser, Oxford University, was a place where 'someone from the Gorbals was in effect a bushman and the Gorbals itself as distant, as unknowable, as the Kalahari Desert'.[53] Thirdly, uprooting creates a yearning for continuity, hence cleavage to the virtues of an imagined community, imagined because although it no longer exists its comradeship and values provide an enduring foundation.[54] Concluding his autobiography, famous football manager Alex Ferguson finds in his tenement boyhood the grounding for his entire worldview: 'I wish I could revisit, however briefly, the sense of community that existed in the Govan of my childhood. It could be a rough world but there were wonderful values at the heart of it. Loyalty has been the anchor

Fig. 7.5 Oscar Marzaroli, 'The Castlemilk Lads', 1963.
Copyright © OPM Marzaroli Collection www.oscar-marzaroli.com

of my life and it is something that I learned in Govan'.[55] The sentiment
was shared by Glasser, who, in a final volume of memoirs, dubbed this
beckoning spirit 'A Gorbals Legacy'.[56] Tellingly, the cover of this book
uses another Hardy image from the 'Forgotten Gorbals' assignment, this
time depicting an older man with his back to camera, walking down a
puddled back-alley. It was probably taken on the same day as 'Gorbals
Boys'.

But there can be no return, at least not according to cultural analysts,
social commentators and autobiographers. When Govan lost its shipyards, its social catalyst disappeared.[57] Elsewhere structures of feeling were
erased along with their physical setting as people were 'shipped out to
housing schemes like penal colonies on the edges of the city or incarcerated in high-rise flats', dispersal heralding the end of community. The
social framework ensuring transmission of values to the next generation
was dismantled.[58] Spring asks, therefore: 'How can one visit the home of
one's childhood?' Only, it appears, by trying to grasp the elusive 'phantom

village' of his title: 'the slums have gone but their meaning remains' leaving only 'an empty sense of belonging'.[59] When communities no longer exist, memories replace them.[60] This in itself can have far reaching effects in transforming the built environment (and people's experiences within it) as their histories are selectively remembered and forgotten in the plans and politics of those engaged in urban renewal.[61] During the 1950s, Gorbals-dwellers were rehoused in huge peripheral schemes like Drumchapel and Castlemilk, where bad design resulted in a lack of communal amenities. Together with continuing crime and unemployment this ensured rapid social deterioration. Photographers caught the apparent reversion to slumdom, Marzaroli's 'Castlemilk Lads' (1963) being arch counterparts of the 'Gorbals Boys'. However, we should remember the degree to which images are not only mediated, but also media creations. In January 1978, just thirty years after 'The Forgotten Gorbals', the *Observer* newspaper published a photo-essay on the dirt-poverty and violence of Glasgow's east end – 'Ghetto city of the poor'. Despite being in a colour supplement, all thirteen images were monochrome, pictures of smashed windows and rubble-strewn back-courts; the text referred to 'a heritage of hardship' giving residents 'a genial stoicism bordering almost upon resignation'.[62] As Damer notes, these images typified a coherent and delimited external stereotype, but one that was 'completely reversed' ten years later with the 'Glasgow's miles better' media campaign. Such manipulation questions the credibility of photographs and leads one to ask: Whose stories should we trust? Meanwhile, much ink has been spilled arguing that while the negative imagery is 'absolutely true' but 'blatantly offensive', the positive is just 'a façade which conceals a complex and harsh reality'.[63] In July 2005, another *Observer* reporter talked to middle-aged men in Possilpark and found a 'hidden underclass willing to work but waiting to die . . . One GP said she had patients who had never known parents or grandparents go out to work'.[64] There is no romantic spirit of community here, only a desperate fatalism. Yet, of course, neither were the residents of the old slums exactly happy with their lot. Lloyd reported from the Gorbals that, 'the local folk say the area is ripe for dynamiting'.[65]

Counter-realities, like counter-memories effect discord. Against the presentist desire of City of Culture image-makers to manufacture a 'spurious communal past' exists the schismatic social geography of troubled neighbourhoods where obesity has replaced the 'gaunt feral look' as the hallmark of poverty.[66] Damer interprets pictures according to imputed motives: Colin Baxter's iconography of the 'new' Glasgow is detached, dreamlike; conversely, the vitality of Marzaroli's ordinary folk transparently reflects a 'strong sense of commitment to his subjects' – 'his

photographs are in good faith, Baxter's in bad'. By the same rather ten-
dentious moral token, Hardy and Lloyd display an authenticity lacking in
Morton and Jarché.[67] In Baxter's imagery:

> The pictures are almost exclusively of buildings, often taken from the air, and
> softened by a light, hazy sun. The transition . . . is from a city of public spaces,
> a city of people at home in the city . . . to a city as *landscape*, a place devoid of
> residents . . . The city-as-landscape does not encourage the formation of com-
> munity or of urbanism as a way of life; rather it encourages the maintenance of
> surfaces, the promotion of order at the expense of lived social relations.[68]

By contrast, since Marzaroli depicts 'ordinary Glasgow people doing
ordinary Glasgow things', like drinking, playing football, shopping,
sitting, his pictures are remembered with affection.

There is also a tension between individual and collective accounts. In
one sense memories, unlike history, are personal and unmediated. But
personal recollections can only be articulated through language, signs and
conventions. Misztal contends that 'memory is the experience of the past
mediated by representation, so it is the construction of images that puts
memories before our eyes and reveals what experience means'.[69] To that
extent, all memory is social memory. Yet if images convey signs, they do
not innately provide meanings, only evidence into which the beholder
might read significance.[70] Remarking upon the current vogue for prints
and postcards of Annan's scenes, Spring notes that 'one generation's
misery incarnate becomes another's consumable style'.[71] But this cannot
suffice to explain the 'Gorbals Boys', who are happy, apparently carefree
youngsters. In the same way that those who got on and got out have
escaped the fate of those currently condemned to living in Possilpark,
their exclusion from the 'The Forgotten Gorbals' article spares them the
sorry posterity of their fellows. Their ordinary mirth finds no place in a
script about dysfunction. Yet their image resonates strongly in the collective consciousness of time and place. Theirs may simply be an evocation
of picturesque poverty. But if so it is problematic, for one is led to ask:
What is the quality that makes it picturesque? How is it that an otherwise
negative experience becomes positively regarded? The answer lies in the
reconnection implied through an affective community of belonging.

CONCLUSION

Considering this desire to reaffirm roots, Samuel identified a nostalgic
anxiety, 'particularly marked among the geographically mobile and the
sociologically orphaned', that has provoked *inter alia* much evaluation of

old photographs.[72] The process has not simply been about reactivating remembrances; rather, it has involved the creation of symbolic spaces. If cities lend themselves to moral abstraction, the slums have been Glasgow's 'visual master-status', and if there is a Glasgow gaze it is recursive and tends to look backwards.[73] However, *Picture Post's* documentary humanism affords access to 'The Forgotten Gorbals' as a knowable community – neither unknowable nor known – whereas the imagined community of retrospect, in its ideological rigidity, forecloses this option.[74] In the analytic space so defined, images are inevitably ambiguous because they fuse past and present. Memories are meaningful because they are 'the central medium through which identities are constructed'.[75] And photographs matter because they are the custodians of memory: without the visual record of the everyday, there are only personal testimonies or constructed histories. Or, rather, images can be *used* to symbolise the past. Thus, photographs collude with memory in identifying a relationship between childhood, values and place, so that to glimpse 'the way we were' is simultaneously to evoke both recognition and loss, albeit the half-known and partially grasped.[76] To this extent, what Hardy produced as part of the discourse of documentary humanism has also been consumed in discursively inflected ways by historians, sociologists, cultural analysts, biographers, Glaswegians and others, each with their own frames of reference.

As the built fabric decays, human resilience is pitted against poor health and social decline. Because of its infamous succession of slum clearance and urban renewal, photographing Glasgow, from Annan onwards, was always about capturing the present as it was about to become the past as layer-upon-layer of communities were reduced to rubble. And while remembering these places means juggling with continuity and discontinuity, to both recognise and minimise the rupture between then and now, memory like the camera lens aims to fix an image but cannot owing to its own fluid character.[77] The role of children is enigmatic here, for whereas older people are often read as the last of their generation, in keeping with the end of an era for a particular framed community, youngsters will live on for many years after the photographic event. The re-appearance of an image therefore acts as a trigger to remembrance when the reality pictured has long disappeared. In its place a myth intervenes – that of the tenement childhood. Understood visually, its coded narratives appear to represent a singular reality about which individuals weave their personal tales, incorporating its neighbourhood ideology. Yet there is no unitary vision, only ways of seeing.

The ontological status of photographs shifts over time from acting as *aides-mémoires* within living memory (via oral accounts) to documents read as testimony of a deeper past. Similarly, their provenance and reception require careful hermeneutic consideration. Bert Hardy's humanism occupies a specific niche within British photojournalism. Its style is certainly not formalist – and, indeed, his Glasgow images contrast directly with Brandt's surrealism – yet despite the apparent spontaneity of 'Gorbals Boys', neither can it be read as guileless naturalism. Whether understood in the context of his immediate assignment, and the 'Forgotten Gorbals' article as part of *Picture Post* in the late 1940s, or as a moment subsequently positioned within the history of documentary photography, or as an image that has struck a particularly deep resonance within popular culture, the image reflects Hardy's desire to expose social reality without resort to the techniques of socialist realism.[78] Nonetheless, its qualities – monochrome rendition, darkly urban setting, tattered clothing – imply a strong, and realist enough social comment.

In December 2000, Andrew Samson, 58, and living in north east England, was reunited with Joan Eardley's portrait of him as a boy when it was sold at auction. Recalling having posed for the artist, he talked of 'being given one shilling and sixpence, and as many cheese sandwiches as he could eat'.[79] In conveying what was foremost in his child's mind this reminiscence re-inscribes something of the subject into the image. Through his remembrance, we sense a different angle to that of the artist, another kind of telling. But now, as for all reflections about childhood, a distance in time has intervened and the experience has been re-contextualised. So too with space – the insider has removed himself from the original locus, by definition altering perspective.[80] In doing likewise, other exiles have eulogised their roots, amongst them famous men who, given some fine tinkering with ages and neighbourhoods, might have been the Gorbals boys.[81]

Meanwhile, in August 2008 a sculpture by Liz Peden, also entitled 'Gorbals Boys' and based closely on 'an iconic snap' taken by Marzaroli, was commissioned as part of the regeneration of Queen Elizabeth Square. It features three young boys wearing their mothers' high heels while playing in the street. One of Marzaroli's original subjects, Ian Docherty, 50, and now a plumber in Motherwell, spoke to journalists at the unveiling. He remarked: 'We used to live in Kidson Street next to the shop that is in the photograph. I remember it well. We just made use of what we had then. Those were the best days.' His mother Betty Docherty, 75, commented: 'The statues are good for Gorbals. Whatever happens, whatever changes, talk of Gorbals doesn't go away.' For her part, the sculptor, aged 53 and a lifelong local resident, 'said the sculpture put the children back on the streets' while the image 'cut right through' the 'big rough and tough' reputation that Gorbals men always had. The Deputy First Minister Nicola Sturgeon went on to say that she felt the installation was 'something which unites the past and the future of Gorbals. Regeneration is about communities'.[82]

Henri Cartier-Bresson once wrote: 'We photographers deal in things which are continually vanishing, and when they have vanished there is no contrivance on earth which can make them come back again. We cannot develop and print a memory'.[83] Yet pictures of children can have lasting emotive power. Consider, for example, Nick Ut's definitive Vietnam War photo of the napalmed girl running naked in terror along Route 1 and its impact upon the course of the war, the American and Vietnamese people, veterans, and, not least, the girl herself. After thirty-five years its legacy remains one of heated controversy.[84] Likewise, the photographic record of Glasgow is vivid and much discussed. So what does the original 'Gorbals Boys' tell us? That it means different things to different people? That nothing seems clearer, yet 'nothing is harder to see once out of its time'?[85] That Bert Hardy was a good self-publicist? Ultimately, what you see is a multiply absent presence: nothing is hidden, but nor does it tell us anything specific. The best we can do is to try to connect the image with its many contexts for, unlike the original photograph, and even for the anonymous pals in the picture, it no longer represents a singular setting, either in the landscape of Glasgow or the cultural topography of remembered experience.

APPENDIX

The Hulton Archive, including *Picture Post* photographs, is now part of Getty Images and is accessible online at http://gettyimages.com. It preserves some 3,544 Hardy images, including 52 from the 'Forgotten Gorbals' shoot. Although cataloguing terms reflect archivists' perceptions rather than photographers' intentions, the most frequently occurring terms used to classify these images suggest Hardy's priorities while indicating their typicality. **Table 1** lists the most common keywords used to index photographs in each of three categories: the 'Forgotten Gorbals' prints; all Hardy prints in the collection; and all Glasgow prints by all photographers. Keywords have been ranked 1–12 according to the percentage of images to which each refers. Those associated with 'Gorbals Boys' are asterisked and show the image to be highly typical of the 'Forgotten Gorbals' prints in that child, slum, street, couple and friendship are among its most common keywords.

The photo is only slightly less representative of all categories, although

Table 1 Comparison of keywords used to classify photographs in the Hulton Archive

Keyword	'Gorbals Boys'	'Forgotten Gorbals'		All Hardy		All Glasgow	
		Rank order	%	Rank order	%	Rank order	%
Group		1	46	1	40	1	35
Child	*	2	42	5	12	4	14
Slum	*	3	38	–	(2)	10	5
Street	*	4	33	7	8	5	12
Couple	*	5	27	3	21	6	11
Playing		6	23	–	(3)	–	(3)
Single		7	21	2	26	2	28
Public house		8	17	–	(2)	–	(1)
Friendship	*	9	12	–	(2)	–	(1)
Clothing		10 =	10	4	20	3	14
Relaxation		10 =	10	–	(2)	–	(1)
Talking		10 =	10	8	7	–	(2)
Black & white	*	–	(6)	6	12	9	5
Uniform		–	(4)	9	6	–	(4)
Crowd		–	(0)	10	6	7	8
Sitting		–	(8)	11	5	–	(4)
Watching		–	(0)	12	5	–	(4)
Urban		–	(6)	–	(2)	8	6
Walking	*	–	(6)	–	(3)	11	5
Dock		–	(0)	–	(1)	12	5
Total keywords	7	67		500		444	
Total images	1	52	100	3354	100	820	100

only 2 per cent of all Hardy images are of slums, and friendship barely scores, suggesting that both categories were unusually characteristic of the Gorbals assignment (Hardy made another visit to Glasgow to shoot 'Glasgow sets out for the Clyde' (Jul 1954), focusing on dockland areas and life on the river); two of his Glasgow images were used for articles on Poles in Scotland (Apr and Oct 1955). Children feature in almost half the 'Forgotten Gorbals' pictures, as do groups more generally, although crowds are absent. Public houses, though appearing in a fifth of the Gorbals images are otherwise surprisingly rare. This kind of exercise gives cause for some scepticism – 'black & white' covers a far higher proportion of images than index entries suggest, as does 'urban'. Nevertheless, comparison between Glasgow and all photographs from other British cities (**Table 2**) confirms the specificity of its visual symbolism:

Table 2   Percentage incidence of keywords: five British cities

Keyword	Glasgow	Liverpool	Cardiff	London	York
Child	14	9	15	8	3
Slum	5	2	1	0.31	0.15
Street	12	8	9	11	4
Total images	820	950	489	30000	22595

Images featuring children, slums and streets are more significant for Glasgow in every case, save a marginally greater proportion of children in the Cardiff photographs. The incidence of 'slum' designations for Glasgow is markedly greater than elsewhere, despite the acknowledged urban deprivation in all these cities. Hardy pictures prevail in *Picture Post* stories about poverty in all except York – 'Life at the Elephant' [London] (8 Jan 1949); 'Is there a British colour bar' [Liverpool](2 Jul 1949); 'Down the Bay' [Cardiff](22 Apr 1950); 'The best and worst of British cities 2: Cardiff' (23 Jan 1954) – but slums signify in the classification of just six images (4 per cent).

Notes

1. As a venerated and enduring representation, the picture is iconic in that a single visual image connotes a predominant impression of the city's past.
2. R. Glasser, *Growing up in the Gorbals* (London: Pan Books, 1986); T. Hopkinson, *Bert Hardy: Photojournalist* (London: Gordon Fraser/Arts Council, 1975).
3. D. Seddon, *RPS Forum – Africa*, http://www.rpsforum.org/showthread. php3?t=393&page=2&pp=15 [#23, 2005] Accessed September 2006.
4. Hopkinson, *Bert Hardy*, p. 9; A. L. Lloyd, 'The Forgotten Gorbals', *Picture Post*, 31 January 1948, pp. 11–16.
5. J. Pitman, 'Glasgow Slums: "The Gorbals Boys"', *Times Magazine*, 1 November 2003, p. 6.
6. G. Jordan, 'The photographs: Plates 1–18', in G. Jordan (ed.),'*Down the Bay': Picture Post, Humanist Photography and Images of 1950s Cardiff*, (Cardiff: Butetown History & Arts Centre, 2001), pp. 28–63 (p. 44).
7. B. Tonkin, '"Icons of the dispossessed": Bert Hardy and the documentary photograph', *History Workshop Journal*, 21, 1986, pp. 157–65 (p. 160).
8. Pitman, 'Glasgow slums', p. 6. Another photograph, also dated 1948 and entitled 'Gorbals Boys', was taken by Roger Mayne. While the backdrop and the ages are similar, this picture includes a dozen boys. Some stare fixedly at the camera; others ignore it and wander with their backs to the viewer; those in motion have the same insouciant demeanour. Much depended on the photographer's technique, and while Mayne's 'bland air of ingratiating vagueness' helped achieve a natural sense, the lack of boundaries afforded by the street clearly limited control over the encircling mob (S. Stevenson, *Photographing Children* (Edinburgh: National Galleries of Scotland, 1993), p. 16).

9. Tonkin, '"Icons of the dispossessed"', p. 163.

10. Ibid. p. 162.

11. See, for example, V. Burgin (ed.), *Thinking Photography* (London: Palgrave Macmillan, 1992).

12. For example, G. Crow, 'Developing sociological arguments through community studies', *International Journal of Social Research Methodology* 3 (3), 2000: pp. 173–87 (p. 76) argues that photographs can be used 'to convey a powerful sense of village history . . . to bring home to the reader aspects of the relationship between work and community which a purely written narrative never could . . . to give a sense of place and people'. They 'help to "place" or "ground" sociological arguments', especially where, despite globalisation, 'the specificities of location matter', hence their inclusion within a number of ethnographies. H. Gans' classic, *The Urban Villagers* (New York: Free Press, 1962) being an early instance, while more recent works, such as J. Foster's *Docklands* (London: UCL Press, 1999) make extensive use of photographs (in her case some 60 images).

13. R. Sennett, *The Fall of Public Man* (London: Faber, 1986); H. S. Becker, 'Visual sociology, documentary photography, and photojournalism: it's (almost) all a matter of context', *Visual Sociology*, 10 (1–2), 1995, pp. 5–14.

14. Hopkinson, *Bert Hardy*, p. 11.

15. Crucially, the new images needed better quality paper to print on than newspapers provided. The flashbulb, allowing ease of access to otherwise dark places such as mines, dim domestic interiors, or streets by night was invented in 1930.

16. S. Hall, 'The social eye of *Picture Post*'[1972], in Jordan, *'Down the Bay'*, pp. 67–72 (p. 71). This discourse had a complicated and often oppositional relationship with social realism, although the latter was to a degree subsumed by the documentary humanism which had emerged as part of the politics of the Popular Front during the 1930s. I am grateful to Owen Logan for this observation.

17. E. D. Gregory, 'Starting over: A. L. Lloyd and the search for a new folk music, 1945–49', *Canadian Journal for Traditional Music*, 27, 1999–2000, pp. 20–43 (p. 32); Hall, 'The Social eye', pp. 71–2.

18. C. Darwent, 'The way we were – photographic legacy of defunct UK periodical, *Picture Post* magazine', *New Statesman*, 25 September 1998.

19. Lloyd, 'The forgotten Gorbals', p. 11.

20. Ibid. p. 11.

21. K. Coates, and R. Silburn, *Poverty: The Forgotten Englishmen* (Harmondsworth: Penguin, 1970). Of itself, the imputation of otherness, requiring research to discover its dimensions, was not radical or novel: compare Lloyd's 'They live four, six, eight to a room, often thirty to a lavatory, forty to a tap. They live in Britain's most abandoned slum' with Charles Booth's 'residuum', or relatively recent New Right sensationalism claiming that 'the underclass' – a behavioural definition foisted upon those living in acute poverty within particular neighbourhoods – 'live in a Britain you would not recognise' (C. Murray, 'Underclass: a disaster in the making', *Sunday Times Magazine*, 26 November 1989, pp. 26–46 (p. 26).

22. Lloyd, 'The forgotten Gorbals', p. 15.

23. Ibid. pp. 11–16.

24. D. Mellor, 'Brandt's phantasms', in M. Haworth-Booth and D. Mellor, *Bill Brandt Behind the Camera: Photographs, 1928–1983* (Oxford: Phaidon, 1985), pp. 71–97 (p. 86). In a 1986 interview, Oscar Marzaroli, while recognising an affinity with

Hardy – 'something of myself in him. The photo-journalist waiting to get in there' – claimed there was 'too much of the poet' in Brandt who 'saw and felt something in the area that wasn't in tune with him' (J. Renton, 'Shades of grey', *Textualities*, 2004–5, unpaginated).

25. Mellor, 'Brandt's phantasms', p. 86.
26. McKenzie's documentary project to record the transformation of Glasgow and other British cities began with the exhibition 'Glasgow Gorbals Children, 1964–65'. J. McKenzie, *Pages of Experience: Photography, 1947–1987* (Edinburgh: Polygon, 1987), pp. 24–35, includes vivid images from this, more akin to the art-photographs of Paul Strand than European photojournalism, followed by a picture of abandoned 1960s flats, taken in 1986 and entitled 'Dereliction . . . all over again!' See also J. McKenzie, 'Gorbals Children', *Portfolio*, vol. 7, 1988. His work includes many images of children, 'Beatle Girl' (1964) being perhaps the most famous.
27. Unlike in Leeds, photographs were not themselves used as direct evidence to justify planned improvements (cf. J. Tagg, *The Burden of Representation: Essays on Photographies and Histories* (London: Macmillan, 1988), pp. 117–52).
28. I. Spring, *Phantom Village: The Myth of the New Glasgow* (Edinburgh: Polygon, 1990), pp. 16, 18. A few Annan images have a haunting emptiness, e.g. '75 High Street, Glasgow', where washing hanging out of windows is the only evidence of human occupation. Nevertheless, children standing in groups, made curious by cameramen, are characteristic of early photography. The street was also an escape from damp, dark interiors and rather more of a social space than today. The proliferation of children in these street scenes was overstated because they saw photographers as a source of entertainment, 'men with magic boxes'. By the mid-twentieth century, children would pursue cameramen to take their picture or to ridicule them, yet, arguably, 'these self-confident, curious groups of children rarely appear in pictures despite their common presence', unless the photographer managed to remain unobtrusive (see Stevenson, *Photographing Children*, pp. 15–16).
29. W. Bolitho, *The Cancer of Empire* (London and New York: G. P. Putnam's Sons Ltd, 1924), pp. 53, 31, 30. Bolitho compares Glasgow to District Six in Cape Town and the Old Port in Marseilles, finding Glasgow 'unrivalled by any exotic' misery because, at least, slums elsewhere 'have sun and air and wind' (p. 31).
30. T. Normand, 'Alvin Langdon Coburn, Robert Louis Stevenson and Edinburgh', *History of Photography*, 29 (1), 2005, pp. 45–59. In this respect, Brandt's formalism created the visual exception.
31. 'River of tragic silence', *Daily Herald*, 3 November 1931; 'The watch on the Clyde for work that never comes', *Daily Herald*, 6 November 1931; 'Heartbreak Close', *Daily Herald*, 10 November 1931; 'Ships, slums and pride', *Daily Herald*, 17 November 1931. All were part of a series entitled 'In Scotland Again'.
32. Serious social problems underlay these observations, although their perspective – and their choice of metaphor – was stereotypical. As one Glasgow historian notes: 'Inevitably the depression exacerbated social problems, especially housing shortages and overcrowding. Certain communities experienced the disproportionate weight of congestion, the most notorious being Hutchesontown and the Gorbals, to the south of the River Clyde. In 1931 almost 85,000 people inhabited the area, which covered only 2 per cent of the city's total territory. It had long been a magnet for immigrants, particularly from Ireland and eastern Europe, and thus demonstrated an unusual cosmopolitan quality for Glasgow. Yet sensationalist journalism embellished

the "facts" of inter-war slum life and perpetuated an unsavoury image of the city that survived for decades. A favourite literary device was the metaphor of infestation, whether by rats, street gangs, immigrants or socialists, to illustrate Glasgow's crowded and corrosive slum environment' (E. Maver, 'No Mean City: 1914 to 1950s'. http://www.theglasgowstory.com/storye.php Accessed June 2009).

33. H. V. Morton, 'Heartbreak Close', Daily Herald, 10 November 1931. This couple were second-generation Irish Catholics, a fact that contributes to their 'othering' by Morton: 'The place of honour is given to a coloured picture of the Pope in the act of blessing the apartment. The corner by the sink is always wet when the wind and rain blow from the east; and if you tap the wall by the bed half a pound of white plaster will trickle out on the floor.' The difficult relationship between alterity and cosmopolitanism is reflected in the work of both Glasser, who had Lithuanian-Jewish forbears, and Marzaroli, who was Scots-Italian and raised in the central Glasgow district of Garnethill.

34. M. Bartholomew, 'H. V. Morton's English Utopia', in C. Lawrence and A. K. Mayer, eds, Regenerating England (Amsterdam: Rodopi, 2000), pp. 25–44 (p. 38).

35. G. Jordan, 'Tiger Bay, Picture Post and the politics of representation', in Jordan, 'Down the Bay', pp. 9–21 (p. 9). Glaswegians display a similar fondness for Marzaroli. See, for example, Spring's reflection: 'If I look through Oscar Marzaroli's grainy black and white snapshots of adults and children or studies of Glasgow tenements, I see exactly the Glasgow of my childhood' (Spring, Phantom Village, p. 101).

36. 'Shadow', Midnight scenes and Social Photographs: Being Descriptions of the Streets, Wynds and Dens of the City (Glasgow: Thomas Murray, 1858); Spring; Phantom Village, pp. 5–13.

37. H. Hendrick, 'Constructions and reconstructions of British childhood: an interpretative survey from 1800 to the present', in A. James and A. Prout (eds), Constructing and Reconstructing Childhood (London: The Falmer Press, 1990), pp. 35–59.

38. L. Abrams, The Orphan Country: Children of Scotland's Broken Homes from 1845 to the Present Day (Edinburgh: John Donald, 1998), pp. 208–9, 166, 102.

39. A. James, Childhood Identities: Self and Social Relationships in the Experience of the Child (Edinburgh: Edinburgh University Press, 1993), pp. 42, 103, 132. The Foucauldian interpretation owes much to D. Armstrong, Political Anatomy of the Body: Medical Knowledge in Britain in the Twentieth Century (Cambridge: Cambridge University Press, 1983).

40. Spring, Phantom Village, p. 16. In 1934 Lewis Grassic Gibbon wrote of 150,000 people in Glasgow living in such conditions 'as the most bitterly pressed primitive in Tierra del Fuego never visioned', 'sub-humans' who 'crawl into childhood in those waste jungles of stench, disease and hopelessness' (L. Grassic Gibbon, 'Glasgow' [1934], in I. S. Munro (ed.), A Scots Hairst (London: Hutchinson, 1967), pp. 82–94 (pp. 84–5)).

41. J. Fisher and C. Oliver, 'A short commentary on the photographs of Oscar Marzaroli', in O. Marzaroli and W. McIlvanney, Shades of Grey: Glasgow, 1956–1987 (Edinburgh: Mainstream, 1987), pp. 207–23 (p. 217).

42. C. Oliver, Joan Eardley, RSA (Edinburgh: Mainstream, 1988), pp. 45, 53, 69, 56. Several pictures depict facial abnormalities such as saddle nose caused by congenital syphilis. Some insight into Eardley's practice is provided by the Films of Scotland documentary, Three Scottish Painters (1963), which shows her at work in her studio with one of the Samson children.

43. Ibid. p. 66.

44. E. Morgan, *The Second Life* (Edinburgh: Edinburgh University Press, 1968).

45. R. Ross, Foreword in O. Marzaroli, *Glasgow's People, 1956–1968* (Edinburgh: Mainstream, 1993).

46. Complementarity between the two media is reflected in Eardley's work, where proof that her vision depended 'on factual sustenance rather than memory or imagination' is sought in detailed similarities between preparatory photos she sometimes took and finished paintings (Oliver, *Joan Eardley*, p. 71). Marzaroli later acknowledged that Eardley influenced him 'more than anyone' (Renton, 'Shades of Grey'). In turn, Morgan wrote a series of what he termed 'instamatic poems' in which he attempted to arrest action and record events in a photographic manner.

47. Cf. D. Parker and P. Long, '"The Mistakes of the Past"? Visual narratives of urban decline and regeneration', *Visual Culture in Britain*, 5 (1), 2004, pp. 37–58, which applies the notion of an urban imaginary to the visual rhetorics through which Birmingham's architecture has been interpreted.

48. Spring, *Phantom Village*, p. 27.

49. W. McIlvanney, 'Where Greta Garbo wouldn't have been alone', in W. McIlvanney, *Surviving the Shipwreck* (Edinburgh: Mainstream, 1991), pp. 163–84 (p. 167). After Gans (see note 12), the 'urban village' concept was especially salient in the community studies sociology of the 1960s (see, for instance, N. Dennis, 'The popularity of the neighbourhood community ideal', in R. E. Pahl (ed.), *Readings in Urban Sociology* (Oxford: Pergamon Press, 1968), pp. 74–92). For literary and sociological implications see C. Craig, 'Fearful selves: character, community and the Scottish imagination', *Cencrastus*, 4, 1980–1, pp. 29–32, and S. Damer, *Glasgow: Going for a Song* (London: Lawrence & Wishart, 1990), pp. 101–3.

50. F. A. Walker, 'The Glasgow grid', in T. A. Markus (ed.), *Order in Space and Society* (Edinburgh: Mainstream, 1982), pp. 155–99, cited in Spring, *Phantom Village*, p. 26. See also F. Wordsall, *The Tenement: A Way of Life* (Edinburgh: Mainstream, 1979).

51. The reference is to A. McArthur and H. K. Long, *No Mean City: A Story of the Glasgow Slums* (London: Longman Green, 1935), a novel written jointly by an unemployed Gorbals baker and a London journalist that gained widespread notoriety – and sales of half-a-million copies – for its raw portrayal of razor gangs, corruption and hard drinking. Pivotal in creating Glasgow's external mythology, the book is now generally disparaged for purveying sensationalist 'underworld' stereotypes. The strength of this slum iconography remains such that some autobiographers feel a need to issue disclaimers. For instance, R. Wilkinson, *Memories of Maryhill* (Edinburgh: Canongate Academic, 1933), p. 2, begins almost apologetically: 'The trouble about writing about a place like Braeside Street is that it was – and still is – very respectable . . . Stories about working-class life in Glasgow seem never to be complete without the Gorbals or Bridgeton or the wild East End.' His Maryhill had 'no slums to call its own', although his father was a long-term unemployed shipyard worker and fervent Communist.

52. R. Bromley, *Lost Narratives: Popular Fictions, Politics and Recent History* (London: Routledge, 1988), p. 40.

53. R. Glasser, *A Gorbals Boy at Oxford* (London: Chatto & Windus, 1988), p. 1.

54. B. Anderson, *Imagined Communities* (London: Verso, 1991).

55. A. Ferguson (with H. McIlvanney), *Managing My Life: My Autobiography* (London: Hodder & Stoughton, 1999), p. 442.

56. R. Glasser, *A Gorbals Legacy* (Edinburgh: Mainstream, 2000). As an obituary notice remarks, Glasser spent his academic career 'campaign[ing] against the destruction of traditional communities and their tried and tested values' (Anon., 'Ralph Glasser: thinker who applied the lessons of his Gorbals childhood to the Third World', *Times*, 10 May 2002).

57. Ferguson's eulogy begins: 'To call Govan a district is an insult. It is a unique entity, a place with its own independent spirit and clearly defined personality . . . But the feeling of being special came from something more basic than civic history. It came, above all, from the working-class pride and energy generated by Govan's worldwide significance as a birthplace of the big ships' (*Managing*, p. 1). By contrast, contemporary Govan has the reputation of being a depressed Wine Alley (see S. Damer, *From Moorepark to 'Wine Alley': The Rise and Fall of a Glasgow Housing Scheme* (Edinburgh: Edinburgh University Press, 1989).

58. McIlvanney, 'Where Greta Garbo', p. 170. B. Misztal, *Theories of Social Remembering* (Maidenhead: Open University Press, 2003), p. 52, citing M. Halbwachs, *The Collective Memory* [1926] (London: Harper Colophon Books, 1950), p. 157, comments that 'the reason members of a group remain united, even after the group is dispersed, "is that they think of the old home and its lay-out". In other words, the spatial image alone, by reason of its stability, gives us "an illusion of not having changed through time and of retrieving the past in the present".'

59. Spring, *Phantom Village*, pp. 5, 3. On his return to the Gorbals, Glasser similarly discovered that all evidence of the places of his childhood had been erased: nothing was left but 'a bit of broken masonry, a jagged piece of railway arch, a gable with only the sky behind it . . . all points of reference gone'(quoted in E. Wilson, *The Sphinx in the City: Urban Life, the Control of Disorder and Women* (London: Virago, 1991), p. 148).

60. Cf. P. Nora, 'Between memory and history', *Representations*, 26 (1), 1989, pp. 7–24 (p. 7): 'There are *lieux de* mémoire, sites of memory, because there are no longer *milieux de* mémoire, real environments of memory'. Oral accounts and photographs are, of course, central to the burgeoning people's museum movement, as is a defining consciousness of remembered community which is used to repopulate imaginatively streets that have long been bulldozed. See, for example, the essays collected in C. Rassool and S. Prosalendis (eds), *Recalling Community in Cape Town* (Cape Town: District Six Museum Foundation, 2001).

61. A. Huyssen, *Present Pasts: Urban Palimpsests and the Politics of Memory* (Stanford: Stanford University Press, 2003).

62. 'Ghetto city of the poor', *Observer*, 22 January 1978, cited in Damer, *Glasgow*, p. 205.

63. Damer, *Glasgow*, pp. 205–6.

64. L. Martin, 'The Sicknote City', *Observer*, 3 July 2005, p. 17.

65. Lloyd, 'The forgotten Gorbals', p. 16. Similarly, ex-residents who have campaigned to have their homes demolished nonetheless talk ruefully of 'some fantastic memories . . . such as the great community spirit there . . . I'll have mixed emotions when I see Capelaw [an Edinburgh tower block] come down' (B. Ferguson, 'Bound to Be a Blast', *Edinburgh Evening News*, 12 April 2005). Subsequent news footage indeed caught such ambivalence on film as the dust clouds were still settling. The article meanwhile suggested that although memorialising took place instantaneously, its objective was to gain closure – 'archive photographs and memorabilia connected with the tower

blocks over the last 40 years is [sic] currently on display in the local St Mark's Primary School to mark their end'.

66. Spring, *Phantom Village*, p. 2; J. Knight, 'The changing face of poverty' [*BBC News Channel*, 26 July 2005], http://news.bbc.co.uk/1/hi/business/4070112.stm Accessed June 2009.

67. Damer, *Glasgow*, p. 7. This emic/etic dichotomy has been used analytically to favour (as emic) or disparage (as etic) particular documentary humanists. Thus Orwell – unlike Hardy and Lloyd – has been criticised for foisting the impressions of an outsider onto an understanding of working-class life in the 'prole quarter' (see P. Wright, *On Living in an Old Country* (London: Verso, 1985), pp. 215–23). C. Baxter, *Glasgow* (Glasgow: R. Drew, 1986). Subsequently, Baxter's compositions have illustrated several Glasgow guides and calendars.

68. D. Mitchell, *Cultural Geography: A Critical Introduction* (Oxford: Blackwell, 2000), p. 8.

69. Misztal, *Theories of Social Remembering*, p. 119.

70. See Nora, 'Between Memory and History'.

71. Spring, *Phantom Village*, p. 31.

72. R. Samuel, *Theatres of Memory* (London: Verso, 1994), p. 352.

73. Damer, *Glasgow*, p. 8. In its relationship with decay, poverty frequently suggests an otherwise forgotten past. Although compositionally they are almost copies of Hardy's 1948 pictures, photographs of children playing on half-demolished walls during the 1960s are popularly regarded as 'reminiscent of the Depression' (R. Kenna, *Scotland's Children in Pictures* (Glendaruel: Argyll Publishing, 1996), p. 15).

74. R. Williams, *The Country and the City* (St Albans: Paladin, 1975), pp. 202–20.

75. Misztal, *Theories of Social Remembering*, p. 1.

76. R. Barthes, *Camera Lucida: Reflections on Photography* (London: Harper Collins, 1984); Jordan, 'Tiger Bay', p. 20.

77. Memory is reflexive and selective, and in attempting to recover what is lost, we may forget what we have forgotten, a process evaluated in S. Buck-Morss, *The Dialectics of Seeing* (Cambridge, MA: MIT Press, 1989), itself an attempt to 'reconstruct' Benjamin's unfinished Arcades Project.

78. Cf. Wolfgang Suschitzky's documentary film *Children of the City* made in Dundee in 1944 (for the Ministry of Information) and concerned with delinquency. Suschitzky's sister, Edith Tudor Hart, was a documentary photographer whose pictures of working people in London and South Wales reflect a strongly social realist approach.

79. Anon., 'Andrew's picture from the past is worth a lot', *Northern Echo*, 5 December 2000. The occasion for the sale was the death of author Naomi Mitchison who owned the painting. Interestingly, Samson commented that he could not afford to bid for the picture, thus demonstrating how far the original depiction remains an appropriated artefact.

80. One anthropological perspective claims that people are 'defined by space and are nevertheless the defining consciousness of that space' (E. Ardener, 'Remote areas: some theoretical considerations', in A. Jackson (ed.), *Anthropology at Home* (London: Tavistock, 1987), pp. 39–54 (p. 39)). Contemporary social and geographical mobility – not to say globalised media awareness – question the adequacy of this observation. The implication is that poorer, less mobile people are more restricted in the resources of self-definition, a circumstance caught in the suggestion that some Glaswegians' pride and 'humane irreverence' is due to the fact that they 'didn't have much more

collateral than their sense of themselves' (McIlvanney, 'Where Greta Garbo', p. 169). Nevertheless, Spring (*Phantom Village*, p. 102) alludes to the metaphorical communities of novelist Alisdair Gray capturing the 'fragmentation of real city life' in ways that 'kailyard' urban village representations do not (see Chapter 4). Note also Ardener's title referring to 'remote areas', not inner-city neighbourhoods, the implication perhaps being that the former are somehow more distinctive.

81. Hardy and Lloyd arrived in the city on the day after Alex Ferguson's sixth birthday; Billy Connolly was a few months younger. These men may no longer be in or close to the picture, yet spiritually they remain of it.

82. A. Campsie, 'Art imitates life as picture inspires Gorbals sculpture', *The Herald*, 30 August 2008.

83. H. Cartier-Bresson, *The Decisive Moment* (New York: Simon & Schuster, 1952), quoted in Jordan, 'The photographs', p. 28. In his eagerness to revivify nineteenth-century naturalist ideas, Cartier-Bresson represents a rather different tradition from Hardy.

84. D. Chong, *The Girl in the Picture: The Story of Kim Phuc, the Photograph and the Vietnam War* (London: Viking, 2000); R. N. Timberlake, 'The myth of the girl in the photo', http://hometown.aol.com/ecperry/myth1.html [1997] Accessed September 2006.

85. Tonkin, '"Icons of the dispossessed"', p. 160.

Chapter 8

Finding ways home

The station is in the middle of a moor. There appears to be no habitation around. In the distance are some hills.

The train stands at the station.

As it pulls away, Renton, Spud, Tommy and Sick Boy are left standing on the plat-form, looking around.

SICK BOY

Now what?

TOMMY

We go for a walk.

SPUD

What?

TOMMY

A walk.

SPUD

But where?

Tommy points vaguely across the moor.

TOMMY

There.

SICK BOY

Are you serious?

They step across the tracks toward the vast moorland. They stop. All but Tommy sit down on rocks or clumps of heather.

TOMMY

Well, what are you waiting for?

SPUD

I don't know, Tommy. I don't know if it's . . . normal.

A group of three serious Walkers trudge past from the other end of the platform, decked out in regulation Berghaus from head to foot. They tramp off towards the wilderness. The boys watch them go. Spud opens a can.

TOMMY

It's the great outdoors.

SICK BOY

It's really nice, Tommy. Can we go home now?

TOMMY

It's fresh air.

SICK BOY

Look, Tommy, we know you're getting a hard time off Lizzy, but there's no need to take it out on us.

TOMMY

Doesn't it make you proud to be Scottish?

RENTON

I hate being Scottish. We're the lowest of the fucking low, the scum of the earth, the most wretched, servile, miserable, pathetic trash that was ever shat into civilisation. Some people hate the English, but I don't. They're just wankers. We, on the other hand, are colonised by wankers. We can't even pick a decent culture to be colonised by. We are ruled by effete arseholes. It's a shite state of affairs and all the fresh air in the world will not make any fucking difference.

The three serious Walkers are receding into the distance.
The boys troop back towards the platform.
(voiceover)
At or around this time, we made a healthy, informed, democratic decision to get back on drugs as soon as possible. It took about twelve hours.[1]

The nation's encounter with modernity has produced alienation at least as much as it has induced a sense of belonging. The trip to Corrour station in *Trainspotting* recounted above indicates a disaffected sense of severance from whatever 'Scotland' and 'Scottishness' might be; and there is certainly no positive attachment to the iconic landscape around Rannoch Moor. We are indeed a long way from Rebus's puzzled but fond recollection of St Andrews where our investigation began. Of course, both examples are fictional, but then so are all representations. In what respect, therefore, can different narratives and images tell us anything consistent about modern Scotland? Does not their very diversity preclude us from advancing anything like a coherent analysis?

Saddled with the tropes of Kailyard, Tartanry and Clydesidism, the sociological analysis of modern Scottish culture has produced a constructionist view that limits the imagination of the nation to 'top-down' representation. This has the virtue of simplifying reality, but by the same token it disguises, indeed misrepresents, the discursive density of individuals' engagement with place and their fellow human beings. The foregoing chapters have therefore tried to establish some elements of the social imaginary through which people understand their country. I have argued that its formation relies upon a specifically modern way of seeing where images function to shore up a sense of identity, and that these, in turn, rely for their salience upon their connection with personal and collective remembrances determined by socialisation. There are ways in which modern memory is distinctive in facilitating accounts that either cleave to modernity as the source of identification or more frequently reject it as the vehicle of dissociation, but, however dispersed or contradictory the evidence, the concept provides a frame of reference through which to interpret Scottish culture.[2] This final chapter attempts to explain how it is 'memory above all that maintains the imagined identities upon which society rests'.[3]

Communities Under Modernity

Associations of human beings are of various types, resting on different principles [of which] two are so radically distinct that confusion has dangerous consequences. There is one type constituted by a common purpose; there is another which consists in the sharing of a common life. It is essential to distinguish these; and I propose to use the terms 'society' and 'community' for this purpose.[4]

Thus speaks John Macmurray, seminal theorist of ethical socialism and 'affective community'. From Ferguson on, the project of civil society has been one that has sought what I have referred to as 'an appropriate ethics to guide us in the public sphere' (p. 75), and as with Ferguson, so with contemporary thinkers such as Maffesoli or Alexander, the answer appears to lie with the maintenance of an impetus of 'democratic vitality'.[5] The inherently collective character of such a social force requires that some sense of community is central to the meaning of society. However, the view from modernity is one that sees society as *gesellschaft*: much of our sociability consists of relationships between strangers, persons with whom we have no connection through kinship, and is thus categorically different from the pre-modern world of ascribed clan ties. This is a perception that underscores the functionalist approach to nationhood, and one which has significant bearing upon the morality of civil society, for according to this view, tradition equates with community whereas modernity begets society.

In several instances this straightforward theoretical dichotomy has underlain further analytical distinctions. For example, the internal colonialist perception of Highlanders and Islanders as socially peripheral and culturally backward 'others' is conveyed in the etic cultural account discussed in Chapter 6. But there are many detractors. Not only does the emic cultural account signify the ongoing significance of identification and self-representation through the local, understood as *both* common purpose and sharing a common life, but the tension between 'society' and 'community' as ways of understanding the nation in general reflects a manufactured vision at odds with the idea of Scotland as an imagined community. Another way of looking at this tension is to compare the social, reflecting a model or view of history and society imposed from above or from outside, with sociality, as emerging from within what Maffesoli would call 'tribes' (see Chapter 2). As Chapter 4 demonstrates, the pervasive ideology that derides the literature of local community as parochial in the pejorative sense fails to grasp the continued significance of the 'parish paradigm', that is, a worldview grounded in the egalitarian mores of the local nexus. To this extent, the moral economies of parish communities are not something that can be dismissed, à la Taylor, as pre-modern or anachronistic because of their limited domain of knowledge and access to a wider public sphere; rather, they co-exist alongside the modern social imaginary and, indeed, determine its efficacy. Any inclusive analysis of social memory must therefore reach beyond an elite model of representation and find ways of interpreting the maintenance of national identity (or, rather, identifications of nationhood) as a kind of deliberative democracy of vision.

The great problem with modernity is that it ushers in liberty, democracy and the triumph of reason at the same time as modernisation destroys social cohesion and the homeostasis of the human and natural environment. The consequences for memory and belonging are profound although by no means simple to untangle, especially when the discourse of nationhood is as dense as it is in Scotland.

Modernity heralds 'a new conception of the moral *order* of society'.[6] An organised imaginary is of the essence. Thus Kenneth Clark speaks of civilisation as depending upon 'those ordered memories that are the basis of morality',[7] while John Grierson claims 'all things are beautiful if you have got them in the right order'.[8] Changes to socio-economic arrangements required accompanying shifts in how culture and morality were entailed in one another. Eugen Weber explicates the tardiness with which the French peasantry adjusted to the idea of nationhood, but it would be inappropriate to apply a logic of slow diffusion in the Scottish case.[9] As late as 1956, Moray McLaren was writing that 'the Scot of today . . . loves the physical fact of his own land "out of an atavistic sense of his possession of it by his own effort"'.[10] The connection between land and place *as nation* had lain deep in the psyche for centuries, and if the coming to terms with Unionist nationhood was a rather abrupt and brutal experience for many Highlanders inured to the loyalties of clan and kin, by the nineteenth century at least, an independent-minded Scottishness was synonymous with the values of the Lowland peasant as exemplified in Alexander's *Johnny Gibb*. But what of the urbanised twentieth century and after? Whereas Taylor understands the emergence of a national social imaginary to be critically dependent upon changes in how people imagine belonging, no such transformation may be necessary where the nation is already perceived as the macrocosmic image of the parish. Similarly, the generation of national identity, from the places on the margin that MacDiarmid advocated as a counter to the imperialist imposition of nationhood by the British metropolitan centre, misses the point that an indigenous, 'from below' version of Scottishness as a way of thinking and doing already prevailed, albeit that this sat (and still sits) uncomfortably with a stereotypical 'Scotland' touted for tourists, hence the relevance of the cultural intimacy thesis. In Nairn's argument, the cultural deforma-tion wrought by Kailyard is responsible for lumpen false consciousness. The parochial mindset may indeed tend toward the sentimental, but in its democratic aspect it could also be said to underlie the morality of politi-cal preference, what McCrone refers to as 'a clear association between being "Scottish" and having social democratic values'.[11] The long-held traditions of locality, together with the pride taken in having a devolved civil society which has delivered the bases for a strong voluntary sector, education and health care system (albeit with the aid of centralised inter-ventions lauded by an alternative Griersonian ideology) run deep. Those relatively affluent voters who nonetheless vote for left-of-centre parties are deemed 'subjectively working-class'. In effect, it is argued, they look back to their parents' values, learned in an earlier industrial era, for moral guidance – an imputed psychology again suggesting that worldviews do not always reflect the material conditions of the present. In this way, 'tradition' is always *part of* modernity. It is what maintains continuity between generations and in the politics of national identity, even if, at times, it categorically opposes some versions of Nationalism. By the same token, society is infused with ideas of community, the very means by which we imagine its salvation.

There is a whiff of the subjunctive about the idea of community because it is always good, always intimate, unlike other forms of social organisation, such as society or the state.[12] Does it therefore follow that idealised communities are the only 'real' communities? Is community simply a moral project that rejects individualism in favour of social solidarity or is it something that is also empirically observable? Are there such things as communities that are real rather than abstract or imagined? Pursuing the logic of Williams' method for a sociology of culture requires a shift from the sociology of knowledge to a sociology of consciousness: 'knowable communities' are past situated, but structures of feeling are emergent and present.[13] We can refer to rural Scotland, to the Highlands as the mythical landscape on which tourist images of Scotland flourish or to the Lowlands as the literary terrain of Kailyardised popular culture. But we can also consider the real, physical places in which people live. In Stenhousemuir, in East Kilbride, in Shotts, in Dundee, Kelso and Fort William, in Stornoway, Aberfeldy and Whithorn, there are populations, institutions, families; kirks and ceremonies; schools and songs; farms and factories. And if the people living there are more than simply individuals going their own separate ways, what kinds of solidarities do they feel and express? To paraphrase Eagleton, are there aspects of their present circumstances that provide hope for realising political ends or, in the absence of such favourable conditions, are they condemned to 'fall ill of longing' – a condition remarkably akin to nostalgia?[14]

'Community' denotes legitimacy; it justifies the way we live, or, rather, the way we should like to live. In the contemporary world, this produces a dilemma, for globalisation has transformed our experience of time and space: whereas pre-modern individuals looked to tradition for guidance, this authority has been replaced by a sense of the future as open and uncertain.[15] The past may be regarded as Arcadia but it is no longer the stable template for Utopia in the future. Moreover, detraditionalisation sees:

> a shift in authority from 'without' to 'within'. It entails the decline of the belief in pre-given or natural orders of things. Individual subjects are themselves called upon to exercise authority in the face of the disorder and contingency which is thereby generated. 'Voice' is displaced from established sources, coming to rest with the self.[16]

As a statement of the condition of late- or post-modernity, this view would render obsolete much of what has been said about the significance of community under modernity. It would also seem to devalue the salience of collective belief in the ideology of progress, and indeed in 'authentic' social memory. Huyssen suggests: 'The current obsession with memory . . . is a sign of the crisis of that structure of temporality that marked the age of modernity with its celebration of the new as utopian'. Paradoxically, the rapid growth in museums and memorialising coincides with 'an undisputed waning of history and historical consciousness'.[17] So too with the structures of spatial stability framing collective life now that lives are increasingly concerned with movement and systems are increasingly organised around 'mobilities' rather than being territorially fixed.[18] The age of globalisation is unlike the era of Grierson's representation of grand state schemes, and if the places where Scots live now are not always the ones from which the putatively national *weltanschauung* is derived, what is anachronistic is the amnesiac assumption that communities are necessarily place-bound or defined by locality. Many are instead networks of moral contingency – 'tribes' to use Maffesoli's coinage, rather than tribes in the genealogical, blood-relation sense. Certainly, the public sphere is not a neutral zone of civil inattention but a discursive space through which claims compete.

It follows that there is no one tradition, or unified morality, or singular conception of nationhood. If the binaries on which modernisation is predicated are flawed, so too are its unities. To regard *the* nation as having *a* culture, some kind of essence distilled by intellectuals and then projected onto political and popular understanding, corresponds to 'an essentialising, an idealising, a reduction to paradigmatic features, of Scotland as *home*'.[19] McCrone argues instead that 'one can identify a coherent body of social and political values which makes Scotland a cohesive society, as well as one with a complex array of social identities', and that culture is only significant in that it 'celebrates and mobilises certain values' which have political utility.[20] Collective identifications are perceived as dependent upon socially constructed representations. There is nevertheless another, phenomenological route by which the experience of being in a particular place produces identity and meaning.[21] Here the relationship between landscape and belonging discussed in Chapter 5 takes on a specific significance.

BELONGING IN PLACE

Alain Touraine argues that faith in material progress has faltered under the fear that 'growth will destroy basic natural equilibria' as humanity breaks with natural being, consequently becoming barbarous.[22] Responding to similar concerns, Neal Ascherson advocates the idea of a Scottish 'cultural landscape' that involves 'abandoning the anthropocentric perspective of the modern West, and returning to the vision of human beings who understood themselves and their imagination as components of the natural world'.[23] At one level, he is simply acknowledging that instead of castles, megaliths and other artefacts being presented in isolation, the heritage industry can do more to evaluate each historical object in its entire context, from the geological to the social – a shift from archaeology to 'total ecology'. But he is also pursuing the programme advanced by Frank Fraser Darling in *West Highland Survey* (1955), a body of work that, he argues 'permanently changed Scottish attitudes to landscape'. Fraser Darling 'forced his readers, his audiences and his colleagues to accept that the landscape of the West Highlands was not "natural" but an artefact . . . He was the first influential thinker in Scotland to insist on a holistic approach to human settlement and its physical environment'.[24] An Englishman who did not move north until he was nearly thirty, his genius was no direct brainchild of the democratic intellect, but his generalist approach certainly appealed to it.

From the standpoint of environmental history, Smout notes that with Patrick Geddes a half-century previously there had been an early and 'special Scottish context for the study of ecology',[25] namely a perspective of 'man-in-nature' whereby, contrary to the conventional, English wisdom, humans were seen merely as the main actors among other animals rather than outside invaders of the natural world. Furthering a model of society based on the interdependent triad of folk, work and place, where 'home' simultaneously embraced nature, nation and region, his espousal of the Celtic revival made him for some 'one of the pioneers of modern Scottish nationalism'.[26] His maverick but influential development of human ecology – an holistic approach to how people might live in and manage their 'near environments' – need not detain us here, save to note that it entailed a shift into town planning that effectively eclipsed this national vision. But it was his view, or, at least, his sentiment and, to a degree that of John Muir before him, that re-emerged with Frank Fraser Darling, whose researches on red deer and seals 'blended science and the romantic tradition', alive as they were 'with descriptive passages about the scenic context'.[27] It is a perspective that finds popular echoes ranging from Gavin Maxwell's *Ring of Bright Water* trilogy, through the 'new' nature writing, to arguments supporting crofting as sustainable land use.[28] Both Geddes and Fraser Darling proselytised 'an attitude of mind to nature',[29] but it is the embedding of people within the landscape as an organic – albeit highly dysfunctional – element that is most significant for our understanding.

Intriguingly, Geddes's sociology developed from Comte and Le Play, thus bypassing, I would argue, the imaginative requirements of an Enlightenment tradition whose sociology was founded in a particular modern conception of progression in the moral order. For him, the crucial construct through which belonging was to be grasped was not the community but the region:

> the region becomes the basis from which is fostered the cultural tradition of a people and that embodies the spirit of place. The customs, practices, and habits of action of a people are distinctive of their region. There is, therefore, a determinate relationship between 'place', 'work', and 'folk'.[30]

Such a privileging of place appealed similarly to writers like Neil Gunn, whose 'description of this magic unity with the landscape [in *Highland River*] is immediately juxtaposed with . . . the "infernal conditions of some Glasgow slums": a hell of "nightmare horror", of a world betrayed by history'.[31] Thus, Craig avers: 'against the temporality of its false and failed histories, the [early twentieth-century] Scottish novel asserts the significance of the geography of the region; against the destructive powers of progress it sets a knowledge more ancient than civilisation, one which is inscribed in and maintained by the particular qualities of its landscape', those of permanence and transcendence.[32] In its ecological harmony, the region becomes the container of 'values denied by the very processes of history', 'an eternal, non-linear set of values'.[33] There are indeed 'associations which are "domestic" and local, which seem to defy history by being related to place rather than time'.[34]

In the mid-twentieth century the writers Neil Gunn and Nan Shepherd wove their novels around the relationship of their protagonists to the spiritual qualities of nature and place.[35] Both also produced revealing non-fiction: Gunn's autobiography, *The Atom of Delight* (1956) delineates the Zen Buddhism underpinning his work, while Shepherd's essay on the Cairngorms, *The Living Mountain* (1977 [written in 1947]), focuses on the sensual, embodied experience of landscape as well as its soulful dimension. These authors share a poetic close to the anthropologists' 'dwelling perspective' or 'memoryscape', in which 'cultural memory is embedded in the landscape' and over time becomes part of it.[36] As de Certeau argues, history here 'begins at ground level, with footsteps' inasmuch as place is constructed from within, rather than by looking at it from outside.[37] Such writing is not just about social relationships in a community or, alternatively, the meaning of landscape to the individual. Instead, it fuses the relationship of the individual and the community in which they interact with the ground in and on which they have their being.

Echoing the inseparability of land and peasant in the novel, and indeed reflecting the cultural accounting found on Whalsay by Cohen and embroidered in Chapter 6, recent ethnographic research among Border sheep farmers, having emphasised the actor perspective – 'the knowledge, understanding and discourse of people that are embedded in their every-day lifeworlds'– concludes that the spatial relationship between family and farm, being and place, is 'consubstantial' such that the one stands for the other.[38] The study cites a dialogue in which one farmer 'uses the name of the farm, which his family tenants and where they live and work, to stand for his family as well as to give a distinct social identity and status within the community'. Since farmers have always been known by the names of their farms in Scotland, this may appear self-evident, but Gray uses the consubstantial identification to argue that 'the family farm is more a way of being-in-the-world than a specific set of people, relation-ships and/or activities whose boundaries can be precisely defined'. Thus, after Heidegger, the essence of family farming must be understood not as a set of measurable attributes, such as kinship relations or methods of man-agement, but as a mode of apprehending, where attitudes, behaviour and things are considered 'family-farmlike', and the farmers' actions should be interpreted as stemming from this ontological disposition. Habitat is thus central to habitus.[39] Theirs is a distinctly practical consciousness, while here too is an ethics of belonging-in-place synonymous with a moral rationale for community. Nevertheless, this unusually strong iden-tification amongst a group whose occupation is particularly land-based and whose settlement in the one area can be traced back for generations cannot be held up as representing the wider mores of contemporary Scottish society.

Other case studies have attempted to analyse the interpenetration of personal, local and wider experiences of belonging in place. In his impact study of the US Polaris base at Holy Loch, George Giarchi borrows Gerard Manley Hopkins' concept of 'inscape', a term that simultane-ously conveys the concreteness of place and the individual's experience of encountering this setting. However, rather than attempting to access solitary ruminations, Giarchi develops a notion of 'social inscape' to analyse the impress of externalities as inter-subjective, 'plural experiences involving the sedimentation of views'. He enquires: 'Are there maps of life inside people which represent both the immediate world and that of the remote world beyond?'[40] Of course there are, but there is some debate as to how these maps relate to one another. Giarchi identifies various 'scapes' or contexts, ranging through 'inscape' and 'social scape', to 'nearer and wider outscapes' whose boundaries are defined in terms of relative access and familiarity. 'Ecological scape', concerns perceptions of liberating or inhibiting environmental factors, while economic, political and cultural 'scapes' are similarly outlined. Thus the perceptual dimensions of community recognise the objective constraints and possibilities of each domain. This spatialisation of understanding, while clearly connecting personal to local to national and international realms, is categorically distinct from the idea of imagined community as microcosm of the nation in which a singular conception of the local is symbolically transferred onto the working surface of the national. Nevertheless, Giarchi's characterisation of the 'historical scape' of the older generation at Holy Loch unmasks a selective forgetting where, instead of being concerned with the threat of radiation and ballistic confrontation, many choose to remember the days when "submarines were here to fight the Germans". These people, whom he regards as 'living in the "inscape of yesterday"',[41] would appear to be engaging in something very similar to our hypothetical *People's Friend* readers, for they are again invoking the remembered past as a source of values. Wartime jingoism aside, it is debatable whether this entreatment of past locality can be extrapolated so as to represent a nostalgic, still less an aspirational view of nationhood.[42]

Like some regional novels, the phenomenological tradition could be accused of choosing 'regional geography over the national past',[43] thereby failing to address the dynamic impact of broader social processes. Nowadays, most people do not share the inseparable sense of life, work and place accorded the fictional figures of Gunn's Caithness or Gray's Border farmers. This is not to deny, however, that many might wish to. Indeed, the desire to repair such severance underpins the whole elegiac thrust of the sociology of modernity.[44] Much has been written about why societies invent their pasts, and often this relates to the assumption that psychological homelessness is a condition produced by modernity,[45] hence the assertion that 'we have constructed heritage because we have a cultural need to do so in our modern age. Heritage is a condition of the late twentieth century'.[46] As Herzfeld avers: 'The very fact that we talk about "the past" illustrates the groping for a reified certainty to which we are all heirs'. Such certainty is found through myths of origin in which 'the idea of a once-perfect reciprocity' becomes something of a guiding ideal, hence perhaps Geddes's plea for a 'return to the human scale of planning'.[47]

CULTURE AND HOME

There is nationality in districts as well as countries: nay, the people living on different sides of a streamlet, or of the same hill, sometimes entertain prejudices against one another, not less virulent than those of the inhabitants of the different sides of the British Channel or the Pyrenees.[48]

It is part of morality not to be at home in one's home.[49]

Nationalism differs from other modes of identity-construction in that it requires a mythologised element of place.[50] The desire to belong in such a way connects closely with the German consciousness of *heimat*. While this word means homeland it also expresses *zusammengehörigkeitsgefühl*, the 'feeling of belonging together'. The term thus synthesises people and place in a communitarian, moral endeavour. A conservative social sentiment expressed as much in Marx's hostility to the alienating effects of metropolitan capitalism upon traditional working patterns and moral solidarities as in Heideggerian phenomenology, or Tönnies' classic dichotomy, this notion of 'a physical topography with specific customs and idioms' and memories 'embedded in its soil'[51] has lent itself to heavily patriotic interpretations and usages, notoriously in its identification with Nazism. Indeed, it alerts us to the important point that social imaginaries are more than ideas since they can and do have significant material effects.[52] As a plea for ecological solidarity, however, *heimat* is not peculiar to this form of nationalism; nor does it depend upon any equivalence between cultural development and political or economic forces. On the contrary, it reflects 'the capacity of borders themselves to take on cultural meaning that transcends their political or economic purposes'. The willingness to regard Germany as 'a nation of provincials' thus indicates 'the struggle of people continually to renew the communities they have formed, not just at the level of political arrangements, but at the level of symbolic depictions [of themselves]'.[53] Crucially, this means transcending both the particularities of region or locality and the generalities of nation by foregrounding a consciousness of what both have in common: 'the effort, for better or for worse, to maintain "community" against the economic, political and cultural forces that would scatter it'.[54] Yet because these forces have in fact dispersed or destroyed real communities, such consciousness is inevitably a fantasy, at best an imagined community, *lieu de mémoire* rather than *milieu de mémoire*. Of course, this in no way limits its emotive value as both a backdrop for ontological security and a force behind nationalist convictions. For example, emigrant journeys traverse imagined homelands as well as physical space: 'through these genealogical journeys, individuals are able to construct meaningful self-narratives from the ambiguities of their diasporic migrant histories, and so recover a more secure sense of home and self-identity'.[55] But it does mean that a good deal of cultural work has to be done if the gulf between the symbolic representation of community and an actually existing Scotland is not to stand revealed through the kind of 'sub-nationalist' kitsch so deliriously debunked by Hugh MacDiarmid in the 1920s or Tom Nairn in the 1970s.

Clifford Geertz defines culture as 'historically transmitted patterns of meaning embodied in symbols – a system of inherited conceptions expressed in symbolic forms'.[56] It follows that the object of study will be 'not hidden subjectivities or whole ways of life, but publicly available symbols'; that is, representations.[57] If, therefore, memory is part of culture, it has to be audited and interpreted from proxy evidence. Accordingly, Olick and Robbins suggest three ways in which societies have tried to solve the problem of modern memory: they have attempted to 'designate sites to stand in for lost authenticity', to 'proliferate new narratives', and to 'abbreviate . . . in the face of insurmountable accumulation'.[58] The representations of *the* national past with which we conjure are thus inevitably ones in which a limited selection of people and places come to stand for history by means of the stories that are fabricated about them. Herein lies not only the utility but also the danger of icons and stereotypes. But if we set aside this assumption of collective accounting, as well we might in the post-modern present, then we are left not with miscellaneous cultural flotsam but something much more challenging.

Agnes Heller contends that cultural memory is 'embodied in objectivations which store meanings in a concentrated manner, meanings shared by a group of people who take them for granted'.[59] It refers to texts, monuments, symbols, ceremonies, festivals, and places; stories and emblems deployed, carried and ratified by the state and its institutions. Interpreting the play and influence of these objectified forms of remembrance is relatively straightforward. However, there is a confused relationship between cultural memory and civil society, understood as 'everything that the state is not':

> within civil society there are institutions and activities which are unable and unwilling to create cultural memory, for they are not in need of a cultural identity creation. Yet there are other segments or institutions within civil society which carry further, although selectively, inherited junks of cultural memory and create a cultural memory of their own. Civil society thus consists of a mosaic of identities and non-identities.[60]

For instance, purposively rational markets have an investment in abolishing tradition, while other interest-oriented activities such as shopping also lack cultural memory; single-issue movements wear their identities on their sleeves (often literally) for immediate, instrumental reasons.

On the other hand, 'families have a cultural memory, objectified in old letters, photographs, family lore etc.' Civil society thus consists both of 'the heterogeneous mosaic of a great variety of different, sometimes even colliding and hostile cultural memories, yet also a heterogeneous mosaic of activities and group formations in no need of cultural memories'. Yet although 'civil society can function without cultural memory', the same does not apply to its participants, for 'without shared cultural memory there is no identity'. Society is not enough:

> Still it seems as if the need for cultural memory were very strong and as if the Weberian slogan about the disenchantment of the world could be one of many failed predictions. The old conceptual differentiation between community and society comes to mind. It seems as if pure society could not deliver the goods which are still kept in store by communities.[61]

If Herzfeld is correct in claiming that members of different social groups within a country 'fashion and refashion their imagined iconicity', by 'deploy[ing] the debris of the past for all kinds of present purposes',[62] then the legacy of egalitarianism could be seen as a manufactured and fragmented consciousness where people draw upon an inventory of signs, symbols, narratives and discourses to create their own sense of self in the same way that, say, youth cultures utilise available resources to fabricate dress codes. 'Scotland' thereby is no more than a 'semiotic bricolage' created by the knowing use (through 'strategic essentialism') of tartan, shortbread tins, or 'See you, Jimmy' hats simply because these motifs distinguish the country from others, and where any link to the past is understood to be at best ironic, so much Auld Lang Synecdoche. Although groups such as sports fans certainly fit this characterisation, much research remains to be done to establish the veracity of such a claim in a wider, everyday sense.[63] It will require, *inter alia*, following Herzfeld's programme of social poetics by attempting to 'understanding the social life of stereotypes from within'.[64] A colleague of mine recently brought me up short by observing that 'students are dismayed by too much irony. They wade through discarded crisp packets rather than shortbread wrappers'. And one can speculate that the effectivity or cultural purchase of pasted-on symbols may be limited in so far as evidence of historical experience is required to legitimate identity claims, through what Calhoun refers to as the conferment of 'temporal depth'.[65] That is to say, they are not comparable with objects like a family snapshot or an heirloom that provides tangible evidence of personal connection, 'something that is kept and passed on, not because it is supposed to have any intrinsic value but because it evokes a labyrinth of memory to which it acts as the clue'.[66]

Although attempts to impose a classificatory logic upon history through the archive or via the media are undoubtedly significant, it would be facile and misguided to assume that 'strong' representations could produce a cultural unity by which the idea of a singular nation might emerge. Documentary records are a scant source of popular consciousness anyway. In accepting the force of socialisation, or for David McCrone echoing Ferguson, 'civil societalisation',[67] in cultivating individuals, I am not arguing for a particular form of territorial nationalism, based on a common culture, any more than one could advance claims of ethnicity.[68] Quite the reverse: to acknowledge the economic, political, social and cultural fragmentation within the country, its diaspora, and civil sphere, and also the absence of a convincingly collective foundation myth, is to realise that there must be many Scotlands.[69] Craig is right to argue that 'There can be no coherent narrative of the nation . . . its narrative spills out over many territories; it cannot be accommodated within the continuities demanded by the genre of a national history.'[70] But I do want to suggest that it is the universe of meanings co-habiting under the canopy of the Scots imaginary that describes the field in which each of us might relate to the place. This requires that we probe beyond cultural memory and into the more overtly subjective domain of the personal.

CONNECTING TRACES

Heller distinguishes cultural memory from what she calls 'traces of the past stored in a kind of collective consciousness ready for recall or hidden in a collective unconscious buried under the ruins of forgetting'.[71] In other words, in addition to the mosaic of competing notions of identity recoverable from diverse historical records or from ethnographic observation, there are the fugitive traces of belonging that do not bear such direct empirical scrutiny.[72] What makes such elusive imprints so significant is that if they do indeed tap into a 'collective consciousness' then they mark points of identification whereby individual impressions may be connected to a societal vision. If an analogy with interpreting the photograph may be made, reading the artefacts of cultural memory resembles Barthes' *studium* in that these objects and images allow for a culturally informed reading, whereas these hidden traces, in their private, personalised recognition of meaning are more like the *punctum*. Importantly, however, Barthes' duality is one of 'co-presence of two discontinuous elements' within the same image.[73] Like the *punctum*, the intensely personalised memory trace may not be communicable in language, and it may also lack reference to any sanctioned cultural memory. However, it may yet find resonance in a sense of belonging to something collectively identified, albeit unarticulated.

Paradoxically, to suggest examples would, of course, be to begin a process of articulation. One thinks here of experiences, often spiritual in flavour, conveyed in the mixed sense impressions of poetry, as in Charles Murray's evocation of longing, from South Africa, for his native Aberdeenshire – 'I want to wade through bracken in a glen across the sea/ I want to see the peat reek rise'.[74] Yet, as soon as such feeling is committed to paper and published, its uniqueness evaporates; we begin to construct the cultural meaning of the feel of walking through bracken, the smell and sight of peat smoke rising. It seems, then, that the poet plays the role of unearthing hidden traces from 'the ruins of forgetting' and, in so doing, transfers them to the archive of cultural memory. Is there then an equivalent process by which historians and others might access this lost treasury?

Unlocking the connection between imagination, memory and belonging requires focus on the relationship between self and society. Because emotions thrive upon oppositions, perceiving a past that is sufficiently distinctive from the present is a psychological necessity. Equally, however, possessing a coherent sense of self requires biographical continuity, in which the individual both lived in the past and exists today, so that 'the past' is simultaneously both part of what we are and where we are not. Elements of it form a framework for interpreting the world and our place within it, but only those aspects that have relevance to our contemporary existential and social context. Thus, imagined communities have a situational value: the couthy stories in The People's Friend hold meaning for older women imprisoned in urban tower blocks; the Knoxian parish republics where the democratic intellect throve inspire educationists and entrepreneurs alike; the loyalty of a Glasgow tenement motivates the football manager; solidarities of World War II galvanise the older generation beside the Holy Loch.

Rather than creating a morality with which one feels comfortable from a selection of ideologies on offer in the present culture, this view would claim that individuals cannot escape their own histories. 'The past' persists as the memory of one's own period of socialisation, a recollection (however warped) of a time and place in which the necessary founding components of one's worldview are to be found. Whether that time and place ever objectively existed is a moot point, a matter for the person defining the situation, not for historical truth. Modern memory seeks to articulate relationships between fragments recalled from lived experience and popularly understood myths or cultural narratives, thus any reference to the past always consists of an admixture of intensely intimate recollections filtered through the shared language of a collectively organised imaginary. Such is the social construction of reality. Beyond this lie unexamined thoughts, forever inaccessible. The modern social imaginary, in contradistinction to all that has gone before (and might come after) conceives of civil society as a performative speech act; that is, 'what constitutes the public is nothing other than the common action of discussing itself'.[75] And in this vision of society as a conversation, much of our dialogue consists of indirect speech in which 'the speaker communicates to the hearer more than he actually says by way of relying on their mutually shared background information'.[76] The best, therefore, that analysis can do is to locate the points where personal remembrance and identification meet something larger, to establish the common ground enabling cultural communication, for if we wish to know what this – or any – nation means to people, we need first to understand how they might be conscious of belonging or, just as importantly, not belonging to it.

Such investigation rightly provokes contention and debate, and much research on memory and memorialisation focuses on the emplotment of particular landscapes, locales, or sites within differing narratives. Yet the 'stories' of Bannockburn and Culloden cannot be disentangled from the battlefields themselves, any more than the meaning of, say, the scheme or farm where one grew up can be understood apart from the place itself.[77] In many instances, however, it is the physical erasure of such real environments that renders them imagined sites of memory, *lieux* rather than *milieux de mémoire*. Ruins – once the homes, fortifications, places of worship, storage, or work of our forbears – are neither, for as Simmel wrote: 'All the uncertainties of change in time and the tragedy of loss associated with the past find in the ruin a coherent and unified expression'.[78] In their enigmatic fusion of loss and reconnection, they provide a catalytic function, signifying both an absent past and, in their continuing existence, a tangible present. The poet Sorley MacLean, writing 'Hallaig' on Raasay, found that the wildness of the place was 'partly a consequence of loss: its spaciousness declared an absence, and its solitude a calamity.' Such a sense of place prompts Macfarlane, walking through the infamous clearance sites of Strathnaver now preserved as a heritage trail to ponder: 'To be in such landscapes is to be caught in a double-bind: how is it possible to love them in the present, but also to acknowledge their troubled histories?'[79] Answering his question requires acknowledgment of the inventiveness of a specifically modern imagination; to whit, the hegemony of a romantic way of seeing. It is not simply that remembrance is tied to place, but that this entailment is 'seen' within the terms of a particular way of appreciating the 'beauty' of landscape. The synopsis to a recent illustrated book about the Highland clearances thus reads: 'Stunning colour photographs depict the actual townships as they are today and the landscapes from which so many were banished, each conveying not only the natural beauty and colour of some of Scotland's most spectacular scenery, but also capturing the spirit of the places that witnessed such traumatic and shattering events.'[80] The rural romanticism of such 'spectacular scenery' finds, as we have seen, its ugly complement in the denigration of the detritus of industrialism.[81] Place and memory are bound together in the recognition of loss by the physical existence of the ruin. But picturing this signifies an absent presence: the image of a moment past, vanished from sight, yet immortalised by its very capture. The trace, then, prompts visualisation.

MEMORY PICTURES

The simplicity of the Isles life particularly close to the mainland is disappearing and modern conditions with their resultant haste are gradually taking its place. The single wire of a crude aerial is to-day not an uncommon sight beside the cottage on the wind-swept moorlands. The lone cottager to-day looks into the whirling vortex of modernity.[82]

It is 1933. Within a landscape of apparent tradition, the writer here makes reference to the insidious influence of the wireless, hidden but for the evidence of antennae. The image of 'the single wire of a crude aerial . . . beside the cottage on the wind-swept moorlands' is a powerful encapsulation of places on the cusp of change. The visual media themselves were to embed the signs of modernity into the cultural imaginary, John Grierson's commitment to evoking the modern in films such as *The Face of Scotland* being an explicit attempt to realise the shift from an older order of society to the new; from ruined blackhouses and castles to factories and power stations, each in their different way embodying a spirit of national pride and integrity. Meanwhile, Edwin Muir's image of modern industrialism remains entirely negative and Blake's decidedly gloomy.[83] The 1930s also witnessed heightened efforts to construct the Highland landscape as a touristic 'place for looking'[84] precisely because of its apparent resistance to change, hence the popular Batsford guides and Morton's *In Search of* volumes, albeit that they owed much of their success to the advent of the motor car. Rooted in the eighteenth-century endeavours of landscape painters such as Gilpin and the itinerant journals of Pennant and Boswell and Johnson, this was a continuing romanticisation that found in the twinning of tourism and photography an empathetic combination of two significant offspring of modernity even while it sought to protect such places from its ravages. The connection persists in what MacDonald refers to as the 'process of preserving a particular visual order'. Many current disputes over land use concern the appearance of landscape and the buildings within it, so that, for example, the thatched houses photographed by Strand now enjoy legal protection – 'the value he and Werner Kissling conferred upon them as vestiges of an ancient material culture, now statutorily prevents an owner from any alteration of the original features'.[85] Conservation and preservation are thus tied to visual rather than functional attributes.

The way is thereby cleared for a de-coupling of the relationship between place and history, and with this the devaluation of memory. The philosophical obsession with representation that began in seventeenth-century Europe has become 'the vision machine' of postmodern culture in which contemporary visual technologies disrupt any sense of connection between seeing and knowing, so that images and icons are often mere simulacra, 'heritage' at best a playful reconstruction of what might have been.[86] Given the contingency of modernity and the rise of visual awareness, my approach has been a particularly ocularcentric one. Of course, memories also associate times and places with evocative sounds, smells, tastes and other sensations.[87] But the visual remains peculiarly potent because images possess power by virtue of their relative ease of communicability (in an age of high visual literacy) and sheer volume compared to, say, traces of the recorded voice or memories of particular odours and the meanings so attached.

Undoubtedly, in a postmodern era, 'we interact more and more with totally constructed visual experiences'.[88] For Nora, memory, while attaching itself to sites rather than events 'has become a matter of explicit signs, not of implicit meanings; in this sense it is more a matter of associations, allusions and symbols'.[89] Benjamin's contention that 'history decays into images not into stories'[90] implies that the same may be true of historical subjects, the logic of these arguments being that their remembrances cannot be construed as narrative representations of reality. Yet the issue is not one of historical veracity so much as one of salience. The reason that some images become icons of popular memory while others do not lies in the aforementioned 'epidemiology of representations', their cultural resonance and receptivity by way of our socialisation through particular institutions and forms of knowledge. In this sense what we remember of the nation is what we are taught about Scotland, either in the obvious educational sense or through subtler forms of learning and mediation.[91] Meanwhile, what we can recover of our 'history' depends upon which materials are archived and in what ways. The piecing together of

'Scotland' as a geographical phenomenon from diverse sites also occurs in narrative form through the verbal iconicity of the novel: 'The places visited by picaresque heroes are transformed from accidental locations into ones which have developed a representative significance: the individual traveller thus becomes the bearer of a consciousness of the nation as interconnected space'.[92]

It is not simply that photography, for instance, aims to stabilise memory, but that photographic collections instantiate particular sets of images in specific categories.[93] Cultural memory therefore privileges certain images in the same way that particular names and narratives, and indeed nations are preserved. National identities are sustained by the habituation to and repetition of specific representations via 'a variety of mnemonic sites, practices and forms . . . mythologies, and associated physical places, as ordering principles for articulations of national memory'.[94] If one were to ask a random group of Scots, whose names come to mind when they think of their country's history, it is likely that William Wallace, Robert the Bruce, Mary Queen of Scots, Bonnie Prince Charlie and Robert Burns would feature. And, as Zerubavel points out with reference to a similar exercise conducted in the United States, 'the fact that so many different individuals happen to have the same "free" associations about their nation's past shows that their memories are not as independent of each other's as we might think but merely personalised manifestations of a single common, collective memory. It also underscores the tremendous power of mnemonic socialisation'.[95] Clearly, such 'personalised manifestations of a mnemonic community's collective memory' are not the same thing as 'truly personal recollections', but how are the two to be distinguished when unravelling the meaning of belonging?

Let us continue with the notion of images of national identity. In the first, collective category we might find photographs of Edinburgh Castle and Ben Nevis, while in the second, 'truly personal' one, perhaps a specific house and a snapshot of someone's grandmother. As suggested above, the former may reflect a disjuncture between place and one's personal history; meanwhile, the latter lacks any point of reference beyond the individual's recollection. So it is that the institutional claims of nationalism made by politicians or tourist boards differ from the experiences of nationhood felt by those living within a nation. And if Nora is right in claiming that 'the nation as a foundation of identity has eroded as the state has ceded power to society',[96] then commonly recollected – and, in the museum sense collected – representations have declined in significance. Collective memory is not what it used to be. How, then are the myriad unique, personal memory traces regarded as being about belonging somehow connected to a broader notion of remembrance?

One answer lies in what it is we mean when we identify a sense of belonging, for this implies if not a oneness with, at least an accommodation to, places (including landscapes) and/or the people within them. When individuals connect in this way they are acknowledging something personally felt but also something beyond the personal in that they are only part of the imagined picture, and sometimes stand outside it looking in. And this 'something' is akin to community in that memory acts as a catalyst for yearning, being the mechanism through which a trace of past identification is recollected. It is not simply that what we now see and how we understand it are culturally constructed – this, if you will, is the social imaginary part – but that we identify with the image or sentiment because it reveals the elusive imprint of a lost past from which our moral present takes root. This pulse of reconnection can only be felt if our mental picture supposes the dichotomous way of seeing upon which modernity, as the antithesis of tradition, is predicated and by which the modern life course is measured in ages and stages.[97] Indeed, such moments of simultaneous loss and recognition define modern memory just as surely as does the fix cast upon historical perception by the Enlightenment project.[98] Craig writes that 'the Scottish experience of cultural dislocation finds expression in narrative terms in plots of biological uncertainty or familial displacement', which is why the child uncertain of origins or looking for its parents is 'one of the fundamental tropes of the modern Scottish novel'.[99] Here is the metaphor of the modern self, like Cain expelled from Paradise and condemned to wander, in search of who he or she once was, for reconnecting requires much memory work.

In her poem 'Forget It!', Kathleen Jamie recalls a school history lesson. *'Mum!/ We done the slums today!' 'What for?'* replies her mother, *'Some history's better forgot'*, prompting the reflection 'So how come/ we remember the years/ before we were born?' The observation follows that 'this is a past/ not yet done, else how come/ our parents slam shut, deny/ like criminals: *I can't remember, cannae/ mind*, then turn at bay: *Why?/ Who wants to know.'* The guarded shame of a generation about a past they have escaped – or rather wish to have left behind, in mind as well as material fact, but cannot because 'stories are balm,/ ease their own pain' – contrasts with the pride and need to know of their offspring: 'I claim/ just one of these stories,/ razed places, important as castles,/ as my own'.[100] The past is 'not yet done' because it is a necessary part of the present, it provides its very explanation and anchorage. Even as its distance and difference render it 'other', we seek the threads that connect us, tell us where we came from and how we got to be who we are.[101] A photograph like the Gorbals Boys says to the viewer: 'That was childhood, a childhood in another age, when – I remember (if I am old enough) – poor kids (maybe like me) wore tacketty boots; a time and place when . . .' etc. The mental reconstruction of an image of community follows, based either upon personal remembrance or what we have learned, second-hand, about the past. Obviously, in terms of belonging, such a photograph will mean more to some than to others. The viewer does not have to know the scene intimately: we will read into the picture what we think we see (childhood, pastness, poverty); if we know it was taken in the Gorbals, this information might further condition our thinking; if we also grew up in Glasgow, we might be still more influenced, and so on. Like Jamie's schoolgirl we might feel the bond of continuity with our sense of self at one remove. If I look at one of Paul Strand's images of crofters on the Uists, I read into it pastness, isolation, rurality, 'otherness' from the British mainstream. Accordingly, I reveal the force of cultural conditioning. On the other hand, the son of one of the persons pictured sees something rather different. Having purchased the book as a gift for his father he 'was shocked to see they had called him MacLellan instead of MacLean'.[102] His indignation at an apparent misreckoning of kin in South Uist reflects the importance of genealogical and local pride. But both of us share in creating modern memory, as will manifold others, for in the many interpretations that may be given of each photograph inheres what may be understood as its rich and multiple meanings.

Diversity is in the nature of modern memory. However, care should be taken to distinguish such from randomness for, crucially, these meanings can be related to one another. While Nora contends that memory is 'nothing more than sifted and sorted historical traces',[103] it should be remembered that this process of organisation applies not just to cultural memory, but also to our uniquely individual mental recollections, for even these are culturally habituated. When considered according to the common characteristic of being pictures taken in Scotland, images become connected through the shared lens of nationhood; they variously – very variously – *represent* the inventory of how we might see a country. And it is in addressing how they are representative that we interpret identification and belonging. Of course, there is always the proviso that most images, places, or lives lived in those places may have little or nothing explicitly to do with identifying with the nation. Yet this in itself is a statement about what belonging means to people. The chauvinistic pull of *Braveheart* or alienation of *Trainspotting* are complemented by the apparent placelessness of George Blake's Dennyloanhead in the 1930s and of

Fig. 8.1 Paul Strand, 'D. J. MacLellan, South Uist, Hebrides 1954'.
Copyright © Aperture Foundation Inc., Paul Strand Archive.

many a suburban estate today. In this regard, it is the things we do not take pictures of or write about or otherwise publicly discuss that are, or perhaps would be most revealing for, as Blake said, in ignoring the unremarkable we 'miss much of the quiddity of Scotland'.[104] Similarly, in the diffident non-nationalism of many inhabitants, exiles, or strangers just passing through we might access forms of identification that are more appropriate than those conditioned by the weight of belonging to a nation as defined in the discourse of politicians or, indeed, cultural sociologists. The paradox here is that in even suggesting such a possibility a fresh imaginary emerges, redefining and embracing such diffidence as characteristically Scottish. In short, whether one resides there happily, disaffectedly or indifferently or, indeed, not there at all, there is no escape from the imagination of place, however feeble or corrupted this may be.[105] Even placelessness is defined by its opposite. It is this imperative that renders the evocation of 'Scotland', and by extension any nation, central to understanding modern memory as a way of knowing the world. As Norman MacCaig wrote: 'The little plot – do I belong to it or it to me? No matter. We share each other as I walk amongst its flags and tombstones.'[106]

Notes

1. J. Hodge, *Trainspotting: The Screenplay* (London: Faber & Faber, 1996).
2. To the extent that culture shapes social life rather than simply reflecting it, this is a plea for historical sociology as cultural sociology in the sense intended by Jeffrey Alexander's 'strong program' in cultural theory – see J. C. Alexander, 'Cultural sociology or sociology of culture?', *Culture*, 10 (3–4), 1996, pp. 1–5; J. C. Alexander and P. Smith, 'The strong program in cultural theory: elements of a structural hermeneutics', in J. H. Turner (ed.), *Handbook of Sociological Theory* (New York: Springer, 2006), pp. 135–50.
3. D. Sayer, *Going Down For Air: A Memoir in Search of a Subject* (Boulder, CO: Paradigm, 2004), p. 7. See also Assmann's claim that memory provides 'the connective structure of societies' (J. Assmann, *Das kulterelle Gedaechtnis: Schrift, Erinnerung und politische Identitaet in fruehen Hochkulturen* (Munich: C. H. Beck, 1992), p. 293, cited in J. K. Olick and J. Robbins, 'Social memory studies: from "collective memory" to the historical sociology of mnemonic practices', *Annual Review of Sociology*, 24, 1998, pp. 105–40 (p. 105).
4. J. Macmurray, *Conditions of Freedom* (London: Faber & Faber, 1950), p. 35.
5. J. C. Alexander, 'Civil sphere, state, and citizenship: replying to Turner and the fear of enclavement', *Citizenship Studies*, 12 (2), 2008, pp. 185–94 (p. 183).
6. C. Taylor, *Modern Social Imaginaries* (Durham, NC and London: Duke University Press, 2004), p. 2 (my italics).
7. K. Clark, *Civilisation: A Personal View* (London: BBC and John Murray, 1969), p. 284.
8. The quotation provides the opening epigram to Basil Wright's history of film, B. Wright, *The Long View* (New York: Knopf, 1974).
9. E. Weber, *Peasants into Frenchmen: The Modernization of Rural France, 1870–1914* (London: Chatto & Windus, 1977).
10. J. Grierson, Review of M. McLaren, *Understanding the Scots: A Guide for South Britons and Other Foreigners* (London: Frederick Muller, 1956), *Scotland*, November 1957, in F. Hardy (ed.), *John Grierson's Scotland* (Edinburgh: Ramsay Head Press, 1979), pp. 100–5 (p. 105).
11. D. McCrone, *Understanding Scotland: The Sociology of a Nation* (London: Routledge, 2001), p. 124.
12. R. Williams, *Keywords* (London: Fontana, 1983), pp. 75–6.
13. R. Williams, *The Country and the City* (St Albans: Paladin, 1975), pp. 202–20; R. Williams, *Marxism and Literature* (Oxford: Oxford University Press, 1977), pp. 136–41.
14. T. Eagleton, *Heathcliff and the Great Hunger: Studies in Irish Culture* (London: Verso, 1995), p. 242, cited in S. Lyall, *Hugh MacDiarmid's Poetry and Politics of Place: Imagining a Scottish Republic* (Edinburgh: Edinburgh University Press, 2006), p. 13.
15. A. Giddens, *Modernity and Self-Identity: Self and Society in the Late Modern Age* (Cambridge: Polity, 1991).
16. P. Heelas, 'Introduction: detraditionalization and its rivals', in P. Heelas, S. Lash and P. Morris (eds), *Detraditionalization* (Oxford: Blackwell, 1996), pp. 1–20 (p. 2).
17. A. Huyssen, *Twilight Memories: Marking Time in a Culture of Amnesia* (New York: Routledge, 1995), cited in Olick and Robbins, 'Social memory studies', p. 120.
18. J. Urry, *Mobilities* (Cambridge: Polity, 2007).

19. C. Craig, 'Visitors from the stars: Scottish film culture', *Cencrastus*, 11, 1983, pp. 6–11', p. 8. See also C. Craig, *The Modern Scottish Novel: Narrative and the National Imagination* (Edinburgh: Edinburgh University Press, 1999), p. 30: 'The idea of the nation as a single and unified totality is itself an invention required by a specific phase of the development of the system of nation-states in the global development of modernity.'

20. McCrone, *Understanding Scotland*, p. 146.

21. Given the connections between belonging and place, a considerable number of recent studies are in cultural geography. H. Lorimer, 'Cultural geography: the busyness of being 'more-than-representational', *Progress in Human Geography*, 29 (1), 2005, pp. 89–94 (p. 94) notes that: 'non-representational theory' has become an umbrella term for diverse work that seeks better to cope with our self-evidently more-than-human, more-than-textual, multisensual worlds. The term 'emotional geographies' has been used refer to connections between emotions and the socio-spatial concepts of place and community – see J. Davidson, L. Bondi and M. Smith (eds), *Emotional Geographies* (Aldershot: Ashgate, 2005).

22. A. Touraine, trans. D. Macey, *Critique of Modernity* (Oxford: Blackwell, 1995), p. 371.

23. N. Ascherson, *Stone Voices* (London: Granta Publications, 2002), p. 217. See also P. Fowler, 'Cultural landscapes of Britain', *International Jnl. of Heritage Studies*, 6 (1) (2000), pp. 201–12. 'Cultural landscapes' generally signify relict environments, the implication being that human society and the associated land uses of ancient times were more ecologically attuned than in subsequent eras when the relationship between society and nature became increasingly attenuated.

24. Ascherson, *Stone Voices*, p. 222.

25. T. C. Smout, 'The Highlands and the roots of green consciousness', *Proceedings of the British Academy*, 76, 199, pp. 237–63 (p. 247).

26. A. Law, 'The ghost of Patrick Geddes: civics as applied sociology', *Sociological Research Online*, 10 (2), 2005, para. 2.4. Interestingly, Hugh MacDiarmid wrote approvingly of Geddes as a traditional generalist in a specialist age (S. Lyall, *Hugh MacDiarmid's Poetry and Politics of Place: Imagining a Scottish Republic* (Edinburgh: Edinburgh University Press, 2006), p. 45).

27. Smout, 'The Highlands', pp. 255–6.

28. G. Maxwell, *Ring of Bright Water* (London: Longmans, 1960), *The Rocks Remain* (London: Longmans, 1963), *Raven Seek Thy Brother* (London: Longmans, 1969); R. Macfarlane, *The Wild Places* (London: Granta Publications, 2007); J. Hunter, *The Claim of Crofting* (Edinburgh: Mainstream, 1991).

29. Smout, 'The Highlands', p. 259.

30. J. Scott, 'The Edinburgh School of sociology', *Journal of Scottish Thought*, 1, 1, 2007.

31. Craig, *Modern Scottish Novel*, pp. 152–3.

32. Ibid. p. 150.

33. C. Craig, *Out of History: Narrative Paradigms in Scottish and English Culture* (Edinburgh: Polygon, 1996), p. 54.

34. Craig, *Modern Scottish Novel*, p. 158–9. D. Lowenthal, 'European landscape transformations: the rural residue', pp. 180–8, in P. E. Groth and T. W. Bressi (eds) *Understanding Ordinary Landscapes* (London: Yale University Press, 1998), p. 180, suggests that 'the locus of memory lies more readily in place than in time'.

35. The poet Norman MacCaig may be said to have done likewise, particularly in longer works such as 'A Man in Assynt' (1969). However, MacCaig's self-styled moniker of

'Zen Calvinist' was not a serious philosophical claim. As he notes: 'I was on a panel and I was asked what my religion was and I said "Zen Calvinist," just to shut them up' (J. Renton, 'Norman MacCaig: an interview', *Textualities*, 1987. http://textualities. net/jennie-renton/norman-maccaig-an-interview/ Accessed: June 2009).

36. T. Ingold, 'Building, dwelling, living: how animals and people make themselves at home in the world', in M. Strathern (ed.), *Shifting contexts* (London: Routledge, 1995), pp. 57–80; M. Nuttall, *Arctic Homeland: Kinship, Community and Development in Northwest Greenland* (Toronto: University of Toronto Press, 1992), p. 39; G. Carter, '"Domestic geography" and the politics of Scottish landscape in Nan Shepherd's *The Living Mountain*', *Gender, Place and Culture*, 8 (1), pp. 25–36 (p. 32). Carter also considers how landscape figures in the novels of Catherine Carswell and Willa Muir.

37. M. de Certeau, 'Practices of space', in M. Blonsky (ed.), *On Signs: A Semiotics Reader* (Oxford: Blackwell, 1985), pp. 122–45 (p. 129), cited in Carter, 'Domestic geography', p. 320.

38. J. Gray, 'Family farms in the Scottish Borders: a practical definition by hill sheep farmers', *Journal of Rural Studies*, 14 (3), 1998, p. 341–56.

39. Ibid., pp. 345, 355.

40. G. G. Giarchi, *Between McAlpine and Polaris* (London: Routledge, 1984), pp. 12, 11.

41. Ibid. p. 124.

42. As Appadurai suggests, in a very different discussion, 'the suffix *-scape* allows us to point to the fluid, irregular shapes' of various domains of meaning (A. Appadurai, *Modernity at Large: The Cultural Dimensions of Globalization* (Minneapolis: University of Minnesota Press, 1996), pp. 27–47, cited in D. Bell, 'Mythscapes: memory, mythology, and national identity', *British Journal of Sociology*, 54 (1), 2003, pp. 63–81 (p. 80)). Its heuristic utility makes it similarly possible to envisage a 'national mythscape', understood as 'the discursive realm, constituted by and through temporal and spatial dimensions' (Bell, 'Mythscapes, p. 75), a conceptualisation that is categorically different from Smith's idea of 'ethnoscape' as a landscape 'invested with ethnic kin significance' (A. Smith, *Myths and Memories of the Nation* (Oxford: Oxford University Press, 1999), p. 150). See also P. Basu, 'MacPherson Country: genealogical identities, spatial histories and the Scottish diasporic clanscape', *Cultural Geographies*, 12 (2), 2005, pp. 123–50.

43. H. Tange, 'Regional redemption: Graham Swift's *Waterland* and the end of history', *Orbis Litterarum*, 59, 2004, pp. 75–89 (p. 77).

44. There is also much here that would benefit from the application of geographical ideas. See J. N. Entrikin, 'Place, region and modernity', in J. A. Agnew and J. S. Duncan (eds), *The Power of Place: Bringing Together Geographical and Sociological Imaginations* (Boston: Unwin Hyman, 1989), pp. 30–42.

45. P. Berger, B. Berger and H. Kellner, *The Homeless Mind: Modernization and Consciousness* (London: Pelican, 1974); J. Meyrowitz, *No Sense of Place: The Impact of the Electronic Media on Social Behavior* (New York: Oxford University Press, 1987).

46. D. McCrone, A. Morris and R. Kiely, *Scotland the Brand: The Making of Scottish Heritage* (Edinburgh: Edinburgh University Press, 1995), p. 1.

47. M. Herzfeld, *Cultural Intimacy: Social Poetics in the Nation-State* (New York and London: Routledge, 1997), pp. 62, 112. Herzfeld cites Engels' primitive communism and Maine's pre-contractual primitive society as examples of such myths.

48. R. Chambers, *Popular Rhymes, Fireside Stories, and Amusements in Scotland* [1826] (Edinburgh: W. R. Chambers, 1842), pp. 123–4, cited in K. D. M. Snell, 'The culture of local xenophobia', *Social History*, 28 (1), 2003, pp. 1–30 (p. 8). Snell also cites Boswell observing bitter rivalries between Highlanders who recounted 'the outrages with which [their ancestors] suffered from the wicked inhabitants of the next valley' (p. 8, n. 35).

49. T. W. Adorno, trans. E. F. N. Jephcott, *Minima Moralia: Reflections from Damaged Life* (London: Verso, 1978), p. 79 – a sentiment derived from Nietzsche and taken up by Edward Said as reflecting the responsibility of the intellectual exile/exiled intellectual.

50. Bell, 'Mythscapes', p. 79, n. 10.

51. S. Schama, *Landscape and Memory* (London: Harper Perennial, 2004), p. 113.

52. Taylor, *Modern Social Imaginaries*, p. 183, notes that 'social imaginaries . . . are never just ideology. They also have a constitutive function, that of making possible the practices that they make sense of and thus enable'. Similarly, in *The Imaginary Institution of Society* (trans. K. Blamey, Cambridge, MA: MIT Press, 1998), Cornelius Castoriadis argues that 'the real' is formed by human applications of social imaginaries.

53. C. Applegate, *A Nation of Provincials: The German Idea of Heimat* (Berkeley: University of California Press, 1990), Preface.

54. Ibid. p. 6.

55. Back cover text from P. Basu, *Highland Homecomings: Genealogy and Heritage-Tourism in the Scottish Highland Diaspora* (London: Routledge, 2007).

56. C. Geertz, 'Religion as a cultural system', in M. Banton (ed.), *Anthropological Approaches to the Study of Religion* (London: Tavistock, 1966): pp. 1–46 (p. 3).

57. A. Swidler, 'Geertz's ambiguous legacy', in D. Clawson (ed.), *Required Reading: Sociology's Most Influential Books* (Amherst, MA: University of Massachusetts Press, 1998), pp. 79–84 (p. 79).

58. Olick and Robbins, 'Social memory studies', p. 133.

59. A. Heller, 'Cultural memory, identity and civil society', *Internationale Politik und Gesellschaft*, 2001, 2, pp. 139–43 (p. 139).

60. Ibid. pp. 140–1.

61. Ibid. p. 143.

62. Herzfeld, *Cultural Intimacy*, pp. 154, 27.

63. The 'faux photomontages' created by Calum Colvin reflect this process within fine art and have been interpreted as such. However, such arch representation is categorically distinct from the analysis of everyday popular culture.

64. Herzfeld, *Cultural Intimacy*, p. 156.

65. C. Calhoun, 'Nationalism and ethnicity', *Annual Review of Sociology*, 19, 1993, pp. 211–39 (p. 235). Cf. Bell, 'Mythscapes', p. 79, n. 10.

66. W. McIlvanney, *Surviving the Shipwreck* (Edinburgh: Mainstream, 1991), p. 117.

67. D. McCrone (2007), 'Recovering civil society: does sociology need it?', http://www.institute-of-governance.org/publications/working_papers/recovering_civil_society

68. M. Gardiner, *Modern Scottish Culture* (Edinburgh: Edinburgh University Press, 2005), p. 2, argues that 'since Scotland has no state, the question of what it is, is necessarily a cultural one'. And in his conspectus the constituents of this cultural nation are history, philosophy, education, religion, law, sport, languages, parliament, literature, the visual arts and architecture, mass media and music. In all these

areas we can point to distinctively Scottish elements, symbols and traditions. Since formal citizenship – including that conferred upon immigrants – can only be British, people cannot officially become Scottish. Thus 'they have to see their Scottishness or Englishness as a cultural phenomenon' (p. 137).

69. For a critique of various theories of nationalism as applied to Scotland, see S. Bruce, 'A failure of the imagination: ethnicity and nationalism in Scotland's history', *Scotia*, XVII, 1993, pp. 1–16.

70. Craig, *Modern Scottish Novel*, p. 237.

71. Heller, 'Cultural memory', p. 139.

72. See P. Ricoeur, trans. D. Pellauer, *The Course of Recognition* (Cambridge, MA: Harvard University Press, 2005), p. 111: 'An image of the past comes to mind for me. In this sense, it is a passive moment'. Every trace, in effect, is in the present. And the trace will always depend on the thought that interprets it: 'the deciphering of traces presupposes that they were, as we say, left behind. This simple phrase evokes their fugitive, vulnerable, revocable character. In short, it belongs to the idea of a trace that it can be wiped out.'

73. R. Barthes, *Camera Lucida: Reflections on Photography* [1980] (London: Vintage, 1993), p. 23.

74. C. Murray, 'The Alien', *Hamewith* (London: Constable & Company Ltd, 1920), pp. 2–4 (p. 4).

75. S. Crocker, Review of C. Taylor, *Modern Social Imaginaries*, *CJS Online*, Jan–Feb 2005, p. 2 (http://www.cjsonline.ca/pdf/socialimaginaries.pdf).

76. J. R. Searle, *Expression and Meaning: Studies on the Theory of Speech Acts* (Cambridge: Cambridge University Press, 1979), pp. 31–2.

77. See C. Tilley, *A Phenomenology of Landscape: Places, Paths and Monuments* (Oxford: Berg, 1994), p. 27: 'People routinely draw on their stocks of knowledge of the landscape and locales in which they act to give meaning, assurance and significance to their lives. The place acts dialectically so as to create the people who are of that place. These qualities of locales and landscapes give rise to a feeling of belonging and rootedness and a familiarity, which is not born just out of knowledge, but of a concern that provides ontological security.'

78. Quoted in Olick and Robbins, 'Social memory studies', p. 107.

79. Macfarlane, *The Wild Places*, pp. 122–3.

80. D. Craig and D. Paterson, *The Glens of Silence: The Landscapes of the Scottish Clearances* (Edinburgh: Birlinn, 2004).

81. For a sophisticated, multi-faceted appreciation of the latter, see T. Edensor, *Industrial Ruins: Space, Aesthetics and Materiality* (Oxford: Berg, 2005).

82. I. F. Anderson, *To Introduce the Hebrides* (London: Herbert Jenkins, 1933), p. 216, quoted in J. Burnett, '"Into the whirling vortex of modernity": cultural developments in the Scottish Gaidhealtachd, 1935–1965', in R. J. Morris and L. Kennedy (eds), *Ireland and Scotland: Order and Disorder, 1600–2000* (Edinburgh: John Donald, 2005), pp. 175–88 (p. 175).

83. This difference in view is more apparent than real, given that even the stoically optimistic Grierson despaired of industrial decline during the worst of the Depression. Looking back from 1956 he wrote: 'It has been a dark story and the darkest day I think I ever saw was when the sun was shining brightly and there was not a cloud in the blue sky over the industrial town of Coatbridge and for the odd ironic reason that not a single chimney was smoking. When I tried to make a film of it, so bewildered

and angry were the idle men in the streets that I was nearly lynched . . . The main point in time, however, is that a technical revolution as ultimate as anywhere has been undertaken and is now succeeding better than to plan' (J. Grierson, 'The hub of Scotland', *Industrial Scotland* (1956), reprinted in F. Hardy (ed.), *John Grierson's Scotland* (Edinburgh: Ramsay Head Press, 1979, pp. 19–29 (pp. 23–4, 28)).

84. F. MacDonald, 'Geographies of Vision and Modernity: Things Seen in the Scottish Highlands', unpublished D.Phil. thesis, University of Oxford, 2003.

85. Ibid. pp. 379, 380.

86. G. Rose, *Visual Methodologies* (London: Sage, 2nd edn, 2007), pp. 3–4, alluding to R. Rorty, *Philosophy and the Mirror of Nature* (Oxford: Blackwell, 1980); P. Virilio, *The Vision Machine* (London: BFI, 1994) and J. Baudrillard, ed. M. Poster, *Selected Writings* (Cambridge: Polity, 1988).

87. While there exists considerable scope for research into the other senses, the absence of archived sources or published material presents particular challenges. This is less the case with sound, which includes musical recordings and oral evidence, than with smell and touch. Examples of material that might prove useful in reconstructive memory research are P. J. Stollery, 'Fields of Silence', 'Gordon Soundscape', 2005 (Acousmatic compositions on fixed medium) and 'Resound' (sound installation/documentary) – parts of the Gordon Soundscape project; and S. Scroggie, *The Cairngorms Scene and Unseen* (Glasgow: Scottish Mountaineering Trust, 1989), the recollections of a blinded hill walker. See also: S. Nenadic, 'Sensory experiences: smells, sounds and touch', in E. A. Foyster and C. A. Whatley (eds), *A History of Everyday Life In Scotland, 1600 to 1800* (Edinburgh: Edinburgh University Press, forthcoming), Chapter 8; Lorimer, 'Cultural geography'; E. Thompson, *The Soundscape of Modernity* (Cambridge, MA: MIT Press, 2002).

88. Rose, *Visual Methodologies*, p. 4. See also N. Mirzoeff, 'What is visual culture?', in N. Mirzoeff (ed.), *The Visual Culture Reader* (London: Routledge, 1998), pp. 3–13.

89. P. Nora, 'Between memory and history', *Representations*, 26, 1989, pp. 7–25 (p. 22).

90. W. Benjamin, *Arcades*, 476 [N10a, 3], cited in A. Auerbach, 'Imagine no metaphors: the dialectical image of Walter Benjamin', Image [&] Narrative [e-journal], 18 (2007). Available at: http://www.imageandnarrative.be/thinking_pictures/auerbach.htm Accessed June 2009.

91. The changing ways in which Scotland has been portrayed in popular film presents an interesting case study. See D. Petrie, *Screening Scotland* (London: BFI, 2000) and *Contemporary Scottish Fictions* (Edinburgh: Edinburgh University Press, 2004).

92. Craig, *Modern Scottish Novel*, p. 12; Stevenson's *Kidnapped* (1886) presents a good example of such. Fanny Osborne wrote in the Preface, 'The tale was to be of a boy, David Balfour, supposed to belong to my husband's own family, who should travel in Scotland as though it were a foreign country'. She might have added, 'and in doing so lending iconic significance to the places on that journey'.

93. Elizabeth Edwards suggests that this process is driven by fear that archival entropy will lead to the loss of national memory ('Recording our past: memory and the photographic survey movement', seminar delivered in 'Memory, history and society' seminar series, University of Aberdeen, 21 March 2006). See also V. L. Pollock, 'Dislocated narratives and sites of memory: amateur photographic surveys in Britain, 1889–1897', *Visual Culture in Britain*, 10 (10), 2009, pp. 1–26.

94. Olick and Robbins, 'Social memory studies', p. 124.

95. E. Zerubavel, 'Social memories: steps to a sociology of the past', *Qualitative Sociology*, 19 (3), 1996, pp. 283–99 (p. 294).

96. Olick and Robbins, 'Social memory studies', p. 121.

97. As Bruno Latour argues in *We Have Never Been Modern* (Cambridge, MA: Harvard University Press, 1993), the 'great divides' between nature and human, subject and object, science and society are very much a fiction of the 'modern' world.

98. Ricoeur, *The Course of Recognition* (p. 111) sees in this conjoining trace 'the enigma of the presence in an image of an absent thing that this image represents'.

99. Craig, *Modern Scottish Novel*, pp. 111, 110. Family dysfunction pervades popular fiction, not least romantic novels and short stories.

100. K. Jamie, *Waterlight: Selected Poems* (Saint Paul, MN: Graywolf Press, 2007), pp. 43–6.

101. Craig's 'out of history' thesis appears to offer a counter-argument: 'The Scottish "predicament" . . . is not simply the residue of a harsh industrial world, nor the effort of a people to build a better environment than the one they have inherited: it is the total elision of the evidence of the past and its replacement by a novelty so radical that it is impossible for the individual to relate to it his or her personal memories. And impossible, therefore, for that environment to be "related" to a coherent narrative' (*Modern Scottish Novel*, p. 21). *Pace* Edwin Muir, this framework of discontinuity created by rapid industrial and urban transformation may hold true for fiction but is rather less persuasive when applied to the lives of those who lived through and made sense of such change.

102. A. MacLean, Customer review of P. Strand and B. Davidson, *Tir A' Mhurain: The Outer Hebrides of Scotland* [1962] (New York: Aperture, 2002, with preface by C. Duncan), http://www.amazon.co.uk/Tir-AMhurain-Outer-Hebrides-Scotland/dp/089381993X/ref=sr_1_1?ie=UTF8&s=books&qid=1247496684&sr=1-1 Accessed June 2009.

103. Nora, 'Between memory and history', p. 8.

104. G. Blake, *The Heart of Scotland* (London: Batsford, 3rd edn, 1951), p. 101.

105. T. Devine and P. Logue (eds), *Being Scottish: Personal Reflections on Scottish Identity Today* (Edinburgh: Edinburgh University Press, 2002), p. xiii, note that 'some conclusions are inescapable . . . it is remarkable how many contributors refer to the importance of place, landscape and belonging'. This has, of course, long been a concern of geographers – see, for instance, J. A. Agnew and J. S. Duncan (eds) *The Power of Place: Bringing Together Geographical and Sociological Imaginations* (Boston: Unwin Hyman, 1989).

106. N. MacCaig, 'Chauvinist' in N. MacCaig, ed. D. Dunn, *Selected Poems* (London: Chatto & Windus, 1997), p. 139.

Index